The Progressive Audit

A Toolkit for Improving Your Organizational Quality Culture

Also available from ASQ Quality Press:

The Management System Auditor's Handbook
Joe Kausek

The Internal Auditing Pocket Guide
J.P. Russell

Quality Audits for Improved Performance, Third Edition
Dennis R. Arter

The Process Auditing Techniques Guide
J.P. Russell

The Process Approach Audit Checklist for Manufacturing
Karen Welch

*Process Driven Comprehensive Auditing: A New Way to Conduct
ISO 9001:2000 Internal Audits*
Paul C. Palmes

Internal Quality Auditing
Denis Pronovost

Fundamentals of Quality Auditing
B. Scott Parsowith

To request a complimentary catalog of ASQ Quality Press publications,
call 800-248-1946, or visit our Web site at http://qualitypress.asq.org.

The Progressive Audit

A Toolkit for Improving Your Organizational Quality Culture

Robert Pfannerstill

ASQ Quality Press
Milwaukee, Wisconsin

American Society for Quality, Quality Press, Milwaukee 53203
© 2005 by ASQ
All rights reserved. Published 2006
Printed in the United States of America

12 11 10 09 08 07 06   5 4 3 2 1

Library of Congress Cataloging-in-Publication Data

Pfannerstill, Robert, 1951–
    The progressive audit : a toolkit for improving your organizational
quality culture / Robert Pfannerstill.
        p. cm.
    Includes bibliographical references and index.
    ISBN-13: 978-0-87389-662-7 (soft cover, perfect bound : alk. paper)
    ISBN-10: 0-87389-662-9 (soft cover, perfect bound : alk. paper)
    1. Auditing, Internal. 2. Total quality management. 3. Corporate culture.
I. Title.

    HF5668.25.P49 2005
    658.4'013—dc22   2005017090

ISBN-13: 978-0-87389-662-7
ISBN-10: 0-87389-662-9

Publisher: William A. Tony
Acquisitions Editor: Annemieke Hytinen
Project Editor: Paul O'Mara
Production Administrator: Randall Benson

ASQ Mission: The American Society for Quality advances individual, organizational, and
community excellence worldwide through learning, quality improvement, and knowledge exchange.

Attention Bookstores, Wholesalers, Schools, and Corporations: ASQ Quality Press books,
videotapes, audiotapes, and software are available at quantity discounts with bulk purchases for
business, educational, or instructional use. For information, please contact ASQ Quality Press at
800-248-1946, or write to ASQ Quality Press, P.O. Box 3005, Milwaukee, WI 53201-3005.

To place orders or to request a free copy of the ASQ Quality Press Publications Catalog, including
ASQ membership information, call 800-248-1946. Visit our Web site at www.asq.org or
http://qualitypress.asq.org.

 Printed on acid-free paper

Quality Press
600 N. Plankinton Avenue
Milwaukee, Wisconsin 53203
Call toll free 800-248-1946
Fax 414-272-1734
www.asq.org
http://qualitypress.asq.org
http://standardsgroup.asq.org
E-mail: authors@asq.org

This book is dedicated to my wife Debbie for her amazing support and patience in this undertaking and the many hours that she got the kids out of the house so I could write, rewrite, and rewrite again. I also appreciate her tolerance of the piles of books and research articles in our living room. It is also dedicated to my little girl, Madeline, who must have wondered what Daddy was doing for so many hours on the computer.

Table of Contents

CD-ROM Contents

File: ProgressiveAudit.xls

In this Excel file are seven tabs of templates that correspond to the seven appendixes in the book:

A—Mfg scrguide
B—Mngr cklst
C—Sup cklst
D—Mfg Eng cklst
E—Setup cklst
F—Op cklst
G—Floor

List of Figures and Tables

Preface

I truly believe *The Progressive Audit* is a book that anyone involved with auditing should read. It is based on my practical experience, most of it working for Briggs & Stratton Corporation, and quite a bit of outside research. To get new ideas, I read from numerous sources on quality management systems and audits during the development of this methodology. When you work 25 years for the same company, especially one that dominates the marketplace and is a world leader, you develop bias. I wanted to learn how others approached developing their internal audits to gain a broader perspective.

I believe the activities and tools discussed in this book have had a significant effect on improving the quality culture at the three facilities over which I have responsibility. I can say this because I have worked closely with the various facilities for over 14 years, so I have been able to see the change over time. There have been other management initiatives as well as a strong emphasis on quality within the corporation, but the progressive audit methodology described in this book digs down into the core of our systems and that's where you can understand and influence quality.

This book is not just about auditing but also about management strategy, employee involvement, and raising the level of the organizational quality culture. I believe the audit must provide an understanding of the level at which the quality culture exists so management can implement improvements. It must uncover the various subsystems that exist within organizations and also raise the level of understanding in the workforce. You can have great training programs but unless you directly involve the employee, it just doesn't seem to stick.

The Progressive Audit is about a methodology to implement a sound internal audit program, how to get employees to actively participate in it, how to drive quality system concepts throughout all levels in the organization, and how to manage it so you're not doing all the work. The management team owns the program, which provides quantitative results that can be compared year after year, and includes strategies for moving toward the future while auditing the present.

In closing, I want to make some general comments about the book, which is written in three parts. In Part I, I will discuss concerns and issues with auditing and why there is value in an internal audit program. In Part II, there is discussion on key system concepts and the culture of an organization, with my focus on the ISO standard. I feel it is important to ensure that the reader and author have a common understanding of the systems that are to be audited because there are varying opinions and degrees of implementation. In Part III, I will discuss the internal audit in detail. Many of the concepts presented are proven methods that have been around for a long time; in this book, they are revisited and bundled in a methodology that truly adds value to the organization in very specific ways.

Acknowledgments

This book would not have been possible without the input, concepts, and actions of my friends and associates. I would first like to thank Paul Kondracsek, my good friend and our director of quality for his forward-thinking ideas about quality systems, audits, and customer satisfaction. Our internal audit would not be where it is today if not for the hard work of Mike Enoch, former divisional quality engineer, in supporting its implementation throughout the division. I would also like to thank quality managers Arnold Jansen, Sean Gregory, and Daron Wilson for their strong commitment to quality and tremendous support for this program.

I would like to thank Cindy Holland, one of the original lead auditors, for her many contributions, such as the concept of using checklists, and Ken Elliott for first coming up with the idea of using our supplier survey as the format for the internal audit. I would like to thank my first boss when I started in the field of quality, Don Kernwein, who truly understood systems and was instrumental in our understanding of the ISO standard. I would also like to thank Sherry Gay, our systems coordinator, for reviewing the contents of this book and making suggestions for improvement.

I would be remiss without including Roy Kerr for our many hours of discussion on quality systems, especially processes, which were really a learning session on my part. I also want to recognize my friend Bill Palmer, a professor at Murray State University, for his concepts and ideas related to Deming, our in-depth discussions on management, and opening my eyes to the practical side of statistical process control. I also want to recognize the following individuals for their contributions: Bruce Bowlin, Heidi St. Louis, Mark Melloy, Greg Wyatt, Kurt Martin, Christy Williams, Jaime Bunton, Dan Halbert, Mike Lehn, Rodney Bohannon, Jon Cowley, Ken Carson, Rick Johnson, Jim Korich, and my current boss Larry Bartling. Finally, I would like to thank my former boss, Joe Wright, for his encouragement and support in implementing this program as well as our many hours of fruitful discussion.

Robert Pfannerstill

Part I

Does The System Audit Need to Change?

This book is really about continuous improvement. To explain what I mean by that statement, it's really a story about realizing that I didn't much care for the way I did internal quality system audits. I didn't see much difference in the methods other quality managers used nor did I find a single publication that had a practical solution. There were plenty of good resources available offering various techniques and formats, but there didn't seem to be any that explained in common language how they implemented an audit program. I found quality magazine articles defending internal audits, others suggesting improvements to the audits, and a number of them just plain criticizing the audits. What struck me was that many people did not like doing them, especially me.

I didn't always feel this way, because I had personally experienced the positive benefits of an internal audit program when someone else did it. But over time, as we achieved registration to the ISO 9001[1] standard for all the manufacturing facilities, we felt the quality systems in place were meeting our needs. The overall system was not as much of a priority anymore because the focus was on specific aspects of the system, such as customer satisfaction and product quality. The internal audit became simply a means of satisfying a requirement of the standard. Management changed its approach to conducting them, moving the responsibility from corporate to the facility, and that is when I began my love/hate relationship with internal audits. The truth is that even when I disliked them the most, I still believed there was value in performing them.

In our organization, the internal audit started many years ago because we were pursuing ISO 9001 registration. In the early days, it was performed by corporate. I liked it when the corporate guys would come down to the plant for the annual internal audits. I would even look forward to it because the audits were something new; we were always making improvements, and I wanted to show them off. I liked the interviews because I learned from them and they were challenging. I also liked the fact that they would tell me we were doing some things really well because it was recognition.

Management then made a decision to put more accountability for the systems at a level closer to the facilities, so the internal audits became a divisional responsibility. Our divisional quality manager made the annual trek to the regional facilities to conduct the audits, but it still was a positive experience. One reason was his knowledge and understanding of systems, because he was the driving force in the corporation for achieving ISO 9001 certification. The other reason was I didn't have to worry about doing it.

The change that really stirred things up in our division occurred just after I became the quality manager of one of the plants. My predecessor, who became the new divisional quality manager, believed in having others involved in the audit. During his first year, he requested a manufacturing manager to assist him with the audit. By the second year, the quality managers were charged with doing their own internal audits. The division would provide assistance for areas requiring independence, but the movement was clearly to involve more people in the process.

It had been so easy to rely on a corporate or divisional manager to do it. As a quality manager, all I needed to do was a quick review of my quality manual and some prepping for the departments in the plant. I would set up the tours so we could show the auditor our best departments, but also let him see a few areas where work needed to be done so we would get some opportunities for improvement. As a seasoned veteran, this whole scenario wasn't a big deal because the main objectives were to satisfy the ISO 9001 requirement that we did an internal audit and to verify that our systems were followed.

Now, because of a directive from management, I needed to establish my own internal audit for the plant. Instead of merely prepping for the audit, I had to conduct it, except for divisional quality doing the areas under my direct responsibility. I had mixed feelings about the initiative. I thought the concept of putting responsibility at the plant made sense, and I actually looked forward to doing it. I had previous experience in audits because I had conducted supplier surveys for many years, so doing my own audits shouldn't be a big deal. The problem was that I also had a lot of other responsibilities, little time, and a facility with a thousand employees that made over three million engines a year.

The easiest thing to do was model my audit program after what I had seen others do, so I borrowed the checklist from the divisional guys and did my annual internal audit a few weeks before the ISO audit. What I also did was perpetuate the concept that the audit is just to satisfy the ISO quality system requirements and verify systems compliance. My intent was to add value to it, but time constraints and other priorities got in the way. That's when I realized the internal quality audit needed to change.

1

Do We Believe the Systems Audit Is Important?

Let's begin with a basic premise repeated in most quality publications: quality systems audits are important to any good quality system. This is written in numerous quality-focused books and articles, and any good quality manager will publicly proclaim it. Just like verifying the status of our financial situation by reviewing budgets and balancing our checkbook, we need to review, analyze, and make recommendations on the status of the quality systems we implement. This seems like a practical and logical conclusion. Quality system audits, in some form or another, verify that our systems are documented, implemented, and effective. Depending on the efforts taken from the results of the audit, it can also be a tool for continuous improvement activity.

The question is "do we really believe this?" If we don't balance our checkbook, we may get by for a while. Eventually we will need to come to grips with the fact that we have excess if we're lucky, but in some cases, we are lacking and must not only find the money to cover the checks but also pay fines for our misdeeds. However, if we don't take personal responsibility for verifying that the checkbook is correct, we can still rely on the bank to send us a monthly statement verifying the compliance of our "bookkeeping." The bank will provide key information whether we balance our checkbook or not.

In this same regard, there are also feedback mechanisms in organizations that provide an effectiveness measure of our quality system. Customer complaints, product defects, customer evaluation reports, internal defect reporting, and various other measures provide very important information about our systems. If business is going well and our feedback mechanisms are telling us systems are working, quality system audits verifying that we're doing what our systems say we should become more a matter of reviewing procedures and cleaning up "loose ends" once each year. The quality systems audit becomes a "thing" the quality department does and manufacturing managers look at this activity as merely a necessary evil.

Let's look at the checkbook scenario again. Relying on the bank is okay if you almost always carry a balance, but what if you run pretty tight or make a simple mistake? By the time you realize it you could be in a big mess. This could become really painful if you're facing bills that are due and have big overdraft fees, plus a royal headache trying to figure out what you did wrong. In this case, balancing the checkbook may be a necessity, or you can take preventive action by applying for a charge card so overdrafts will be transferred and no overdraft fees will be initiated. Ultimately, you can audit (balance your checkbook) or rely on the feedback of the bank statement; it depends on where you get the most value (or least pain).

Auditing a checkbook against a monthly statement is obviously minor compared to auditing an organization's quality systems. Although used as an illustration of a concept, balancing your checkbook is really not auditing but more like 100 percent inspection because you need to look at all the checks that came in to know what's outstanding in order to balance it. If your wife maintained and balanced the checkbook, you could audit how accurate and timely she was in that task; you could also be sleeping on the couch.

PURPOSE OF THE AUDIT

There are many purposes and methods for conducting quality system audits and most techniques have been around for years. Audits can be used to determine if a project is on track, that product meets internal requirements, that product received by a customer meets requirements, and that procedures, whether defined in a document or through training, are followed as intended. The methods used vary depending on the task. If product-related, you will most likely be measuring samples with some sort of gage, although you may use visual inspection to verify that certain features are present. If it's a project, you may use the project time line to verify that it is on track while you review documents to determine if key activities were performed and successfully completed.

A quality system audit is also used to verify that we're following our procedures as intended. There are a number of ways to do this. Many organizations have customers that come in to perform quality systems audits (called second-party audits). Organizations may also contract an independent company to send in auditors for the purpose of registering/certifying to a standard such as ISO 9001 (third-party audits). We can perform the activity ourselves through the internal quality systems audit (first-party audits), which is the subject of this book. In all cases, the organization will be measured against some type of standard. This will most likely be the organization's quality management system. It can also be the customer's standard, defined in some sort of supplier manual. In the case of third-party audits, it will be an industry standard or regulation.

In its purest sense, the internal quality systems audit should review the quality manual against a recognized standard to provide assurance that all areas are properly addressed. Once this is completed, the audit then verifies that all requirements in the manual are implemented within the organization, identifying any deficiencies for resolution. This means that we must first and foremost police ourselves. The second- and third-party audits then become a verification of our internal activities, if the organization is subject to them.

When first implementing a new standard or significant revision to an already implemented one, there is a significant focus on updates and training, and the internal audits play a critical role in verifying effectiveness of the efforts. However, after the dust settles and systems are in place, the focus changes. Since we already have more immediate-response mechanisms in place to tell us the organization is running properly, the internal audit becomes an activity that is akin to an annual checkup. If the organization has outside auditors coming in, they may determine the degree of effort devoted toward internal audits based on the external audit results. If there are no second- or third-party audits, it is really up to management to maintain the focus, or angry customers will do it for them.

Some quality managers face this scenario in organizations on the verge of chaos, sometimes with customers that would rather smash you in the mouth than give you a break. These days, this does not necessarily mean significant failure rates because the expectation for zero defects is far greater. In this scenario, key systems are failing to identify or control to the necessary degree and allowing some defective product to reach the customer. If a quality systems audit is performed, it is specific to the issue and most likely driven by a corrective action. There is strong motivation for the organization to identify the problem and take specific action because the customer is breathing down its neck. Once the issue is resolved, we can go back to relying on immediate-response mechanisms to gauge the effectiveness of our systems.

To broaden this discussion, there is a vast array of business climates with varying degrees of discipline for developing and following quality systems, and the customer ultimately drives much of it. I don't necessarily mean customers are demanding that you implement specific quality methods, although this is the case in a number of organizations. It is more the fact that organizations must be profitable, and in order to do that, you must satisfy the customer as efficiently as possible. If your systems allow defective or unreliable product out of your facility, costs will escalate, your reputation is diminished, and you allow the competition an opportunity to gain market share. If you never ship defective product because you have added redundant inspection operations with expensive auditing programs, your margins will be so thin that you will not be profitable.

The critical factor is the decision top management must make in choosing the most effective quality management system that supports the organization's strategies and ensures quality of the product line. Even if the customer dictates this, management must still make decisions regarding how to most effectively implement that standard. Once the system is implemented, the critical factor is how close top management wants to be to the systems. Do they put emphasis on internal audits to assure that the systems are correctly defined and effective, do they rely on measures, or do they delegate responsibility to the quality director or manager and let them report on results?

TOP MANAGEMENT COMMITMENT

There is much written about the importance of top management commitment to developing an effective quality management system. Deming and Juran emphasized this in their lectures to the Japanese in the 1950s and it is still written about and discussed today. In later sections of this book, I have quoted a number of sources related to the importance of this commitment to quality. The question that begs to be answered is "why after all these years is there still the general perception that top management is not as committed as they should be?"

According to management theory research, "study after study has shown that managers work at an unrelenting pace, that their activities are characterized by brevity, variety, and discontinuity, and that they are strongly oriented to action and dislike reflective activities."[2] In this same paper, one study of British middle and top managers revealed that they worked without interruption for about a half hour only once every two days. As we have often heard or read, managers are the movers and shakers of organizations, and studies show that rather than rely on formal management systems, they prefer informal communication with information that is in their heads.[3]

I believe this leaves us with the point of view that while a good quality management system is still considered essential for the rank-and-file workforce, management prefers to not constrain themselves by specifically defined procedures.

How many organizations have well-defined quality procedures for upper management? Executives from various industries know the key quality systems in the organization but do not necessarily quote them as their reason for doing something. Financial and other government regulations are well recognized because those requirements affect the bottom line, in addition to serious consequences if they are not followed. Upper management's primary role is to ensure organizational performance through profitability while complying with regulations, laws, customer needs, growth strategies, community involvement initiatives, and a myriad of other initiatives. They must have financial and other performance summary reports so they can take action to achieve their targets.

In "Why Some Companies Aren't Making the Change," Phyllis Naish laid out reasons why she felt companies were not upgrading to the ISO 9001:2000 standard, based on her experience as a consultant.[4] She said the biggest factor was money due to the cost of transition expenses and registration fees, meaning a lack of return on investment. Customers told her the new ISO standard dictates activities that do not provide value and clients say they are already "meeting customer satisfaction requirements but do not want to take time away from meeting those requirements to document their customer satisfaction."

If those organizations derived value from the ISO standard and audit this would not be the case. This is an important point. In management's mind, the quality systems audit was a method to verify compliance and obtain registration. Some procedural details are uncovered but overall system improvement in the sense of performance is not achieved. Therefore, the underlying message from management is that there is little or no perceived value in the ISO certification audit process except in satisfying the requirements of the customer. This can be demonstrated by the fact that after two and a half years of exposure to the ISO 9001 upgrade, 40 percent of registered companies were delaying the upgrade.

If we look at the relationship of upper management with the organization, initiatives are accomplished through people more than systems. Even periodic reports on financials require a controller or an assistant to do a presentation so that probing questions can be asked because they are ultimately accountable for performance. If something needs to get done, they will put someone on it rather than trust a system to make it happen. The reliance is clearly on people rather than systems until you start getting closer to the product. I believe there are some basic reasons for this.

First, they just don't have the time to really understand the entire system so they have meetings and discussions with the people in charge to know the system status. Upper management spends a tremendous amount of time in meetings, on the phone, or skimming over e-mail and reports.[5] Because of this need for direct communication, the second reason is trust. Top managers must have someone who has knowledge of the important issues so they can obtain reliable information for decision making. Finally, they must have a person in place so there is accountability. They must have someone ultimately responsible for ensuring that the data are correct and properly interpreted. If something gets out of whack, someone in charge must resolve it and provide feedback on the status.

I am not saying that top management has disregard for systems; on the contrary, I think they see systems as essential. I don't believe for one minute that any manager would not see value in having a systematic way of doing things. The problem arises when responsibilities are delegated downward to the point that specific knowledge of systems and any weaknesses are off their radar.

Since organizational performance is critical, one way of showing management commitment is through resources, whether capital or labor. When an organization has a high-level position like a vice president or director of quality reporting directly to the president, it can show a strong commitment to quality. That position provides a voice for quality in the high-level strategies and board meetings. If that position is several levels removed from the president, performance measures are probably more recognized than audit results on specifics of the quality management system.

DIFFERENT POSITIONS
HAVE DIFFERENT PERSPECTIVES

The answer to the question of whether we believe quality system audits are important depends not only on whom you ask but more importantly on their previous experience with them. If an organization has an effective internal audit program and implements opportunities suggested by second- and third-party audits, those involved with the audit will likely see great benefits. If the internal audit program is solely for compliance to a standard, there is most likely resistance to suggestions from independent auditors as well, and it is looked at as more of a dictate than an opportunity to improve.

Different positions will have different perspectives of audits. Top management should want to know if their systems are well defined and implemented. They should also want to know if effectiveness measures are accurate and reflect on the systems. You would think they would demand audit report summaries for review; we know there are mixed reviews on this one.

A vice president or director of quality reporting directly to the president should see great importance in third-party audits. I believe they should also be the driver of internal audit programs to identify strengths and weaknesses within the organization so they can develop future quality strategies. If structured and implemented properly, the top management team will find great value in them.

Quality managers further removed from top management find value in the internal and third-party audits because they recognize that the organization could be better through adherence to the systems. They know that some of the systems aren't followed as defined, so it is important to find out how far the departments have strayed. Audits can identify those issues and hopefully bring enough attention to get management to resolve them. Audits also help them to clean up loose ends and encourage a review of the manual.

Supplier quality personnel have strong beliefs about the importance of sound quality systems but I have found mixed feelings about audits. That is because they have seen a vendor receive excellent audit results only to have serious performance issues with that same supplier. They will also tell you they have faith in the results of some but not all audits depending on the team that conducts it.

Operations managers have a good feel for overall system performance from their various feedback mechanisms, so they may not feel systems audits are necessary if they have had no experience with effective programs. They wear their manufacturing hat that says if the equipment is running properly and they are staffed to do the maintenance activities, the productivity numbers will look good. If the reject numbers are low and quality isn't screaming, life is good.

Finding value in audits really depends on a person's previous experience with good versus bad system audits and the commitment to the directives of those systems. I happen to believe that the internal audit can have a tremendous influence on a manager's perception of the quality system. If an organization doesn't perform audits, it sends the message that the quality system is not valued enough for the organization to make sure you are using it. A similar message is sent if it is a weak audit program that only looks for compliance to a standard. If an organization has a well-defined audit program, the message sent is that it is important for the organization to know if the system is understood, implemented, and effective.

The challenge then is identifying what makes for a good versus mediocre internal audit program. In the next chapter, I will review some important issues that I believe relate to the prominence and value of systems audits. Much of this relates to the development of supplier quality in larger organizations, which I believe has been a key driver for the increasing emphasis on third-party and internal audits.

In the second part of this book, I will discuss quality systems concepts because people hold varying degrees of understanding and interpretation. I believe we should have a mutual understanding of systems, and one way to do this is to discuss some key concepts in this book. Quality systems audits are useless unless there is a defined system to audit. This seems very obvious, yet some books on auditing assume that the reader understands what is meant by the quality system. More importantly, there is also the assumption that the author and the reader have the same understanding of a quality system, so this must be addressed as well.

ENDNOTES

1. ANSI/ISO/ASQ Q9001:2000, *Quality Management Systems Requirements* (Milwaukee: ASQ Quality Press, 2000).
2. Henry Mintzberg, "The Manager's Job," a paper published in a text by Joyce S. Osland, David A. Kolb, and Irwin M. Rubin, *The Organizational Behavior Reader,* Seventh ed. (Upper Saddle River, NJ: Prentice Hall, 2001).
3. Ibid.
4. Phyllis Naish, "Why Companies Aren't Making the Change," *Quality Progress* (September 2002).
5. Ibid.

2

Increasing Demands on Quality Systems and Methods

In the previous chapter, we discussed beliefs about quality systems audits based on prior experience and position. It is clear that auditing product has been a proven tool of quality for many years, but when it comes to auditing systems, there have been varying opinions on the value it provides and the degree to which this can be accomplished.

Logic will tell you that if we have an important system established, we must have some way or another to verify if it is being followed. We must also know if it is working. Some argue that measures are sufficient, while the ISO 9001 standard will say that you need to conduct an internal audit of the system, in addition to a third-party audit, to verify that it is properly implemented and meeting the requirements of the standard. In the one case, you assume the system is properly implemented because the measures are showing that it is working, while the latter method requires investigation to make a decision based on fact.

Quality systems audits have been around for a long time in the form of external audits of suppliers, but the focus on third-party and internal audits has increased dramatically in the past 10 or 15 years primarily due to the ISO 9001 standard. Twenty-five years ago, our organization didn't perform internal quality system audits, yet now we have an entire methodology for this task. This is not to say other organizations were not conducting internal quality audits at that time, but it was not common practice in industry until it became a requirement within a widely accepted standard (automotive standards use ISO 9001 as their foundation).

I believe the internal (first-party) and third-party audits can bring tremendous benefits to organizations, because they have for ours. But there is much disagreement from management on this subject, as reflected in the opinions of surveys of quality professionals. The problem is that significant improvement in mature systems has not been dramatic but gradual, and must be viewed over time, even in years and decades.

With upper management's focus on performance, verifying compliance to systems is probably not high on their list of priorities. Their argument is that the efforts and cost to perform audit activity should be minimized because the results don't justify it. It is the lesser of two evils; not doing it will mean losing registration and ultimately the loss of important customers. Since there are other more timely measures telling you if the key systems are operating properly, performing internal audits becomes primarily a compliance activity.

HISTORICAL VIEW OF QUALITY SYSTEMS

Historically, some organizations embraced systems audits but most did not. Japan led this pursuit many years ago by developing registration to a national quality standard while the rest of the world resisted, eventually following years later. I believe history proves that the ultimate driving force behind widespread implementation of systems audits, whether third-party, external, or internal, was the customer.

In the middle of the twentieth century, Japan was trying to recover from World War II. With the help of the U.S. government, much effort was going into revitalizing a weakened nation with severely limited resources. Since the perception of the world market was that Japan produced inferior quality, Japanese industry leaders believed that they would need strong product specification standards as well as quality standards to reverse this perception. The major Japanese industries worked with America to develop consistent product standards and studied the writings of quality gurus W. Edwards Deming and Joseph Juran and the translated works of Armand Feigenbaum.

The task was huge because the government and the major industries were not just focused on a few corporations but rather on raising the perception of Japanese quality for all industries in the country. Although in Part II we will go into this in more detail, it is significant in the history of quality that they put such a national focus on the quality movement, and standardization "was a key vehicle for consolidating the quality movement."[1] Japan created the JIS (Japanese Industrial Standards) and then developed a system registration against these standards through third-party audits.

Utilizing this methodology, companies could develop their quality systems and register them through JIS certification. Japan not only developed a national focus toward ensuring quality but also systematically raised its level within the entire country through registration to a quality standard. According to Garvin, their national quality movement required a common language, disseminated through massive training programs for all employees from the executive to the operator.[2]

In the United States, the story was dramatically different. While much of the world was rebuilding from World War II, America was providing the products and materials. We could not build enough to satisfy the consumer, so effort was clearly focused on mass production. Industry standards were important for commonality, but the focus on quality standards was not to the degree as seen in Japan. This mind-set thrived for many years until the competition forced us to recognize their importance.

In Japan, they were persistently building their expertise in quality as they focused on standardized work methods, constantly improving based on best practice. In the United States, we were fighting against standards in the form of laws and tradition, creating a cultural focus on the message of the "anti-establishment" and freedom of choice. The good news is that this created a culture of innovation that propelled us farther into the techno-future than we could have imagined. The bad news is that it also created some resistance to well-defined systems in the workplace.

In the 1970s, competition from Japan rose to prominence. While America was producing at an ever-increasing rate, gas prices were skyrocketing. Detroit still had the mass-production mentality of the 1950s. What they offered the American consumer was style and power. Japan offered good gas mileage and raised the bar on product quality and reliability. In just a few years, American automobiles that were once admired for style and quality were starting to be considered inferior to Japanese models, along with motorcycles, air conditioners, and major appliances.

As we moved from the 1970s to the 1980s, American industry seemed overwhelmed by the competition and fears spread that we would lose our industrial base to Japan. They competed on price and quality to such an extent that manufacturing in this country was desperate to learn the quality methods that had made Japan successful. Books on quality systems and methods became popular because the competition produced a better alternative for the consumer; it was driving us to change.

Some organizations embraced quality systems while others promoted "Buy American" campaigns. Unions told the nation to just "not buy it," but the consumer was driven by a desire for value. America was an innovator, so many put their faith in technology. Companies did try quality circles and empowering employees, but to many, changing the culture in the workplace was too slow. Companies looked to robots rather than the operator to standardize work methods. They needed change fast in order to compete or they would lose more market share. But the focus was more on creativity than systems, and I believe that the disdain for standards and rules from the 1960s was still alive and well.

Even into the later 1980s when the ISO standard was released, it was viewed with skepticism in American industry while embraced in other parts of the world. Automotive companies created their own standards for suppliers, who eventually joined together to create the AIAG (Automotive Industry Action Group) standards in the QS-9000 series, while the auto manufacturers themselves focused on innovation and technology.

FOCUS ON IMPROVING SUPPLIER QUALITY

Prior to the major OEMs (original equipment manufacturers) recognizing the international standards, many suppliers would have external customer audits at regular intervals if they had a large customer base. Most large corporations had dedicated personnel responsible for this task. Multi-member audit teams were regularly sent to their suppliers to spend the good part of a week auditing the quality system. They would divide up to scrutinize engineering, manufacturing, quality, purchasing, and management. This required key plant personnel tied up for hours and sometimes days at a time, explaining their systems and showing documentation to prove the activity occurred, not to mention all the hours of preparation.

I became a supplier quality engineer in 1990 and remained in that position for nine years, the last four at a senior engineer level. I worked with numerous component suppliers of our organization. Larger companies we surveyed had quality personnel dedicated to entertaining regular customer audits and assuring that their system would pass. Customer audit teams ranged from seriously dedicated to the occasional walk-through. The underlying value was verification that the supplier met the requirements so business could be conducted.

Many supplier plant and quality managers candidly felt that system audits, both external and internal, were a necessary evil to satisfy customer demands. The reason they felt this was because so many of their resources were tied up in preparation and support of those audits. I heard stories of half-day customer audits and afternoon golf outings. Some quality managers played the role of a salesman, only their product was a system of quality tools so they could pass the survey and continue doing business.

In my company, audits were called supplier surveys. The purchasing agent (buyer) and supplier quality engineer would team up and typically spend one day at the supplier's facility auditing the quality system. For more complicated components and processes, we would also include a product engineer. We utilized a scoring guide with bulleted questions resulting in a scored rating, which allowed us to classify them as excellent, good, conditional, or unacceptable. The guide was based on quality standards in a supplier manual issued to each supplier. In my experience, we could tell within one day if a supplier had a good quality system or not.

I recall performing audits on smaller companies with workforces of approximately 50 employees. These companies would entertain teams consisting of four to six auditors from larger corporations auditing their system for nearly a week. This occurred because it was a mandate from their customer's quality system to ensure that the suppliers met requirements. We all struggled with this because most systems had not evolved to the point of flexibility to address smaller companies. The directive in the industry seemed to be simply ensuring that the audits occurred.

In the height of this community audit activity, you could see that a change was imminent because the many audits were not adding any value to the product itself; they were merely verifying conformance. Over time, many of the larger suppliers became experts at the audit and would have all the documentation so well organized that our presence was a "ho-hum" event. Many developed excellent systems and hung numerous awards on their walls, yet all of these efforts were not necessarily assuring defect-free product, and huge resources were spent within the manufacturing industry to send their teams in for assessments.

We sometimes had serious issues with suppliers that had quality awards on their wall from customers. I remember an incident where one division in an organization was performing a survey because of poor performance while the other division arrived with great fanfare to award them a "Best Supplier" plaque. Clearly, a good quality system did not mean good quality product. A change in the methodology was in order.

Movement Toward ISO

Management began questioning the value of performing systems audits. Companies began moving away from their own external-customer audits to a third-party assessment so they embraced registration to ISO. According to a study published in *Quality Progress,*[3] the four most common reasons for using the ISO standards, in order of importance, are:

- Customer or marketing demands

- Needed improvement in processes or systems

- Desire for global deployment

- Company not focused

In this study, 85 percent were using the international standard because of marketing or customer demands. In other words, only 15 percent of the respondents moved toward the ISO standard because of internally driven reasons, such as improving their own quality systems. This was also supported in a 2004 survey of registered companies, in which 82 percent said registration was mandatory for doing business.[4] The underlying value was the need to satisfy the customer if they required ISO, and if they didn't, the majority chose not to register. What drove the customers to initiate demands for compliance to the ISO standard?

The audit was considered important by the customer to ensure that an acceptable quality system was present. However, it was a sizeable undertaking to coordinate the personnel required to manage a large supplier base. When the European community recognized the ISO standard as a must for doing business, the standard swiftly gained credibility. Management had found a new and less expensive way to obtain value from audit activity.

Throughout industry, management began to realize that costs of maintaining their supplier quality department were considerable. They concluded that a common standard was a good, cost-effective idea, and the ISO 9000 series gained prominence. As the standard gained exposure, companies began to realize the value they would gain through registration. It would reduce large travel expenses and free up valuable resources, previously committed to the customer audits, to focus on product improvement rather than system conformance. Quality system requirements had "boxed them in" to auditing commitments, and now this new standard would free management from what was now perceived as a non-value-added activity.

Suppliers could also change their focus from entertaining numerous customer audits to defect reduction and product improvement. Instead of dedicating guides for multiple audits throughout the year, they could focus on the ISO certification. This new approach in quality management added value to business and seemed like a win/win situation.

Then in 1992, General Motors executive Ignacio Lopez dramatically changed the customer–supplier relationship, and costs became the big driver and growing mantra in the industry. He became known as the man who initiated the culture of price cuts. In that year, he demanded price rollbacks from GM suppliers and tore up existing contracts.[5] It was called the "brutalization" of the industry.

In 1993, Lopez bolted for Volkswagen, taking GM trade secrets with him. GM CEO John F. Smith Jr. appointed Rick Wagoner the role of peacemaker to sooth the angry supplier base. Lopez left behind a group of enraged suppliers, upset at his tearing up of contracts and other aggressive tactics.[6] He also left $4 billion in price concessions. Wagoner sought cooperation and listened to suppliers' concerns but gave back few of the concessions.

Piece price had always dominated the focus, but it seemed to increase in intensity now. It was a quick and easy way to improve the bottom line, if you had enough clout. Since the customer was focused on costs, customer satisfaction became cost reduction. The drive to reduce costs in many cases refocused the emphasis of the supplier from quality systems to improving operation efficiencies and technology in order to survive.

The middle 1990s saw the introduction of difficult times for supplier quality. Although we still valued supplier partnerships, there was a growing emphasis on price by the purchasing department. This was expected considering the growing global competition and the strategy of the automotive industry, but it created conflicts.

Demand for Low Costs

In many ways, there seemed to be a dichotomy of interests. On one hand, quality was demanding lower defect rates through improved technology, in addition to asking for registration to the ISO standard so we wouldn't need to add costs by performing audits. On the other hand, purchasing was quoting other sources and demanding that suppliers drive down costs. In some cases, organizations were forced to rely on ISO or QS (automotive) registration because it severely challenged resources to audit all the new suppliers that were being added. Both were preaching partnerships, which came to mean charge-backs, sharing in warranty costs, low piece price, and low defect rates. In more recent years, the dialogue has not changed; only the purveyors of this model have gotten more creative and the competition more intense.

General Electric Company CEO Jack Welch has been recognized as the CEO of the century, even of the millennium, by many business publications. He has been regularly quoted, his tactics studied in business courses, and he is a best-selling author. Let's look at what "Neutron Jack" did regarding relationships with suppliers. In January 1998, he stressed the need to globalize production to remain cost-competitive. This was a regular topic in his annual pep talk to GE's top managers but this time he also insisted that they demand suppliers follow suit.[7] He was now preaching supplier partnerships meaning overseas facilities to drive improvement to his bottom line.

Welch had cut costs for the last decade as he shifted production and investment to lower-wage countries. He created a new paradigm in industry that many were following.

Under his guidance, GE's U.S. workforce plunged by nearly 50 percent while foreign employment doubled. After those marching orders were given in 1998, the Aircraft Engines (GEAE) unit of GE told dozens of suppliers to cut prices by 14 percent. GEAE's operating profit had grown 80 percent in the four years prior to the new demands, so continuous improvement was literally "continuously squeezing more." The bar had been raised, and not only was the supplier base expected to reduce costs, but now they had to redefine their business strategies by relocating to lower-wage countries.

In forcing suppliers to relocate overseas, this meant the supplier base had to install its processes in another country to reduce costs yet ensure that they met the same quality requirements. There is obviously no grace period for the learning curve. Rather than create a quality culture over time, they would need to do it almost overnight. This global philosophy was forcing manufacturers to reevaluate the efficiencies and effectiveness of both their processes and their systems, with no degradation of quality. To uproot a company or build a relationship overseas without affecting quality requires excellent controls and standardized procedures.

In March 2001, a *Business Week* article titled "Dark Days for Detroit's Suppliers" again detailed efforts to reduce costs through supplier price reductions.[8] In this article, DaimlerChrysler ordered parts manufacturers to accept a five percent price cut by January 2002 followed by an additional 10 percent over the following two years. The article went on to suggest this as the last "fatal squeeze" on parts suppliers that had been going on for the last decade. Many suppliers refused to cave in on the cuts and some were opening their books to Chrysler executives and pleading "show me where I can get five percent."

It is obvious that there are a couple of key issues at play here: top management commitment to performance and a highly competitive environment. An appropriate old saying is "actions speak louder than words." In this case, the clear direction from management is that supplier partnership means better value to maintain and improve their bottom line. Performance means low costs and high value: for purchasing its piece price, for quality its no warranty and rework cost, and for upper management it means meeting their targets with no "surprises." It also means that the competition is willing to step in given the opportunity, whether in this country or overseas.

The large corporations are the big drivers in industry since they have such impact on numerous other industries in their supplier base. They have moved to a "continuously squeezing more" model (see Figure 2.1) that is cyclical and very focused on value.

For many years, quality has been a marketing tool and offensive strategy in proclaiming better or best quality in comparison to competitors. It's now also a defensive strategy in not having substandard quality in the eyes of the customer. Quality management systems have become critical to management for one key reason: you must know you have control of your product because with all the competition, if you slip up it will be detrimental to your business.

However, since quality lives in this environment of "continuously squeezing more," quality is also under pressure to find better and leaner methods of accomplishing its tasks. The customer has alternatives so they can present strong demands, resulting in the

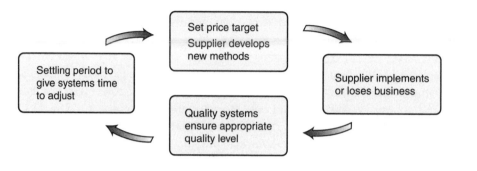

Figure 2.1 "Continuously squeezing more" model.

supplier's management pushing lean because of the pressure on cost. That's why there was such a push for reliable third-party assessments; they lean up the quality department, yet the organization can get the same or a better-perceived benefit. They also tend to put certain aspects of the quality system ahead of others in importance. Let's explore this further.

The concept of quality in terms of defects and reliability of product has changed to the point that it is now simply expected. We have moved from percent defective to parts per million defect rates and are now swiftly heading for "no defects allowed." Quality systems traditionally focused on defect correction through root cause analysis and the eight-discipline problem-solving methodology. These are effective for solving special-cause variation, but in most cases, parts per million defects tend to be due to common cause variation, which demands more sophisticated methods. FMEA (failure mode and effects analysis), design of experiments, and process improvement, in addition to problem-solving methods such as the Six Sigma methodology are tools for consistently reaching those high-quality levels.

One result of this change is the necessity of design change and process control. In essence, this means eliminating special-cause variation. It also means controlling normal variation to the point that it is well within required specifications. This goes well beyond performing a 50-piece capability study to verify that the product meets requirements. It requires real-time demonstrated control of the process so any change or influence on that process can be reacted to prior to it resulting in nonconforming material.

The other result is a strong focus on error-proofing techniques that provide both suppliers and their customers with confidence that product will be 100 percent defect-free. This is necessary in processes that cannot be controlled to prevent defects from occurring. Where in the past labor could be added for 100 percent inspection purposes, it is now only a short-term activity because it is not a statistically valid solution. Even if that inspection is using functional or hard gauging, it is not completely effective to reach no-defect levels because the operator could simply miss the defect. Automatic gauging or production fixtures that will not allow nonconforming product to move on in the process are the only effective means.

The ideal situation is a stable system, which occurs when a product changes little. The processes can be stabilized and previous errors in the system can be resolved through process improvement or error-proofing. However, this is not reality. Quality has become a prominent word for management as a big part of an overall strategy for pursuing value, but based on history, the big driving force is always the consumer.

Consumer Demands for Quality

The interesting point here is that rather than being an outspoken and demanding consumer, he or she drives improvements in quality and value by their ability to purchase and having an alternate choice. What is the customer demanding? I believe the ultimate customer, the end user, expresses demand for value through three avenues:

1. A strong desire for or a keen interest in change

2. An ability to exploit the marketplace

3. A willingness to be exploited by the marketers

The consumer wants change because the marketplace has presented so much innovation and change in the last 50 years and at such an accelerating rate. Products offer solutions like convenience, improved safety, new looks through better materials and styling, improved availability, and at lower costs. The marketplace has created a tremendous appetite for change in the consumer. The end user has learned to expect and demand it.

Through innovation and change, the marketplace has also created accessibility to information. Just investigate buying a car. Any number of Web sites allow you to compare prices of used vehicles, tell you problems that particular model had, and offer you an opportunity to bid through an auction site to get the lowest price. Buying a new car was a dreaded experience years ago. The consumer was at a disadvantage because they didn't know about quality or what they would end up spending. Now they investigate quality and performance history, compare all the available options, and review the dealer's costs, all in a few minutes on their home computer.

With less expensive purchases, consumers tend to buy based on positive past experiences or to fill an immediate need or whim, which increases the importance of name-brand recognition. Marketing plays a significant role because companies can now collect volumes of information on consumer buying habits and trends. They know what the consumer wants, where he or she is headed in the future, and how they must present information to get their attention. They can move consumers by creating a need for a product or service. In other words, the consumer has a willingness to be exploited because they ultimately benefit from it.

Managing Change

The challenging factor becomes desire for change and from the marketing perspective, product enhancements and differentiation. While industry and its supplier base have driven quality to higher levels through design change and process control, the ideal situation would be product stability. This is not possible because competition for the purchase of the product means innovation, flexibility, and enhancements. This forces industry to build the ability for change within their systems.

To accomplish this, there should be well-defined interfaces between marketing and product design. Management must have long-range planning abilities to not only address capacity and profitability of the organization, but to provide the equipment and resources to meet those changing needs. This places great emphasis on advanced product quality planning and strong systems for new equipment integration methods. This also includes methods for flexible manufacturing and excellent change control systems.

Change and high quality, with the significant pressure of continuously squeezing more, demand significant improvements in the move from second- to third-party quality systems audits. They must go beyond verifying compliance to a broad standard. The standard itself must refocus to put greater emphasis on the important systems and techniques necessary to meet today's demands.

EMPHASIS ON PERFORMANCE

ISO 9001:2000 has moved to a focus on process and measures, discussed in more detail in later chapters. This addresses the need for integrated systems that are developed around important activities. Requiring measures with results brings the concept of performance into the audit. Companies must now show that their systems are effective; through quantitative measures the automotive industry has taken this upgrade and used it as a foundation of their requirements for advanced quality planning, measurement analysis, process control, equipment and die qualification, and product approval methods. Improvements have been made to address these critical issues in an attempt to ensure value from registration to the standard.

We have discussed the change from external-customer audits to third-party audits because it offered opportunities to refocus resources. However, there is also the underlying perception that systems audits do not offer value but are rather a necessary evil in the quality systems we have created. Unless they also focus on performance and those critical systems necessary to ensure high quality, there is a low perception of their value to management.

Even the move to third-party audits is suspect because after they pushed for registration to ISO, many companies continued to conduct their customer (second-party) audits. This was because they had serious concerns about the ISO standard and the capability of the registrars to identify performance issues. There have been significant upgrades in the ISO 9001:2000 standard addressing many of these concerns through emphasis on performance. However, there are still certain aspects of the quality system that demand greater emphasis.

Customers can communicate specific demands on performance and systems to the supplier. Unless they formally visit the supplier, they must rely on a third party to affirm that these critical systems are in place. In cases where heightened requirements are needed, there may always be a need to prequalify a supplier through assessment teams. Once qualified, registration audits may be sufficient given an emphasis on strong performance measures.

ENDNOTES

1. David A. Garvin, *Managing Quality* (The Free Press, 1988): 185.
2. Ibid., 195.
3. Charles A. Cianfrani, Joseph J. Tsiakals, and John E. (Jack) West, *The ASQ ISO 9000:2000 Handbook* (Milwaukee: ASQ Quality Press, 2002): 3.
4. Dirk Dusharme, "ISO 9001 Survey," *Quality Digest* (July 2004).
5. Theresa Forsman, "Dark Days for Detroit's Suppliers," *Business Week* (March 5, 2001).
6. Kathleen Kerwin and Joann Muller, "Reviving GM," *Business Week* (December 1, 1999).
7. "Welch's March to the South," *Business Week* (December 6, 1999).
8. Theresa Forsman, "Dark Days for Detroit's Suppliers," *Business Week* (March 5, 2001).

3

Is There Value in the Internal Audit Program?

In researching material for this book, I found 10 articles specifically addressing internal audits in their title, published over the last four years in *Quality Progress* and *Quality Digest* magazines. I was interested in getting some overall idea of the changing perceptions of the audit in addition to specific concepts and ideas. Breaking them down into some general topics, I found the following:

- 20 percent discussed auditing to the ISO 9001:2000 standard.

- 10 percent discussed using precedents to provide more consistency.

- 70 percent began with the assumption that we needed to improve the audits.

  - One said auditors had no respect and deserved it.

  - One suggested we need to devote more time and effort to get benefits.

  - Five specifically stated we need to add more value to audits.

In the article "Internal Auditing: The Big Lies,"[1] audits and auditors "enjoyed the same level of regard as a dead otter." The author suggested they deserve it because of a reputation for nitpicking, not listening, speaking in unfamiliar terms, and performing tasks without relevance to the organization. Although humorous, the article's perception of internal auditing concerns does border on the trivial.

The author stated that the majority of auditors base their auditing on certain principles they do not question nor understand. The primary "lie" is that auditing should be focused on compliance. Most audits focus on two areas: do the procedures meet the standards? and are the procedures implemented? Unfortunately, this scope is limited and does not provide information related to the usefulness of the activities for the organization.

The quality manager knows the quality systems and has a general idea of which ones are functioning well and what areas are in need of work. He or she reviews information every day to know if there are serious concerns. The internal audit becomes an opportunity to publicly state these nagging deficiencies and hopefully get management support to improve the system. If there are big issues that everyone already knows, they will be identified through other means such as defect reporting and corrective actions. The result is that issues found during the audit are more procedural. Production managers typically do not lose sleep over procedural issues.

The internal audit can become a necessary evil because of ISO requirements, offering its primary value in uncovering those loose ends that need to be corrected. Since a good quality system will have strong feedback mechanisms to identify serious issues prior to any devastating effects on the customer, annual "clean-up" audits become a tool only to the quality department. These loose ends become discussions of interpretation and misunderstanding, which generates the perception of nitpicking.

The quality manager or someone knowledgeable in quality will methodically audit the quality system, just prior to the registrar, to ensure everything is in place and functioning. This satisfies the requirement and updates the manual against the system, but it loses its sense of value because the results are not necessarily relevant to upper management or the organization. Seventy percent of the articles I reviewed felt that audits need to be improved and provided suggestions and techniques. The question is how do you do that?

If the quality manager is tasked with the audits as well as implementing the quality system, the workload makes it challenging to derive benefits beyond just implementation itself. A 2003 survey of quality professionals revealed that quality managers led the effort for the transition to the ISO 9000: 2000 standard. Of those working more than 40 hours per week (91 percent), a quarter of the respondents added at least 10 hours to their workweek as a result of the standard.[2]

SEARCHING FOR MORE

In 1998, during that first year of owning the internal audits, my goal was to add real value to our facility. I had audited all areas just prior to the ISO audit and identified some opportunities for improvement. I had all my documentation in order, including an audit plan, so the audit could have been considered successful. The ISO audit went well and the auditor was satisfied with my internal audit results; on paper it looked thorough, almost impressive. The management team was happy and my boss was satisfied. In fact, the registrar recognized some areas in our system as being very good so the surveillance audit was very positive. I was not satisfied.

I knew my internal audit was primarily walking around with the plant manager asking a lot of questions, per the checklist I had borrowed from one of the other divisions. It was enlightening for us because we found some areas that didn't operate quite like we thought, so I ended up tweaking the procedure. It was a concern for others because they didn't know what we were doing. Although I told the managers ahead of time, it was not well planned.

The other concern was that I had to do it. The way the checklist was written, you needed a pretty thorough grasp of the standard because it was adapted from it. Whoever performed as the lead auditor needed that ISO knowledge, or there would be a lot of blank stares on some of the sections. When I looked back on the success of our earlier programs in the company, one contributing factor I remembered was the independence of the entire process. I began wondering what other factors contributed to its success, so I began my investigation into a better methodology by going through files of our earlier corporate audit program.

In the 1980s, our company faced challenges to the business plan. We were, and are today, the largest manufacturer of small internal combustion engines in the world. All manufacturing operations in the early 1980s were in Milwaukee, Wisconsin. We had challenges from the high cost of labor and logistics because we were centralized in a northern state, removed from a customer base predominately in the south. A strike with the union ensued, which hurt business with the OEM because we didn't get them product. I was a laid-off hourly worker thinking I would never be called back, but after the strike was settled, I was again working because we were so far behind schedule. Although the workers in Milwaukee felt things couldn't be better, management was forced to develop plans to open a facility close to the customer.

In the mid-1980s, Briggs & Stratton opened the Murray, Kentucky, facility, and shortly after opened a second manufacturing plant in Poplar Bluff, Missouri. Both utilized the focus factory concept, with highly efficient operations and a skilled workforce. They also modified the quality systems from Milwaukee to better suit their business plan. By the time the mid 1990s arrived, there were three more focused factories in Rolla, Missouri; Auburn, Alabama; and Statesboro, Georgia.

During the later part of the 1980s, corporate quality initiated an internal quality systems audit. The ISO standard was officially released in 1987 and concerns arose in the engine business related to our international customers requiring it and the marketing advantage of being the first to be registered; there was also the obvious opportunity to improve our systems. The plan was to identify needs based on the results of the internal audit, update our systems to the new standard, and achieve registration. That was the goal for quality.

ALIGNING QUALITY SYTEMS

The value in the internal audit was to prepare our organization for the upgrade to ISO, but also to understand our systems and ensure that the key methods were implemented and operating effectively. Management knew the numbers looked good at the regional facilities, but there was no sure way of assessing the state of the quality systems without performing audits. The audit results allowed management to assess the various facilities and choose the best candidate at that time for the initial ISO registration, which was one of the regional plants.

We changed our audit methodology by involving divisional managers in the process to provide greater focus; those managers would be closer to the culture of the various plants in their division. The plant quality systems and manuals were updated to reflect the standard as well as improve some of the methods. The end result was that, in 1993, the

Poplar Bluff facility was the first small-engine manufacturer in the world to achieve ISO certification, with the remaining facilities registering within four years.

As I looked at the bigger picture, I realized that there was value to the corporation beyond assessing the plants for the best candidate for registration. In the years prior to building the regional facilities, all of quality reported to the same manager. This allowed the company to have one quality management system for the corporation. As the manufacture of engines moved away from the north, the reporting structure changed. Procedures and methods were revised until we had variations of our quality systems between the divisions and between the plants themselves.

The commitment to upgrade to ISO and to performing the corporate and divisional audits motivated all the plants to pull their systems together under one methodology. There was tremendous value in this because we standardized our systems by identifying the better methods within the various facilities and implementing them throughout the organization; in a sense, we implemented an internal best practice. There was also value for management because they could identify systemic issues and develop plans to improve the corporation as a whole.

Over time, our systems did improve to the point that few issues were ever found during the audits. There were always opportunities for improvement, but my understanding as well as others' was that we had sound systems, in many cases going beyond requirements, so the internal audits became more of a quick once-over to make sure everything was in order. I feel many companies are at that point, which is why there are a number of publications offering new and better auditing methods.

PROPORTIONAL TO UNDERSTANDING OF SYSTEMS

The value in the audits was proportional to our understanding of the systems. In the early days, the corporate audits offered us an opportunity to compare the facilities against a common standard and identify needs. The plants needed this support to raise their level of understanding. In our division, the methodology slowly changed and we moved audit responsibility from corporate to the division and finally to the plants. In a sense, it was a transfer of knowledge that allowed the transfer of responsibility.

After personally experiencing the various stages of systems development and changing audit responsibilities, I have come to the conclusion that the ideal situation is plant responsibility with higher-level oversight and control. In smaller organizations without a corporate office, this is not a matter of choice. This approach takes advantage of the concept of knowledge transfer and responsibility at each facility while providing an umbrella to ensure consistency of systems and the opportunity to best practice the systems of value.

The challenge in implementing this is instilling understanding of systems at levels removed from the actual operations. Corporate offices tend to have different priorities than manufacturing plants. This even occurs within one facility where those in the office don't understand what it's like on the shop floor. I believe a strong internal audit program can break down those barriers, but there first must be an understanding of the purpose of the systems and their relationship to management and the culture of the workforce.

To improve the audit, you must delve further into the systems to identify the critical aspects that must be understood by the organization. Once you understand those key aspects, you can build an effective audit program. For the purposes of this book, we must discuss systems concepts and some aspects of management theory to understand the reasons why the methodology suggested here is successful. That is the discussion in the next section.

ENDNOTES

1. Dewitt L. Beeler, "Internal Auditing: The Big Lies," *Quality Progress* (May 1999).
2. Larry Adams, "More Work, More Pay," *Quality* (July 2003).
3. Ibid.

Part II

The Challenge of Understanding the Quality Management System

Although the purpose of this book is to present concepts and tools to improve the internal quality systems audit, it is important to investigate and understand what is meant by the quality management system and the term *quality*. There are obvious reasons for this. To perform an audit, you must have criteria on which to base the audit. This is the quality management system, though the audit can also be focused on other management systems or specific activities as well. To implement a quality management system, you must have a clear definition of what you mean by quality. There should be a standard and a quality policy as a foundation on which the various quality methods and processes are based. Otherwise, it is a system without a true purpose.

There is another important reason for investigating core quality management concepts in this book. Through discussion of these concepts, we can begin to formulate strategies for increasing the value of the audit. Today you can read articles, books, and research on the audit; the information is extensive in its descriptions of the audit purpose and process, with areas of agreement and disagreement. Much of it proposes to provide new insight into obtaining more value-added audits, enhancing continuous improvement, or improving effectiveness, and some even explores the notion of combining them with the financial and accounting audits as a means to finally gain upper management support.

The shortcoming of this approach is that we are left with many good ideas and the challenge of determining how to apply them to our system, because they don't necessarily discuss the systems they are auditing. There is also the underlying assumption that we have agreement with the authors on the practical implementation of quality concepts. Logic would tell you that this is not necessarily the case. If there were differing opinions on something as specific as the audit process, we could conclude that there would also be differing opinions on the systems they will audit. If the audit truly becomes a means of evaluating effectiveness and driving continuous improvement, the auditor must understand core concepts since he or she must audit the defined system as well as the effectiveness of it.

There is a definite relationship between what we define as quality, the system we develop to ensure it, and how we measure the effectiveness of that system. If we don't have a consistent definition of quality within the organization, we may think we have agreement when the basis of our discussions is not the same. If our definition is inconsistent, the system we use to ensure it will be ineffective. Finally, our measures may show incorrect or inconsistent results if we don't have a precise definition of quality.

Unfortunately, there are so many requirements and demands placed on the management team of the organization that little thought is given to the root beliefs on which the quality systems and activities are founded. We keep very busy carrying out all the activities, not stopping to think if our purpose for doing them may have changed. The result is that we are doing things for the sake of doing them, and this can consume resources that we can't afford to waste in a competitive global environment. We must introduce a catalyst to force us to think about why we are doing what we are doing; this is the internal audit.

4

What Is Quality?

Ihave always grimaced when I read this in an article or book. As the old saying goes, "I wish I had a buck for all the times I have seen this." So why do I include it again if it has already been covered in other literature? When the term *quality* is mentioned, everyone seems to have a different definition for it. Unfortunately, that is one of the problems we have in quality; there are so many definitions of it and they are not consistent. This isn't so important between different companies but within one organization it is, especially if the definition is different than the customer's. The key point in this section is that the term *quality* is a foundational concept that we build on, so we must be clear on its meaning. Otherwise, you risk building an entire system around something that has different meanings.

There are very basic definitions such as "meets customer requirements" or "conformance to specifications." The quality gurus have defined it with concepts of fitness for use (Juran), the loss a product causes to society after being shipped (Taguchi), and the total composite of product and service characteristics of marketing, engineering, manufacture, and maintenance through which the product in use will meet the expectations of the customer (Feigenbaum). There can be any number of sound definitions for quality but the only one that really matters is how you define it in your company based upon the expectations of the customer, and how that is integrated into your business. Quality is defined by the results it achieves and what you need to do to get there.

The reality is that the definition will be somewhat unique for each company, even though the wording may be similar. Key attributes deemed important regarding quality in my company might be significantly different at yours. For example, if you are in a job shop with one-piece product flow, conformance to specification probably means strict adherence to very detailed specifications for highly skilled employees. If you are in high-volume manufacturing, which is my background, consistency in work methods and error-proofing are far more important. If we don't define some specifics of what we mean by quality, we think we are discussing the same thing and have agreement when in fact, we are miles apart.

The customer will have the most significant impact on your definition of quality; it depends heavily on the product and its ultimate effect on the consumer. If it is a medical device or safety related feature, government regulation demands specific controls and tests to ensure a high level of quality. Highly technical products with high end-user costs will demand greater detail in the level of control. Much of this has been in place for years for these companies so those industries tend to have more sophisticated quality systems driven by the demands of the marketplace.

Quality has become an important marketing tool and the level of expectation of the consumer has risen because of this. People just won't purchase a product or service perceived to have lower quality anymore unless there is some overriding attribute such as low cost, given that the product still fits their need. They accept trade-offs but their ability to compare value and make a wise choice is better than ever because of easy access to product information and comparison studies. A company must have a clear strategy based on knowledge of their position in the marketplace, and their definition of quality must support this.

IMPORTANT TO DEFINE

It is important to define quality within the organization because, otherwise, employees will have varying meanings. If the employee is ultimately responsible for his or her work, which should be the case, they must clearly know what is meant by quality. Work instructions or visual aids should define the specific attributes to be monitored and controlled. Training programs provide an understanding of the importance of following these requirements. Unfortunately, we don't always communicate the "why" to employees so they don't realize the impact of their decisions. In a sense, management inadvertently gives them free rein to develop their own reasons and perceptions of quality, creating a subculture different than what is believed to be the case from the top.

Defining quality within middle management is more difficult because how it is defined has great impact on something they are very concerned about and that is performance. For example, if a mandate comes down through top management that they must strictly adhere to the new quality system, resistance will occur if the definition is merely conformance to requirements. Adherence will be difficult to enforce since middle managers realize that quality is not well defined because there is a subculture out there that operates under a different system.

In my experience with various organizations, strict adherence to all requirements is not a widely practiced discipline because experience and practice over time reveal that certain characteristics are important while others do not cause customer complaints or performance issues. This is the philosophy of "if it ain't broke, don't fix it." We also may have so many specifications in large organizations that we don't know even what they all are.

INFLUENCE OF THE SUBCULTURE

The subculture grows in organizations because specifications will not be changed for various reasons. Requests from manufacturing to make the design consistent with the process are denied because of theoretical stack-ups, external requirements, and lack of resources, or pure opinion that it should be done another way. Product design is also aware of the subculture and reacts accordingly by specifying tighter tolerances because manufacturing tends to run a little outside the spec.

Operations management and employees know that engineers specify tighter tolerances because experience tells them they usually don't have problems if certain parts exceed limits. For this reason, manufacturing struggles with meeting some of the specs. That's why production control has a cartoon hanging in their office with a caption that reads "there comes a point in time when you need to shoot the engineers and get on with production." When quality is not clearly and consistently defined, you have the product development subculture shown in Table 4.1.

Upper management doesn't know or act like they don't know that the subculture exists. They tend to believe in systems for everyone else and expect them to follow them. This is because by nature of their position they must have gone outside the system to create new value and draw attention to their exceptional performance to rise to that level. They tend to believe that if they state it, it happens that way, and don't want to hear that there are "subsystems" with their own sets of norms in the organization. They want to feel that they are in total control.

Middle management is really in the middle, per their title, and is afraid to raise this issue because of management by objectives (performance reviews) and peer pressure not to let the "cat out of the bag." There will need to be explanations of how things got this way, making the easier path to simply continue to manage the subculture while maintaining performance objectives. Operators and hands-on technical personnel only know they need to get product out the door so they run as best as they can with the tools management gives them.

Many people at the operations level of the organization believe the subculture to be the reality that the defined quality systems are a necessary evil whose purpose is to satisfy some government or financial requirement and provide jobs for the quality

Table 4.1　Product development subculture.

Project review	Test results	Conclusion
Tollgate meeting with upper management	Initial design failed test	Manufacturing did not run product to specification
Update meeting with manufacturing facility	Initial design failed test	Engineering set the tolerances too tight for the process

department. Quality is defined in great detail in some areas where we have confidence that it is followed as stated. It is not defined very well in other areas because:

- We have inconsistencies and we don't want to get caught in an audit.

- We can't get everyone to agree on one method.

- We aren't sure what we should do.

Quality must be defined because it forces us to deal with the skeletons in our closets and honestly exchange ideas and methodologies to develop the best practices within our organizations.

Although this scenario may be extreme, it does exist in all organizations to some degree. The challenge in organizations is consistency of understanding and intent. Top management is clearly responsible for developing the organization's definition of quality. They must address how quality relates to the customer, the management team, and the employees. Most importantly, they must ensure that it is adhered to and take appropriate action when it is not. The quality policy is the vehicle for defining quality, the quality management system comprises the methods and techniques for carrying it out, and the measures and internal audit are the means of ensuring that it is appropriately practiced and effective.

AUDITING FOR UNDERSTANDING

A quality audit should investigate where quality is defined and the relationship of the definition to the quality system. Has top management really defined the term *quality?* Defining quality requires a lot of discussion and disagreement to come to a final decision. It can be ignored and you can still have a quality system. However, your organization is then supporting the quality subculture by not clearly defining what it really means.

Has management communicated its definition of quality throughout the company? The goal should be a consistent and accurate understanding of quality throughout the organization, both in management and on the shop floor. Auditing for understanding in the workforce will not only reveal if quality is more than a phrase on a badge but will identify what various subcultures exist. This becomes valuable information for management and employees on how to integrate the message of quality into the organization. This in turn identifies the quality audit as an important tool that adds value to management decision making.

5

The Quality Policy

Many organizations identify their high-level business strategies in a mission statement, which is a declaration of an organization's principles, purpose, and objectives.[1] It defines what the firm believes to be its uniqueness while also providing inspiration to all the stakeholders. It's what they post on Web sites, print in the annual report, and hang on walls. They may have one for the corporation as well as one for each division. Ultimately, its intent is to provide an overall belief and purpose to influence decision making.

Quality's mission statement is the quality policy. According to the ISO 9000 family of standards, the *quality management system* is defined as a system to establish quality policy and quality objectives and to achieve those objectives. Just as an organization utilizes its mission statement as a focus for business strategy, it also needs a focus for its quality commitments and ideals. This should be the quality policy. According to clause 3.2.4 of *ISO 9000:2000 Fundamentals and vocabulary,* a quality policy is the overall intention and direction for quality within an organization, which is formally expressed by top management.

I have gone through a transition in my life. In the past, I would read mission statements or quality policies and wonder if anyone really meant it. Maybe you think that now. Defining a high-level statement about quality looks nice in a manual or on a Web site, but how do you put it into practice? Much time is spent discussing wording to ensure just the right meaning and then it sits in a document, like an ideal to look toward but not something you do on a daily basis.

In graduate school, we had a class on strategic management. The grade was determined by class presentations by each team analyzing two organizations for their competitive strengths. This included understanding their mission and performing a SWOT analysis (strength–weakness–opportunity–threat), a financial analysis, and finally recommending strategies. It started to dawn on me that many successful companies actually took this mission statement seriously. It became obvious when you looked at their strategies and performance because they fit well in the mission. The professor discussed this in some detail with the class, identifying strong and weak statements. The message sunk in.

The quality management system and all the tools, decisions, and actions that we take must be founded on a common theme. I firmly believe that and so do the recognized experts in the field of quality. This is because it is a must in the ISO 9000:2000 standard, and before ISO it was promoted by such esteemed quality minds as J. M. Juran.

Organizations need to drive a stake in the ground regarding their meaning of quality. Per the standard, it should be the "overall intention and direction for quality within an organization . . ." and make the bold statement to the world as to what they will commit. The audit needs to look for this statement of quality because if it isn't there, quality commitment is not defined. The quality policy should also align with the mission statement and core principles of the company. There can be a quality manual with procedures but without a quality policy, there is no statement of focus or commitment aligned with top management. The management review process may evaluate the quality management system for suitability, adequacy, and effectiveness but for what?

The ISO standard requires a customer focus, continuous improvement, and measures of effectiveness. The purpose of the quality policy then is for management to sit down and say (my example):

> We will meet and exceed the customer's expectations, provide the best value in our products and services, and create a work environment that promotes employee involvement and growth while continuously improving our operations.

The audit then needs to investigate and report on what the quality policy means at the different levels of the organization and how management determines that it is meeting what it has committed to in the policy. It must also align with core business strategies or it simply becomes an exercise in supporting the quality department. If the company's core strategy is to move all operations overseas to better compete globally, what value is the policy statement "create a work environment that promotes employee involvement and growth while continuously improving our operations?"

The audit can provide value through investigation into just what is meant by the various statements made by top management. It brings into focus true intent and promotes alignment of core strategies and everyday practices. In a sense, it forces management to "put its money where its mouth is."

Some authors suggest policies hanging on the wall, posted on employee Web sites, or affixed to badges as evidence management has communicated the policy. An auditor can walk around asking different employees what the quality policy is. If employees can quote, summarize, or read it from their badge it is evidence. I think there needs to be more.

When I conducted employee orientation classes as a quality manager, I spent time discussing the quality policy and what it means. I also told employees they needed to remember some basics, so that if our ISO auditor would ask, they could correctly respond. Managers in department meetings review the quality policy with employees and discuss what it means. Does this satisfy the standard? Management has conveyed its intent and communicated it to the organization. But can you really find evidence that it is implemented and effective?

Management should perform an analysis of the external and internal environment to have reliable information, so it can formulate appropriate mission statements on which its strategies are based. In the same sense, the quality policy should also arise from this analysis. There will be key factors that the organization feels must be addressed so that it is successful. These factors will help define organizational objectives.

With greater understanding of the purpose of these high-level statements, improved alignment and consistency of subsequent activities occurs and more value is obtained from the audit. Management should not only formulate the statement of its intent and meaning of quality but also define what objectives it will use for aspects of the policy statement and how it will measure them. There is obvious value in defining quality, but organizations must go further and determine how they will ensure that they are addressing each aspect of the policy. In an audit, how would you verify these statements taken from the above policy example?

1. Meet and exceed customer expectations.

2. Provide the best value in product and services.

3. Create a work environment promoting employee involvement and growth.

4. Continuously improve operations.

"Meet and exceed customer expectations" means the organization has methods to identify what the customers expect. They would also need a mechanism to monitor their efforts to ensure that they are meeting that commitment. To better define this, I would suggest some sort of matrix breaking down the policy and stating what means will be used to measure that objective (Table 5.1).

How do you "provide the best value in products or services?" This would assume you had a means of analyzing the competition since you want the best value. You would also need a good method of turning marketplace needs into specifications that in turn become outputs of the process. You would also need a method of measuring your services. What about promoting employee involvement and growth or continuously improving operations? These could also be displayed as in Table 5.2.

Since the quality policy is both a definition of quality and a commitment, management should be able to break down each key phrase into clear objectives and measures. If they can't, then it is difficult for them to argue that they comply with the policy. Unless you have some means of analyzing the competitor's products, how can you offer

Table 5.1 Quality policy matrix.

Policy	Objective	Measure
Meet and exceed customer expectations	Customer satisfaction	Customer ppm's Customer satisfaction survey Consumer marketing research study

Table 5.2   Quality policy matrix.

Policy	Objective	Measure
Provide the best value in product and services	Analyze competitors' products	Results of competitors' product compared to ours (plus/minus)
	Provide value with customer service	Customer response time
	Develop product designs that meet a need	Consumer research panel
Promote employee involvement and growth	Promote team environment	Participation in company teams
	Employee satisfaction	Employee survey
	Employee growth	Completion of training programs and participation in educational reimbursement programs
Continuously improve operations	Increased productivity	Productivity and operations efficiency
	Cost reduction goals	Cost drivers (scrap, rework)

the best value? You cannot state that you promote employee growth unless you have some means of monitoring your training and educational activities.

This exercise of breaking down those high-level statements allows management to better understand how well they support their commitments. They are no longer simple slogans hung on a wall to satisfy customers and auditors. They are fundamental statements of intent, based upon analysis of the external and internal environment, that provide focus for strategic planning and decision making. For auditors, this exercise provides a means to verify and document that the policy is implemented and effective, depending on the results. For top management, it provides a tremendous opportunity to integrate quality management into the strategic planning of the organization.

ENDNOTE

1. *Webster's New Millennium Dictionary of English* (Long Beach, CA: Lexico Publishing Group, 2003).

6

The Quality Management System

Discussion of the quality management system is complicated to say the least. There is an enormous amount of literature and research on this subject as well as a number of systems, standards, and variations of those standards. Opinions are easily found but developing an understanding of the underlying concepts and requirements of a standard and quality system is a slow process that takes effort and study. When first exposed to parts of it, there is an apparent logic that almost makes it seem easy to comprehend. Unfortunately, understanding part of the system is seeing only a piece of the puzzle, and you miss the big picture of the whole.

It is important that the auditor understand the purpose and important aspects of the system since the team will be auditing activities and processes against them. If the system is certified to a quality standard such as ISO, they must audit the quality management system to that standard to verify that all requirements are satisfactorily met and also audit to ensure that the underlying business principles are correctly addressed by the system.

The purpose of this chapter is not to discuss specific requirements of the quality management system, although some will be discussed. That is better left to other sources specifically focused on the subject because the subject is a book in itself. Instead, I felt it important to look at the quality system in general. My intent is to review general aspects of the ISO 9001 standard with discussion on the process improvements and also investigate some perceptions about standards. There are two important reasons for this approach.

First, because this is a book about auditing, we must obviously understand what we are supposed to audit and why it is important. As stated earlier, there are differences of opinion about quality systems and I feel we must have an understanding of the basics. In fact, we should always go beyond just learning the standard and system. It is important to understand the background and subsequent experiences that validate the importance of the quality system requirements.

Second, understanding some of the common perceptions about the standard and quality system will help us better focus on certain aspects that others in the quality

Table 6.1 ISO matrix.

ISO 9000	Dec. 1997	Dec. 1998	Dec. 1999	Dec. 2000	Dec. 2001	12/1/2001 9001:2000	Dec. 2002	12/1/2002 9001:2000
World total	223,299	271,847	343,643	408,631	510,616	44,388	561,747	167,210
Percent growth		21.70%	26.40%	18.90%	25.00%		10.00%	276.70%
Countries	126	141	150	157	161	98	159	134

profession have identified as a concern. Generally speaking, we all have similar problems and there are opportunities in learning from other successes and failures.

Regarding ISO 9001:2000, there is strong, consistent growth in acceptance of the standard worldwide (Table 6.1). The top 10 countries for growth in 2002 were China, Italy, Spain, Japan, Hungary, the Czech Republic, India, Switzerland, and the United States.[1]

Practically speaking, this steady growth would indicate recognition that it is a standard upon which a quality system can be built to meet quality objectives and satisfy the needs of the customer. From an OEM perspective, the standard offers an ability to assess international organizations for potential business activity without the necessity of performing extensive supplier development. From a supplier perspective, there is the perception that ISO registration provides a ticket to enter the global marketplace.

ISO AND QUALITY SYSTEM STANDARDS

Recent industry publications have been trying to address a growing confusion regarding which quality system should be implemented. *ASQ Quality Progress* (July 2003) had a cover page showing a restaurant menu listing various systems and included an editorial that discussed this confusion among its members. The issue contained articles describing seven systems listed on the menu, including related references, to address this lack of understanding. In fact, in a survey focused on the transition to ISO 9001:2000, respondents stated that even after 95 percent attained registration, 44 percent felt they needed additional help in interpreting the standard.[2] I believe this emphasizes the importance of clarifying key principles and concepts.

All organizations need a quality management system. It defines all activities that are important and agreed upon to ensure the quality of the product or service. This logic is far from unique to business. If the foundation of your house is poor, it will settle, the doors won't shut, and you will see cracks in the walls. In education, years of education build upon each other so that you have knowledge of the advanced concepts but also the basics upon which they are built. In quality, once you have established the foundation, you can then refine it with more specific activities such as Six Sigma or lean manufacturing methodologies.

The ISO 9001 international standard states very specifically what is required for a sound quality system. Over the years, there have been many arguments against various aspects of the standard, but it is used worldwide and has become a basis upon which other systems have been built. Its value not only comes from the fact that it has been developed and revised by experienced, knowledgeable experts through a working group called ISO Technical Committee 176, but because it is recognized as a common standard throughout the world.

The earlier ISO 9001 versions, prior to the 2000 release, were based on 20 elements. These were requirements where the organization had to demonstrate compliance during the certification or registration process, conducted by one of the many independent and certified organizations of registrars. These 20 elements were specific clauses in the standard that defined the quality system, management participation, customer relationships and contracts, supplier relationships, controlling the process, design and development, document and record control, continual improvement, management review, and internal audits. It was first released in 1987 and the European Community recognized it as a requirement for companies to do business in 1989.[3]

Between 1994 and 2000, the ISO 9000 series contained nine basic standards consisting of three requirement standards, a terminology standard, and five guidelines to the standard. With the 2000 release, there are now four core standards[4]:

- ANSI/ISO/ASQ Q9000-2000, *Quality management systems—Fundamentals and vocabulary*

- ANSI/ISO/ASQ Q9001-2000, *Quality management systems—Requirements*

- ANSI/ISO/ASQ Q9004-2000, *Quality management systems—Guidelines for performance improvements*

- ISO 19011, *Guidelines for quality and/or environmental management systems auditing*

Exploring the Eight Quality Principles

In the mid-1990s, ISO Technical Committee 176 researched a large amount of literature, including the various international quality awards. The result was the development of eight quality management principles. These are not new, for if you have read Deming or Juran you will find these in their opinions going back many years. But what the principles do provide are criteria that they held all of the clauses in the standard. Although these specific principles are not directly written into the standard, they are the foundational principles on which the ISO 9001 standard and ISO 9004 performance guidelines are based[5]:

1. Customer focus

2. Leadership

3. Involvement of people

4. Process approach

5. System approach to management

6. Continual improvement

7. Factual approach to decision making

8. Mutually beneficial supplier relationships

There is a strong relationship between the various principles and how they work together to provide a sound quality system. Let's look at customer focus, which is important since you must understand customer needs. Although there is obvious value in focusing on the customer, what does that really mean? Some organizations feel it means saying they have a customer focus to everyone who comes through their door. They show proof by sending out a five-question survey once each year. Is this really a customer focus?

The standard says customer information is received in the form of customer satisfaction, which is basically their perception of your organization's performance and commitment to satisfying their needs. One primary measurement tool is the customer satisfaction survey. The standard says this information also comes in the form of customer feedback, which is a measure of your performance for the customer that you can track to determine if you're getting better or not. There are also customer complaints, which relate to corrective action activity. For the purposes of this discussion, we will briefly look at feedback.

Principle 7, factual approach to decision making, states that you must develop specific quantifiable feedback, whether the customer gives you this information or not. This forces the organization to determine "how to measure customer satisfaction so you know you are succeeding." This principle moves beyond opinion to the reality of factual information.

In addition, you must have leadership (principle 2) to allocate the necessary resources and provide overall company direction. In other words, the leaders must develop a means to obtain this information from the feedback data and then determine what to do with it through objectives and goals. Leadership also means accountability, so management is responsible for taking appropriate action to deliver and obtain results.

You must also show continual improvement (principle 6) because to delight the customer, you need to continue to improve. This clearly puts the emphasis on the organization to develop effective and accurate information that reflects the needs of the customer, and it is sound logic because industries that don't change and improve eventually disappear. It also reinforces the concept of goals and the accountability of the organization in meeting them.

Leaders set direction but satisfying the customer requires others to be on board, which is the involvement of people or principle 3. Although it is important for employees to know the customer's specific requirements, they must also know the feedback. This prevents a company from just posting data and saying they met this requirement.

They must show positive trends and to do this they must involve the employees in meeting this requirement through team efforts to analyze the issues and take appropriate actions to improve.

This leads us to principle 4, the process approach. This is a significant change from the previous standard and has caused anxiety and confusion, but simply means to define the processes you use to accomplish key activities. In this example, the organization should define its "process" for getting customer feedback. This means developing a method to obtain this important information about the customer, organize it, and report it. A process approach says there is a defined, organized method to collect and report customer data.

Principle 5 is systems approach to management and a system is a group of processes and activities. This principle suggests that it may take more than one process to have a customer focus, so management must organize the appropriate processes to ensure that customer feedback is turned into positive results. You may have sales, engineering, manufacturing, and quality all working together through interactions or interfaces of various processes and activities to achieve results.

You will also have a corrective action program that controls how teams are coordinated to develop action plans and resolve specific issues. You may have a continuous improvement process where teams look to the future and determine where the organization needs to go, developing necessary strategies and action plans to achieve those goals. You may also need to develop stronger relationships with key suppliers (principle 8) since you must ensure the quality of purchased product. Although each principle is important by itself, their relationships and interactions are critical to ensure that they all work together to achieve overall organizational objectives that are focused on the customer. Although this is one brief example, you can see the relationship of the management principles and how they work together to provide a sound quality management system.

Customer Satisfaction and Feedback

The ISO 9001:2000 standard has a strong focus on measuring customer satisfaction and feedback. It addresses the argument against the earlier standard that you could be registered but still not meet the needs of the customer. During the registration audit, companies are now required to show their customer measures. Since the focus is on factual information, there must be a sound method for obtaining these measures. It is no longer acceptable to have customer surveys alone; there must be good, consistent feedback measures. This leads to a commitment by management to really understand what the customer wants in terms of quality and take specific action to meet it. Along with this, to show improvement the organization must show positive trends and goals. If you have negative trends with no actions addressing them, you will have a major nonconformance.

Our customer measures for quality for the original equipment manufacturer (OEM) were historically based primarily on results of surveys and the number of complaints and returns. As a plant quality manager, I would receive some periodic reports from a few OEMs on the defects they found, but there was no consistent quantitative data. Our improvement activities were primarily taken to address specific customer complaints because we used this as one of our key satisfaction measures.

During our management review, I would present the number of complaints and the results of a satisfaction survey. In reality, both measures were based on the mood of the customer (OEM) because that determined if they wanted to write a complaint or what issues they could recall to note on the survey. If operations were going smoothly they might decide to just make a call on an issue but not formalize it in a complaint requiring a response. It was more of a heads-up than a demand for action. I'd follow-up internally with an analysis, depending on the call, but typically heard nothing else so I considered the matter closed. I would occasionally call the customers or talk to sales, but overall I would say the customer seemed satisfied with our product.

The year I accepted the position of divisional quality manager, the corporation determined to upgrade to ISO 9001:2000. The increased customer focus in the standard brought the realization that our feedback measures were not adequate. It's not that we had unsatisfied OEM customers and unhappy end users of our engines. Rather, we had accepted a certain level of product quality because the low-percentage defects were hidden, preventing us from making significant improvements. During this period, our largest customers began requesting regular quality meetings. They had also realized the benefit of consistent factual information as a measure to drive continuous improvement of their product.

The results were consistent, historical information driving improvement and established mechanisms to communicate this and ensure management support. In turn, each facility used this information in their management reviews to drive improvement and monitor activities. Feedback summary information was reported, resulting in a closed-loop, continuous improvement process. All of these efforts were related directly to the foundational principles that are incorporated into the requirements of the standard.

THE ISO PROCESS APPROACH TO SYSTEMS

A significant change to the standard relates to the process approach (principle 4). The quality management principle is defined as follows:

> Process Approach: *a desired result is achieved more efficiently when activities and related resources are managed as a* process, *where process is defined in ISO 9000:2000 clause as: a set of interrelated or interacting activities which transforms inputs into outputs.*[6]

All organizations have various processes that can be defined. The confusing side of this approach is the amount of detail you use to describe them. In other words, at what level does a process need to be defined to provide value yet not be described in such detail as to result in unnecessary information? In addition, unless an organization realigns itself around processes, you will still have departments, cost centers, or profit centers to deal with and people assigned to areas along those lines. Redefining this structure into a process mind-set can be challenging.

By definition, a process can be a drilling operation, a manufacturing cell that contains the drilling operation, a department that contains both the manufacturing cell and the drilling operation, or the entire facility that contains all of these processes. Although a drilling operation has inputs and outputs, it very likely would not make sense to define this with a process map if it only plays one small part in the overall process.

The systems approach (principle 5) plays a key role in understanding this to ensure that it adds value to the organization. It suggests a hierarchy of activities from a high level and broad scope down to very specific details, depending on how far you want to "drill down" into the organization. Systemic thinking also brings in the concept of overall organizational needs as well. Basically, the systems approach establishes logical and practical relationships between key activities that ultimately are focused on the satisfaction of the customer and the success of the enterprise.

Component of Process

The process must have an objective or purpose that adds value to the organization; otherwise, it may be better defined by a procedure or work instruction. The quality management system then becomes a defined relationship of multiple processes, including more specific details (procedures and work instructions), for the purpose of ensuring quality through meeting the intent of the quality policy.

In general, all processes have the following components:

- Suppliers (principle 8—mutually beneficial relationships)

- Inputs

- The specific activities of the process (sequence), including controls

- Outputs

- Customers (principle 1—customer focus)

- Relationships or interfaces with other processes (principle 5— systems approach)

- Objectives of the process

- Measures of those objectives with goals to monitor effective performance of the process (principle 7—factual approach to decision making)

- Process owner (principle 2—leadership)

- Process team members (principle 3—involvement of people)

Process measures can present a challenge and are something that needs to be explored by the auditor; do they measure the process or are they a measure used by the process owner and team? I have discussed measures during an ISO audit only to find they really weren't effective. For example, when we first registered to the new standard, we used productivity as one measure for our human resources (HR) process. We felt that performance management and a sound training program would result in improved productivity.

The logic made sense until the auditor asked if HR had a productivity measure for their area. After some weak arguments on our part, we realized that basing a measure for HR on the productivity of other departments wasn't valid. Even though HR may have had an effect on productivity, that number was so heavily influenced by production and labor that it would be difficult to determine the effect of training or performance evaluation.

The other problem with measures is determining whether you are measuring performance or conformance. To illustrate this, we used meeting our project time lines as a measure of the advanced quality planning process for new product introductions at the plant level. It was important for the customer that we met our deadline but the measure was really more for conformance; did we meet the dates? When we discussed our real objectives, the real goal was a product with no defects that met our budget and the promised date. The time line measure was not performance data because if we met the date but the product was defective, the actual performance of that process would have been poor.

The Process Map

To depict a process, we use a process map. As a quality manager, I defined as the continuous improvement process our team meetings where we reviewed key department measures on a regular basis against the goals set through the long-range plan. Team emphasis and empowerment of employees has been a significant part of our organization's philosophy for many years and has contributed to the success of the organization. Included in the process steps or sequence are the team meetings, analysis of data, investigating and developing improvement to meet the goals, planning for future improvements, and reacting to internal and external complaints through corrective action. Corrective action is the formalized method used to solve problems.

You don't want excessive detail in the process map because that creates confusion for the users of the quality manual and unnecessary work for the owner of the manual. It also becomes tedious during the internal audit when verifying that the processes are operating as defined and are effective. The simplest but most effective approach I have found is to use a basic flowchart approach (Figure 6.1) for the process and add in the necessary sequences of activities so it becomes a process map (in this map I did not include suppliers or customers).

This map relays the important information about the aspects of the process: inputs, the sequence of key activities, the output, objectives, and measures. It is better to not define goals on the process maps because they are specific and change annually, based on results of both management review and long-range planning activities. This would require the majority of the processes in the manual to be updated on an annual basis, a time-consuming and non-value-adding task. Rather, the process owner not only "owns" the specifics of the measures, but also the specific goals for each measure.

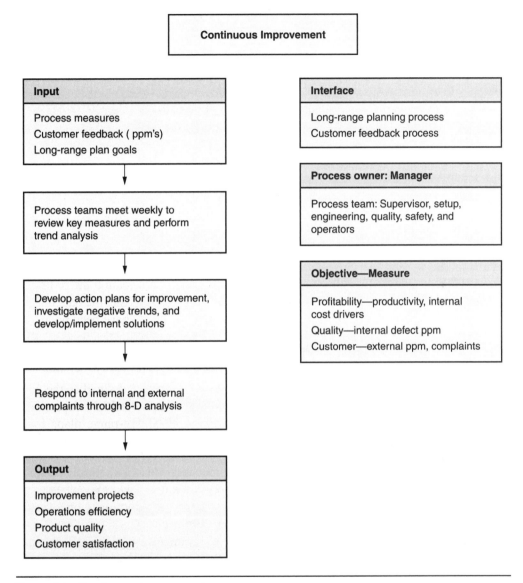

Figure 6.1   Continuous improvement process map.

The interfaces, if important for the process, are also noted on the map. The logic is that if the user must be aware that there are other influences on the process that must be considered, the interface is defined. If those relationships are not important to the function of the process, it is not necessary to show them. Practically speaking, the quality manual should be developed for the occasional user because they will only use it when they want to understand all the necessary activities related to a task they want to accomplish. For this reason, the process map shows the key steps, identifies the related processes, and references important procedures that must be reviewed as well.

Required Documentation

In the quality management system manual, all of these important processes are defined through process maps along with your quality policy and procedures. In the previous ISO standards, there were many procedures required for the manual. The committee put much thought into reducing the requirements for documentation with the ISO 9001:2000 revision. It now requires only six documented procedures:

- Design control

- Control of documents

- Control of nonconforming product

- Corrective action

- Preventive action

- Control of quality records

- Internal quality audits

The standard changed its position on documentation requirements because they decided that companies should determine what is necessary for their organization, not have it dictated by a standard. You could literally have a complete quality management system with some key process maps and the required six procedures, if management and the employees understand the non-defined aspects of the system. In the internal audit, a manager can explain the system and if the employees understand and follow it as described by the manager, you are in compliance.

Most quality managers still document procedures as well as processes. Experience tells you that the activity of defining the process or procedure adds value simply because it forces you to understand all its aspects in order to write it down and may also reveal unnecessary activity. Also, well-written maps make it fairly easy to train employees, as opposed to a manager telling everyone how things should occur.

Many of the processes and activities defined in the quality manual reflect what normally occurs in everyday operations of the organization, so there is no need to refer to the manual. However, though they are common activities there is always the potential of drifting from the original intent. The quality manual serves as a reference of how things should be done and a means for the occasional user to find all the necessary procedures and documents to complete an out-of-the-ordinary assignment as well. One purpose of the internal audit is to verify that these documents remain accurate.

Relationships and Interfaces

In regard to the total system or the relationships and interfaces between key processes, one way to approach this is through an overall plant or facility process map (Figure 6.2).

The overall plant map shows the high-level relationships of the various key processes including overall objectives and measures for the facility. In this scheme, the

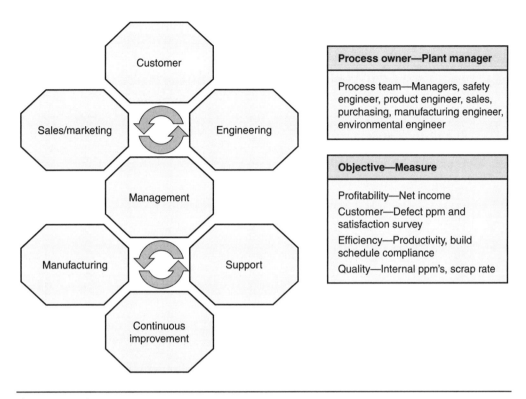

Figure 6.2   Plant process map.

customer has an interface with sales/marketing and engineering to define the product specifications through understanding the customer's needs. That defines the relationship. These groups in turn interface with the management process to relate those specifications that define the needs of the customer to the process of producing a product that meets them. Management has an interface with manufacturing, continuous improvement, and support processes.

Each high-level process is then broken down into key or subprocesses. For the purpose of this book and the related auditing documents that are included, the following high-level processes are broken down as follows:

- Management process
  - Long-range planning
  - Advanced product quality planning
  - Management review
- Manufacturing process
  - Production planning
  - Purchasing

- – Manufacturing
- – Shipping
- • Continuous improvement
  - – Continuous improvement teams
  - – Corrective action
  - – Preventive action
  - – Auditing
- • Resources
  - – Quality
  - – Maintenance
  - – Safety
  - – Environment

QUALITY STANDARDS AND MODELS BEYOND ISO

We have discussed some of the important concepts behind the ISO 9001:2000 upgrade, especially the focus on process and measures. This will be key in our discussions of the internal audit in the next section. Since all quality systems are based on standards, whether formalized such as through ISO registration or simply building the system based on selected aspects of defined methodologies, it is important to consider alternative concepts in our discussion.

Automotive Standards

The automotive industry used the ISO 9001 quality standard as the foundation of its system for its supplier base. They added to this through greater focus on specific aspects of advanced product quality planning (APQP), production part approval process (PPAP), measurement systems analysis (MSA), and process capability requirements (SPC) in the QS-9000 system. These are very formalized methods used to ensure purchased part quality from the sizeable supplier base. In the years following implementation of the QS standard, concerns developed regarding the relationship of the standard to international automotive standards and the quality of the product, so the standard was upgraded.

In 1996, the International Automotive Task Force (IATF) was formed to pull together the various systems: the three European standards, consisting of VDA 6.1 (Germany), AVSQ (Italy), and EAQF (France), and the North American QS-9000 into one automotive quality system. This group consisted of BMW, DaimlerChrysler, Fiat, Ford, GM, Renault,

PSA (Peugeot-Citroen), Volkswagen, and several industry trade associations including AIAG (North America), ANFIA (Italy), FIEV (France), SMMT (UK), and VDA (Germany).[7] In April 2002, the automotive industry rolled out ISO/TS 16949:2002, which will replace QS-9000 in 2006. It again uses the foundation of the international standard, ISO 9000:2000. This is a strong support for the upgrades because all automotive companies globally recognize ISO.

I have suggested previously that one prime motivator for moving to a recognized standard was to reduce the resources required to maintain the supplier base. There was a measurable benefit in having another party audit the supplier. In the automotive initiative to globally implement ISO/TS 16949:2002, the focus of the audit has changed from elements, as in the older standard, to the process audits prescribed by the ISO upgrade. The third-party audits will have greater focus on customer-oriented processes and evaluate overall company performance against specific automotive requirements. It is stated in the ISO/TS standard in very clear terms that a company must define, understand, and document its customer's requirements.

The IATF emphasized that customer specifics are as important as the TS requirements. In addition, DaimlerChrysler, Ford, and GM have again defined PPAP, FMEA, MSA, APQP, and SPC as part of their requirements, following the QS-9000 format.[8] By creating a significant focus on customer requirements and evaluating performance against those requirements, it is believed the weakness of the previous standard has been addressed: correlating registration with quality of output, which is integrated with customer satisfaction and feedback.

A GM representative stated at the seminar, "ISO/TS 16949 is focused on quality system capability for achieving product realization goals with the customer—performance is critical."[9] He later stated, "The certifying body's role is crucial in making sure the certificates have value . . . this process must have integrity, or we'll be trying something else until we find something that does work." The goals of the IATF are to have a single global automotive industry standard as well as a reduction in the need for second-party audits. The automotive industry is planning on holding itself accountable to the standard as well, emphasizing the perception of value in the improvements. The one key ingredient in this change is incorporating results into the equation.

Malcolm Baldrige

The Malcolm Baldrige National Quality Award (MBNQA) has offered a model for performance excellence since 1987 when Congress established it. Per the Web site, applying for the award offers the opportunity to "examine your organization critically and identify strengths and opportunities to improve" and goes on to say "award applicants say the Baldrige process is one of the best, most cost-effective, and comprehensive performance assessments you can get."[10]

The purposes of the award are recognition of achievements in quality and an increased awareness of quality improvement techniques. NIST states that the ISO standard covers less than 10 percent of the Malcolm Baldrige Criteria. They also state that the ISO standards provide an efficient quality conformance system and that registration "determines whether a company complies with its own quality system."[11] The 2005 award categories are as follows:

1. Leadership

2. Strategic planning

3. Customer and market focus

4. Measurement, analysis, and knowledge management

5. Human resource focus

6. Process management

7. Business results

To apply, an organization will typically write a detailed multipage document describing all its activities related to the award criteria. A team of experts reviews each application (minimum of 200 hours), and those selected for on-site visits receive 1000 hours of review and scrutiny. The application process is quite demanding and requires a significant commitment from the organization. Much planning and literally years of work go into implementing a system that meets the requirements of the award.

For this reason, a small percentage of organizations actually apply, an even smaller group receives on-site visits, and only a few receive the award. Since the first awards were issued in 1988, 58 organizations have been recipients. If you look over the list of award recipients, only a few organizations are repeat winners. This suggests that former winners may have found the process valuable at one time but no longer consider it worth the effort to repeat. Although some consider the criteria a tool for performance excellence, they don't continue to use it for quality improvement.[12]

Many states have utilized the same criteria for their state quality award programs. These programs provide an opportunity for organizations to improve and test their systems in a less stringent environment at the state level, potentially moving to the national award level. Past winners of the award have followed this pattern. One important point is that even at the state level, the numbers of applicants are small.[13] This was my observation as well in investigating the Kentucky quality award.

It is suggested that the real value of the MBNQA lies in the fact that many companies use the criteria to audit their own organizations for their continual improvement efforts.[14] This is a benefit claimed on its Web site. Past winners comment that, in writing a 50-page application, they learned much about their organization. However, criticism is leveled at the award for moving away from quality toward performance (450 out of its 1000-point award). Schonberger suggests the older Baldrige was concerned with improving processes for the customer's benefit while the new one, with its focus on results, assumes that processes are running well because the numbers are good.[15]

Schonberger goes on to suggest that the reasons for the change are related to compromises among four interest groups: the quality community, executives, the investment community, and the news media. While quality is still focused on customer satisfaction, executives fund the award and are more performance-oriented, thus the greater emphasis on results. The investment community is looking for short-term results, and the media also like to promote results since most don't understand the mix of quality measures.

It is most interesting to note that Schonberger also suggests that as Baldrige moves away from quality, the ISO standard is now more focused on process improvement and customer satisfaction. In fact, ISO itself supports this performance-focused concept through ISO 9004:2000, which is part of the ISO 9000 standard and offers a guideline for performance excellence, but you cannot be registered to it. It is offered as a guide to support ISO 9001 foundational principles and build upon them to promote enhanced performance of the organization.

Other System Options

There are other systems options as well. One of our customers, intent on improving their internal systems as well as their supplier base, hired consultants to facilitate a series of seminars focusing on the concepts of Deming. The message sent out was that they were moving to the Deming system of quality management. Although I was not part of that group, the sessions were not just for our benefit; the customer participated as well.

Some organizations use Philip Crosby's methods; Crosby is considered to be one of the gurus of quality, made famous by his book *Quality Is Free* written in the 1970s. He was an executive vice president of a major corporation that promoted high-level quality positions in organizations. He had the attention of upper management but, unfortunately, much of the benefit of his concepts was obscured by the zero-defects mantra and the posted slogans that other recognized experts spoke so strongly against.

I have been surprised in reading some articles and letters to the editor suggesting Six Sigma or lean manufacturing as the quality systems of choice. Although these methodologies offer important concepts for quality and organizational improvement, they don't provide a companywide system to ensure quality. An organization must have a basic quality system on which to build more specialized methodologies. There may be immediate needs for solving complicated problems or improving efficiencies, but you cannot lose sight of the importance of a sound quality management system.

ENDNOTES

1. "ISO Survey Reports Registration Growth," *Quality Digest* (September 2003).
2. Dirk Dusharme, "ISO 9001 Survey," *Quality Digest* (July 2004).
3. Ceyhun Ozgur, Gary E. Meek, and Aysegul Toker, "The Impact of ISO Certification on the Levels of Awareness and Useage of Quality Tools and Concepts: A Survey of Turkish Manufacturing Companies," *Quality Management Journal* 9, no. 2 (2002).
4. Charles A. Cianfrani, Joseph J. Tsiakals, and John E. (Jack) West, *The ASQ ISO 9000:2000 Handbook* (Milwaukee: ASQ Quality Press, 2002): 17–18.
5. Ibid., 36.
6. Ibid., 12.

7. Karen Whitmore and Caria Kalogeridis, "ISO/TS 16949: Here at Last," *Quality Digest* (October 2002).

8. Ibid.

9. Ibid.

10. "Why Apply?," www.Baldrige.nist.gov.

11. Ibid., "Frequently Asked Questions."

12. Kennedy Smith, "The Baldrige Revisited," *Quality Digest* (March 2004).

13. Garry D. Coleman, Eileen M. Van Aken, and Jianming Shen; "Estimating Interrater Reliability of Examiner Scoring for a State Quality Award," *Quality Management Journal* 10, no. 3 (2002).

14. Garry D. Coleman and C. Patrick Koelling, "Estimating the Consistency of Third-Party Evaluator Scoring of Organizational Self-Assesments," *Quality Management Journal* 5, no. 3 (1998).

15. Richard J. Schonberger, "Is the Baldrige Still About Quality," *Quality Digest* (December 2001).

7

The Quality Culture

The quality management system provides a relationship between various disciplines that the organization determines will, if followed, ensure that its definition of quality is met. Though all these interrelated activities and documents come together as the quality system, there obviously must be something more. The level of understanding and depth of commitment of leadership determine how that focus on quality is driven down throughout the organization and assimilated by the employees.

Leadership is influenced by the writings of recognized leaders in the field of quality, the research and interpretations of academia, and the published success stories. It is strongly influenced by various industries, such as automotive, in the effort to drive improvement and efficiency throughout the supply chain. It is ultimately influenced by the desire to satisfy the end user of the product.

This concept of a quality culture is an important issue to understand for organizations. That is because quality leadership and quality culture have a strong relationship but exist at different stages of development within the organization. Uncovering it may mean identifying those various subsystems that exist and affect quality in the organization. The levels of understanding and implementation will vary between industries, divisions, facilities, departments, and shifts. Those levels are determined by management commitment, which is influenced by the industry and the customer.

Unless the culture of quality is aligned with the management of quality, the anticipated results will not be achieved. Investigating and understanding the culture means identifying a set of values and beliefs rather than just a set of tools, techniques, and systems.[1]

For comparison, all professional football teams play by the same rules, only a few win the right to compete in the playoffs, and only one ultimately wins the Super Bowl. Some teams seem to be in the running for the top prize more often than others. The consistent winners don't always have the best players or the best coaches, but they have the best team. The rules are the same for everyone, each team uses systems and strategies that the other teams study, but it comes down to desire, organization, and culture that lift one above the other. New coaches study the various methods and practices of historically successful teams and work as assistant coaches for successful college and professional programs. Because of this, they, in turn, learn to implement and improve on these successful practices. Successful programs breed successful programs, but they are usually determined by the coaching staff and some strong leaders on the team.

HISTORICAL PERSPECTIVE

There are great lessons to be learned by looking at a brief historical perspective of quality in regard to culture. Deming, Juran, and Feigenbaum had great influence on the Japanese because Japan was hungry for concepts and direction in quality improvement. Those men provided the ideas and techniques, like they did in America, but something more occurred to create such a transformation. They implemented those important concepts like top management involvement, a sound quality system, and employee involvement throughout all levels, but so did some of the companies in the United States. Why did this movement affect so many Japanese companies?

According to Garvin,[2] the national focus on the quality movement was one of the most distinctive features of the Japanese revolution. Success stories were quickly published and new ideas were rapidly implemented. The "overwhelming impression is one of unity and purpose, with the entire nation moving en masse toward the goal of improved quality." Garvin felt much of this could be traced to the Japanese Industrial Standards (JIS) and the Union of Japanese Scientists and Engineers (JUSE). He suggested, "standardization was a key vehicle for consolidating the Japanese quality movement."

Immediately after the war, the Japanese began efforts toward standardization. They developed the Japanese Standards Association in 1945 and within one year it was joined by a government body, the Japanese Industrial Standards Committee, and began publishing a monthly standards journal. In 1949, the Industrial Standardization Law was passed and within one year after release, they issued the first Japanese Industrial Standards.[3]

Standards are built from a common knowledge base with the ultimate goal of raising and maintaining a level of quality. Because they are put in writing, it forces agreement, but more importantly, decisions are based on scientific methods of proof or historical fact. Then what is left is the challenge of enforcing the standard.

A unifying practice was critical to instituting these standards: certification. Most Japanese firms in the 1950s and 1960s felt it was important to obtain JIS certification so that the consumers would have confidence in their product.[4] The Ministry of International Trade and Industry (MITI) coordinated the process. They verified production methods and product characteristics through an assessment by audit teams to ensure that effective quality systems were in place. It was these efforts, promoted by the government, that ensured the national quality movement in Japan.

Culture is a learned behavior, whether it's in the home, on the shop floor, or in the classroom. The American Society for Quality Control (now the American Society for Quality [ASQ]) came into existence in 1946, the same year that the JUSE was founded. While ASQ primarily focused on technical issues and its audience was practitioners rather than top management, JUSE addressed a broad spectrum. Its training programs targeted top management, quality professionals, managers, and shop-floor employees. These were massive programs conducted throughout the nation that raised the level of awareness and understanding of quality methodology.[5]

Postwar Japan found itself a defeated nation, exhausted of resources and capital due to the war effort. The economic situation and global perceptions of poor quality became a catalyst that ignited a national focus on raising the quality culture in Japan. In addition, since Japan is a small country with limited natural resources, there is a great need to become increasingly more efficient in production. Improved quality meant less waste, so all of these factors became a strong drive toward taking the quality cause very seriously.

In our discussions of the ISO standard, it was proposed that one reason for some perceived ineffectiveness of the pre-2000 version was the fact that it did not require clearly defined objectives and measures. Although "good" companies did this, there was no way of measuring quality performance. Japan set its intent during postwar rebuilding activities on establishing standards and then certifying organizations to these requirements. It was clearly of national importance to set objectives in the form of the standards. The certification process became a national measure to control the process of raising the level of quality within the nation. This is a simplification of a complex topic but true in its basic sense.

The United States was not only victorious in the war, but its postwar industries were thriving and dominating the marketplace. The motivation for America was getting more products out the door to satisfy the hungry consumer. It seemed to be doing things right. It had mastered mass-production techniques and the level of quality seemed to be satisfying the customer. The key concern was product innovation and getting goods into the hands of more and more consumers. It was many years before a need arose in some industries to begin certifying suppliers to an agreed-upon standard. The national importance of certification to ISO in America was driven by the European proclamation that it would recognize the standard in 1989, not because of a national commitment to quality.

Garvin suggested that the following forces were behind the profound quality improvement initiative in Japan: centralized leadership and direction, top management involvement, and the desire to elevate quality to an issue of national importance.[6] In contrast, I would suggest that the quality culture in postwar America was focused on the following: decentralized leadership to open up more national competition, top management focus on meeting increased demands for volume and variety of products, and maintaining American dominance as an issue of national importance.

As we move ahead some 50 years to the 21st century, the world has undergone dramatic changes. "Made in America" slogans have disappeared because most American companies purchase components or import finished goods from overseas. Everyone realized the slogans were a temporary effort, promoted by unions, to encourage consumers to support local industry and resist the onslaught of Japanese goods. Ironically, Japanese retailers now display "Made in Japan" slogans to resist the first big push of Wal-Mart stores in their own country.[7] Japan has slashed prices, built mega-stores, and is working to eliminate the middleman from forcing some of the highest prices in the world in its strategy to resist Wal-Mart.

The enticement of huge revenues from the global marketplace has created formidable competitors in what were once considered backward and underdeveloped countries. Competition has created a buyer's market where the consumer now has their choice of low-cost, high-value alternatives. Huge industries have been brought to their knees because they were slow to react or their strategies were not correctly aligned with the marketplace. Successful companies learned from history and benchmarked those strategies that resulted in success.

Although approached from a national perspective, top management was intimately involved in bringing the new ideas of Deming, Juran, and Feigenbaum into Japan. Not all Japanese companies bought into these new concepts but the significant potential players in the global market realized they needed to take action to survive. This change first occurred in top management because they identified a need and a gap in their own systems. They realized they needed to raise the level of understanding and awareness in the labor force, so training and education programs were implemented. To define their management philosophy, they developed the quality management system. To determine their effectiveness, they implemented measures, and more importantly, a system of registration through quality system audits.

The purpose of these programs was to impact the quality culture of the organization because management realized that it had to be raised to improve the level of customer satisfaction and overcome current perceptions of poor quality. Since it occurred as a united strategy across many of the large organizations, it, in effect, raised the culture in Japan. Since it became a national movement, pockets of success were widely promoted and it became a sustainable movement. There is ownership by top management of the quality culture. Determining how well the management philosophy is implemented is through analysis of the culture.

UNDERSTANDING CULTURE

In understanding organizations, the culture is generalized by phrases like organizational climate, rites and rituals, or simply how things are done. It is an important concept because it becomes the appropriate standard for what employees say or do or for their value system. New employees feel anxiety until they understand the culture and fit in. Culture is a differentiating factor between successful and unsuccessful companies because successful ones typically have a more highly evolved culture. Culture can be multidimensional such as disciplined, quality-oriented, and customer-focused. It is a living, breathing organism that affects the success of an organization and also becomes a means to define the level of understanding in the workforce. Defined by one of the most influential authors on culture (E. H. Shein), it means (quote)[8]:

- A pattern of basic assumptions about how the group copes with the outside world and about how members should act within the group.

- These assumptions define how members should perceive, think, and feel about problems.

- These assumptions have been invented, discovered, or developed by the group out of their experience.

- The group sees these assumptions as valid.

- The group thinks these assumptions are important to teach to new members.

Identifying the current state of the organizational culture will have enormous benefits to management because it will reveal the effectiveness of their management system. Understanding the organization in the context of its culture will also put emphasis on rooting out the various subsystems in existence because they will want to know if those systems are effective or counterproductive. Most importantly, it defines an important aspect of the organization so strategies can be developed to raise the level to meet future needs. Finally, having an effective measure of the culture will allow the organization to measure the effectiveness of strategic initiatives.

If we look at culture from the perspective of management and the investment community, there is a relationship of culture to corporate performance, identified by the research of Kotter and Heskett (quote)[9]:

- Corporate culture can have a significant impact on a firm's long-term economic performance.

- Corporate culture will be an even more important factor in determining the success or failure of firms in the next decade.

- Cultures that inhibit strong long-term financial performance are common, and they develop easily, even when employees are reasonable and intelligent.

- Although tough to change, corporate cultures can be made more performance-enhancing.

Organizational culture can be an asset or a deterrent to company initiatives. One could argue that its value comes from the fact that it is difficult to change, which makes it difficult to imitate. A Conference Board study (1994) of North American and European companies found 32 percent were successful in changing the "vision, values, and culture."[10] A 1996 survey found only 10 percent of corporations were successful in instituting a new management style.[11]

CULTURAL CHANGE

There are many factors affecting cultural change. Leaders of change efforts may not have the influence necessary to gain commitment from mid-level managers and supervisors. The choice of personnel to lead these efforts is based on availability. The more valuable and influential employees are too important to pull off their job so those with less experience head up the efforts. Even with top management support, a weak leader will be ineffective.

If top management does not have a good understanding of the culture, change initiatives may be chosen that are not suitable for the organizational climate. In environments where resources are limited, disciplined problem-solving methodologies will fall short of expectations if those charged with implementing the program are not relieved of other responsibilities. The concept of Six Sigma means devoting personnel to a limited number of projects so they have the time and any additional resources necessary to carry them through to completion.

There may be a lack of trust in management initiatives because in the past, many changes were introduced only to fail from lack of support and commitment. Communication is critical to implementing change. Unless management has developed a good medium for relaying important information, changes to the norm will result in suspicion. Employees are told there will be large-scale informational meetings followed by group training sessions to implement the new quality program. As they settle in their chairs for the presentation, one can hear them whisper, "have you heard anything about this . . . no one ever asks any of us what we think?"

Kotter and Heskett found that the length of time to accomplish the change was a significant factor. In a study of 11 large organizations attempting a major cultural change, including General Electric, British Airways, and Xerox, the length of time ranged from four to 10 years. They also found that successful changes might erode over time because new managers did not understand the strategy or because the reason for the success was forgotten.

In small organizations, one or two people are highly influential. New owners can make immediate changes, both good and bad, because it is a small and close working community. This also applies to new companies. They start off small, become successful, and as they grow, results decline because they don't know how to perpetuate the successful culture. Also, the culture will change as a reaction to management decisions.

Following is an example of a reactionary change. Southwest Airlines has been recognized as one of the best companies to work for and Herb Kelleher, their CEO until 2001, has been a motivational speaker at various conventions. Their organizational culture is studied in MBA textbooks because they have been able to "create a successful strategy through strong leadership, a unique and favorable corporate culture, and excellent employees."[12] The textbook goes on to state that these competencies make it difficult for the competition because they can't be easily imitated. This combination contributes to an attractive cost structure supporting its reputation as the most consistently profitable American airline.

If we move ahead a few years, a *Wall Street Journal* article discussed the conflict between management and its flight attendants, arguably the purveyors of its unique culture to the general public.[13] According to *WSJ*, the flight attendants union was asking for assistance from national mediators because dialog was growing bitter after 16 months of negotiations. The attendants began running ads in 13 major markets for Southwest saying, "Working for free . . . Isn't that just 'plane' nuts?" They also held demonstrations at airports, around the time Southwest announced its 30th consecutive year of profitability, to call attention to the fact that members are required to clean planes and do other tasks without pay.

As stated, the culture makes "basic assumptions about how the group copes with the outside world and about how members should act within the group." In this case, the flight attendants were highly motivated and known for making flights enjoyable and humorous. This turned into vocal demonstrations reacting against management because of perceptions that although they contributed to the company's success, management did not recognize it.

Developing a strong quality culture is difficult but it plays a significant role in a successful quality program. Implementing the ISO 9001:2000 standard points toward the emphasis on management involvement, measures, effectiveness, and customer focus. To meet these requirements, middle management and supervisors must participate in quality initiatives to show improvement in the measures. In addition, customer focus will not be evident unless there is a commitment of necessary resources by management and a high level of concern by those interacting with the customer. Although three years seems enough time to implement, if the culture is not sufficiently advanced, it will take longer.

ENDNOTES

1. Kim Cameron and Wesley Sine, "A Framework for Organizational Quality Culture," *Quality Management Journal* 6, no. 4 (1999).
2. David A. Garvin, *Managing Quality* (New York: The Free Press, 1988): 184–86.
3. Ibid., 185.
4. Ibid., 185.
5. Ibid., 194.
6. Ibid., 197.
7. Ann Zimmerman and Marin Fackler, "Wal-Mart's Foray into Japan Stirs a Retail Upheaval," *Wall Street Journal* (September 19, 2003).
8. Martin E. Smith, "Changing an Organization's Culture: Correlates of Success and Failure," *Leadership and Organizational Development Journal* 24, no. 5 (2003); referenced the works of E. H. Shein, "Organizational Culture and Leadership," Second ed. (San Francisco: Jossey-Bass, 1992).
9. Ibid.; referenced works of J. P. Kotter, *Leading Change: An Action Plan from the World's Foremost Expert on Business Leadership* (Boston: Harvard Business School Press, 1996).
10. Ibid.; reference to K. Troy, *Change Management: An Overview of Current Initiatives* (New York: The Conference Board, 1994).
11. Ibid.; referenced P. Mourier and M. E. Smith, *Conquering Organizational Change: How to Succeed Where Most Companies Fail* (CEP Press, 2001).
12. Michael A. Hitt, R. Duane Ireland, and Rober E. Hoskisson, *Strategic Management: Competitiveness and Globalization,* Fourth ed. (Cincinnati, OH: Southwestern College Publishing, 2001): 193.
13. Melanie Trottman, "Southwest Seeks Mediation in Talks with Attendants," *Wall Street Journal* (September 16, 2003).

Part III

Analyzing and Improving the Quality System—The "Progressive" Audit

The previous section discussed relationships between the audit and the quality system, but the main purpose was to discuss the concepts of quality policy, quality management system, and quality culture. This is important to ensure that the person developing the audit and the auditors have an understanding of the important aspects of a quality organization. We must realize that organizations are very complex and it is an enormous challenge to adequately identify the important activities and the relationships between the various processes. In this same regard, it is also challenging for those charged with developing and implementing the audit to develop an audit program that will be effective. Both require a significant commitment of time and resources; one is typically up front and the other is ongoing.

Developing a quality management system manual is a huge time commitment, but it occurs once, and afterwards, it is only modified for upgrades. That is one reason why the upgrade to ISO 9001:2000 has raised concerns by many companies. As described previously, quality managers are pulled in many directions and struggle with this task because it demands so much time. They must not only work with the various departments to upgrade to the new requirements but also properly define the new activity in the manual. The various departments can and should develop their own process maps and procedures, but there still needs to be continuity within the entire manual that will fall on someone, usually the quality manager. Unfortunately, for many, it is used once each year for the audit (internal, second- or third-party audit) and then it simply takes up disk space until the next cycle.

Developing and implementing the internal quality systems audit is approached from a different perspective. Those responsible must interview, review documentation, and observe activities to determine if the quality management system is consistent with the intent of the organization. Since ISO now requires fewer procedures and less documentation than in the past, auditors also may be required to first determine what that system is through those interviews and then verify whether it is implemented. All areas must be audited on a regular cycle, typically annually, according to the standard. The unfortunate but typical case is that internal audits are more or less a quick refresher on the system, carried out just prior to the ISO audit.

In this final section, I will describe in detail the "progressive audit" process with a focus on how to derive value from this activity. This approach is not new. Much has already been written in this regard, with many good articles and books developing concepts for audit format, checklists, techniques, terminology, and suggestions for adding value to the audit. In fact, the upgrade to the ISO standard itself has resulted in greater focus on continuous improvement, so text on the standard invariably addresses the audit as an important tool for achieving a better system.

What I feel is lacking in publications about audits are details of how one can derive this value. Important concepts about audit teams are developed, but I don't feel the literature goes far enough on the enormous benefits of team-based auditing. It is my hope that, based on practical experience, I can offer some new insights into the audit process, including tools and techniques that will gain management's attention and move the audit to its rightful place as a critical tool for organizations.

8

Confessions of a "Last-Minute" Auditor

In my previous life when I first became a quality manager, I was a "last-minute" auditor. Before that time, I participated in last-minute audits to learn the trade, but once I became the quality manager, I inherited responsibility for the system audits so last-minute audits became my torch to carry. It was a stressful activity bred from the perception that resources were limited and audits were a necessary evil. It was constrained by lack of understanding of quality system development and naïve confidence that everyone understands fully what he or she is supposed to do.

Like any good audit, the last-minute audit has its purpose and scope. It is designed to review all the requirements of the standard against the activities of the organization, utilizing a minimal amount of time and resources, so it can meet the requirements of the ISO standard; that is, perform internal audits on all areas defined in the standard. The audit plan, since it occurs just prior to the audit, requires short-term commitment from the management team and results in surprised auditees because it is not communicated well on the shop floor. The audit results, with this approach, will satisfy the requirements but offer few opportunities for improvement.

The underlying management philosophy here is that there is limited value in the activity. When prompted by the scheduling of the ISO audit, the internal audit season arrives. Once the internal audit is performed, people find value in being questioned on their interpretation of the quality requirements for their area. There is a level of satisfaction in performing the internal audit because the organization feels "ready" for the third-party audit, but the value is greatly diminished because management sees it primarily for compliance and as a tune-up.

To better understand, let's look at objectives and measures, which are not new to businesses. Organizations have had financial-related ones for years to improve profitability. In my company, quality-related ones were improved due to the upgrade to the ISO standard. Where in the past we monitored our defects and customer complaints, after the upgrade it became a very formalized process reported in meetings occurring weekly, monthly, quarterly, and annually. It received upper management attention and resulted in significant improvements in the quality of our processes and our engines. Market share increased, profits improved, and so did customer satisfaction.

The quality measures forced us to investigate what we would have considered to be minor issues in the past, due to the management commitment to improve. We reduced product defect issues and customer use issues. This was not all a result of our own motivation; we got a strong push from our largest customers as well. We now had the data and details to measure our success but in some cases, the customer was driving us to a higher level of quality. The point is that this necessitated understanding, and any issue became an opportunity to improve the end product and ultimately, customer satisfaction and trust.

Management has internal objectives and measures to provide a sense of control over the operations. Internal accounting audits are critical, primarily to ensure that the financial numbers are correct, and the law requires them for publicly held corporations. Great commitment and support by upper management had gone into detailing and auditing the systems to ensure that the reporting mechanisms are correct and monitored. If you look at quality management systems, however, there has not been the same focus. The operations numbers gave management a sense of control such that audits became primarily a means of verifying compliance and nothing more. This assumed that the means we used to develop the systems were sound.

MAKING ASSUMPTIONS

In developing a quality management system, you make certain assumptions. You assume that the manager of the area developing the process map or procedure understands his operations well enough to define the area correctly. You also assume that all supervisory personnel managing that area understand its operations so there is reasonable consistency between shifts. Assumptions are made regarding appropriateness of measures, consistent and proper use of the various process control mechanisms, knowledgeable and well-trained employees, and no misinterpreted numbers nor subsequent inaccurate reporting.

One big assumption is that people really understand. The concept of defining systems through process maps and procedures can be reviewed countless times with the management team and department personnel only to find that they still "don't get it." Sometimes it may be intentional because they want to get the quality manager out of their area by agreeing to some change. Most of the time they do not read the details, nor do they understand their role in the quality management system as well as they think.

I am not suggesting that defining organizational systems isn't taken seriously because I believe it is. However, I believe there is a certain disconnect between managers, supervisors, technical support, and operators. The quality manual reinforces the need to define our activities, so we must dedicate some resources to define them. If an appropriate amount of time and energy is not spent on this task, the result is a system that represents how we would like the area to operate rather than reality. In most cases, the best system lies somewhere between the two.

Let's briefly look at the process of developing a simple procedure. The quality manager meets with the manager of the area and discussion occurs to define what needs to be accomplished. The manager may set up a meeting with his subordinates to get additional details but many times he relies on experience. In many cases, the quality manager develops the procedure and reviews it with the area manager to ensure it is accurate. Ultimately, consensus is reached and the approver group signs off.

In the case of developing a high-level process map, the recommendation typically made is for the area to take on that responsibility. Many organizations will have a team devoted to mapping out the critical processes. Training to understand the methodology is provided and the team then studies the department and defines the best method. When more than one facility is represented by the proposed map there is greater demand on resources to investigate and accurately report on the activities. Trying to develop "best practices" within the organization becomes "best compromise" and the final map is either too general or reflects the more outspoken team members.

What are we trying to accomplish? The ultimate goal is to understand the system and define it in a way that results in the most efficient operations with the output of a high-quality product or service. The reality often is that the goal becomes meeting the standard and getting all this documentation completed by a specific deadline. Resources are limited so shortcuts are taken. As I stated earlier, the systems are developed based on assumptions that leadership of the area has a sound grasp of their operations.

The resulting product of all these activities is the documented quality management system. Although the new ISO standard requires far less documentation, most organizations have added more due to requirements for objectives and measures of quality. Technology has advanced since the earlier "hard copy" manuals so we can now give them a new look. There may be numerous hyperlinks to other documents, and since they are electronic, we can easily add features to make the document more appealing.

We can now create a high-level model for the home page on the intranet, showing continuous improvement circles of the plan–do–check–act cycle. We develop orbs of color identifying the various key areas, all linked so the user can drill down to the specific process maps of that area. Our measures and improvement activities are linked to the maps through PowerPoint presentations and colorful charts. Technology has greatly improved the visual impact of the quality manual.

In many organizations, manuals are becoming works of art, worthy of recognition by the registrar. Their appearance alone gives the impression of a well-organized company. However, it is far easier to develop an impressive manual than it is to create a strong and thriving quality culture. Over time, people believe that those well-organized maps and procedures accurately represent the quality system. They think their presence on a server somehow influences the day-to-day operations of the organization even though personnel rarely reference them.

In previous sections, I referenced articles criticizing the ISO third-party audit as one reason organizations were delaying their upgrades. They suggest that little or no value is derived from this activity. Articles also suggest there is a problem with the internal audits. Books are published because there is a market for information on how to improve this activity. If there weren't issues, there would be less coverage.

The purpose of the internal audit is to investigate, analyze, and report on activities related to the quality management system. Considering the potential for some inaccuracies in our procedures and inconsistencies in our activities, you would think this activity would have significant importance in the organization. Based on what I read in the literature and my personnel experience, it does not.

WHO'S DRIVING THE AUDITS?

My company was fortunate in that it drove its own quality system improvements through internal requirements and eventually, the ISO 9001 registration. I say fortunate because research indicates that greater value and commitment results if improvement is internally driven as opposed to an edict from the customer.[1]

In their research, the authors found externally influenced adoption of the ISO standard showed improved results in efficiency, awareness, organizational control, staying in business, and customer relationships. Companies internally motivated saw additional benefits of improved internal efficiencies and effectiveness, human resource benefits, financial improvements, and increased market share. Their conclusion was that "firms that are determined to improve their internal efficiencies would execute the ISO exercise more seriously."[2]

Our organization drove this activity because we did not experience regular customer audits or direct influence on our quality systems. Instead, there were occasional customer visits to tour one of our facilities. In the past, there was little outside influence requiring specific quality systems, except through requests for corrective actions. This has changed in recent years because the customers are putting more resources into verification.

In the late 1980s, we instituted an annual corporate audit of all our manufacturing facilities. Our VP of quality and the corporate quality engineer established audit standards and rated each facility. It was a welcomed event since we did not conduct our own audits at the plants. This provided focus and attention on quality systems, albeit annually. It also showed upper management support and commitment to the quality systems.

Initially, they used a rating system, which had an interesting effect. Productivity and financial performance numbers drove plant management teams and they had been conditioned to meet goals. In this same regard, quality managers liked the ratings because they provided targets and something to analyze against. When overall quality system scores were given, it tended to energize the management teams to investigate ways to improve for better scores next audit season. It gave them an overall measure of their performance.

In ensuing years, corporate moved away from the scores and simply "certified" the systems, which seemed to result in less improvement incentive. The internal audits then evolved into the divisional quality managers' responsibility, just prior to the time we registered our first facility to the ISO 9002:1987 standard. In 1993, Briggs & Stratton's Poplar Bluff, Missouri, facility was the first vertical-shaft small-engine manufacturer in the world to be registered to the ISO standard. Because we had developed a history of quality system improvements due to the corporate internal audits, we were able to identify Poplar Bluff as the facility with the best chance of success at the initial registration. Of course, once one facility is registered, the knowledge gained can be taken to others and within a few years all Briggs & Stratton facilities were registered and still are today.

The divisional quality managers used a checklist for their audits based on the 20 elements of the 1987 and 1994 standard written in question format. It was useful only for someone with a sound understanding of the ISO standard. It was maintained on a spreadsheet and used throughout the organization. We continued the policy of not using scores because it was felt there was too much focus on the rating and that led to challenges of some audit findings.

THE ANNUAL EVENT

The audits were always annual events, conducted prior to the ISO assessment as a "tune-up" for the plant management team. The logic of this approach was sound but I could see a growing emphasis on last-minute audit methodology. There were strengths to this approach like upper management support, someone independent of operations administering the program, reasonable consistency between the various facilities, and compliance with the standard. The weaknesses of this approach were time constraints to thoroughly audit all areas, lack of involvement of personnel at the plant except as an auditee, and the infrequency of the audit.

An effort was made in our division to involve more personnel outside quality. The attempt was made to perform the audit quarterly at the three plants with the divisional quality manager and one department manager. Rather than wait until "crunch time" before the ISO audit, we could break it down into more manageable pieces. Management felt this would encourage involvement of the management staff. The plan was to alternate various managers for each quarter at each facility.

Prior to the first audit quarter, each plant manager asked for volunteers from his management team. There was not overwhelming enthusiasm for this new concept. The managers worked 12-hour days and their focus was staffing, building schedules, and keeping equipment running. Audits were always a once-a-year task and their knowledge and interest in them were mainly to verify that they met requirements. Each plant managed to find a volunteer or the plant manager volunteered someone.

At my facility, the divisional quality manager spent some time with his "team" reviewing the checklist and standard. The manager selected was very experienced and an excellent communicator. He was also a good friend and I could tell from his expression that it was becoming a somewhat painful experience. He did manage to ask some good questions and provide input into the audit, but I would hardly call it an overwhelming success.

I remember discussing his experience afterwards and he said it was confusing and somewhat boring. He didn't understand the checklist, which was based on the 20 elements. Although it was adapted to a question format, the terminology was foreign and not shop-friendly. He just didn't have any interest in it, only in improving operations, and it seemed he struggled with the connection. His motivation for the exercise was to help us out in performing this task. It was, in his mind, a necessary evil. His work was still waiting for him so there was strong motivation to finish the audit to get back to work.

The strategy for encouraging more involvement was moderately effective but definitely not a home run. The managers were committed to the company and were excellent at their jobs. They became involved to help out the quality department. However, there was good logic behind getting more people involved with this activity.

The first round of internal audits was completed on schedule. The next quarter arrived but customer demands delayed the schedule; the last-minute audit had survived. It was moved around to accommodate various higher-priority meetings and tasks. It finally came down to crunch time and the remaining areas were audited. I look back at that audit season and I see the activity as an attempt to change the culture. Although it started a new way of thinking, the end result was that we scrambled to get it completed.

GETTING MORE INVOLVED

The following year, the strategy was to have the plants take responsibility for the internal audits, further involving managers in the process. Our ISO audit supported this because the plant management team had to become more involved in our quality system. I engaged the help of the plant manager and acted as a facilitator, using the same 20-element checklist. The end result was compliance with the requirement and we found some procedural areas that we could improve.

The primary reason for the change was trying to derive more value from the audit because there was a perception that moving responsibility down to the plants would encourage more buy-in to the quality management system. The primary reason for the lack of success was because management at the plant, as well as corporate, still viewed it as a compliance activity. Although we had the checklist defining all the requirements, knowledge of the standard was important. The burden fell on the quality manager because no one outside the quality department had a thorough understanding of ISO or our entire quality system; they only understood the pieces affecting their area.

There was a sincere interest in moving toward greater involvement of the management team but I didn't know how to get there. The "team based" audit was not well accepted at the facilities because it wasn't perceived as a means to reduce or prevent defects nor improve our bottom line. There were more effective systems to accomplish that.

There was another big drawback to the last-minute audit. Its scope was so broad and the resources so limited that we were moving away from consistent systems between the plants. As pointed out by one quality manager, because we had less direct involvement from one common contact at the divisional level we were becoming less consistent in our operations. This was an important insight. Even though we were all under the ISO umbrella, each facility had its own quality manual and was responsible for its own audit. The three plants within our division were slowly moving in different directions.

As the plant quality manager, I was at a crossroads. We were moving away from someone outside the plant taking responsibility for the internal audits. My counterparts in the other facilities resisted this effort; it meant far more work and commitment to get the audits completed and there was not widespread support. That's when our quality team at the plant formulated the initial concepts of the "progressive audit," with a format based on our supplier quality systems survey, suggested by our supplier quality engineer. It became a team-based concept with responsibilities spread out over a number of individuals, based on an audit scoring guide and a checklist that is easy to use and requires fewer training hours for the audit team to be effective.

I realized that the last-minute audit is ineffective because it demands too much time from the quality manager. I couldn't manage the audit process because I was doing it, and with my other responsibilities, there was simply not enough time to do it well. That was the same dilemma of the divisional quality manager position. Even though we enlisted other managers, we were spread too thin to give the audit its rightful focus and respect.

If I could establish teams, I could manage the audit schedule by spreading out the activities throughout the year. If I could develop lead auditors to manage the teams, it would allow me to review the results with the managers as if performed by a third-party assessment. I realized that a quality manager is too close to the quality systems at their facility to be performing the audit.

ENDNOTES

1. Salleh Yahya and Wee-Keat Goh, "The Implementation of an ISO 9000 Quality System," *International Journal of Quality and Reliability* 18, no. 9 (2001): 941–66.
2. Ibid., 959.

9

The Progressive Audit

W hat is the progressive audit? The word *progressive* was not chosen because it was a catchy phrase. It was chosen because I felt it best described the experiences of others and myself as we began to really understand the many benefits of a strong internal audit program. I came to the realization that there was so much more to be gained from this activity than what we were currently achieving. The last-minute audits were providing value as a quick refresher before the ISO audit and to clean up those loose ends, but true appreciation for this activity was sorely lacking, especially on my part.

The progressive audit is all about attitude, and attitude correlates directly with culture. It means getting everyone in the organization to realize their role in the quality system but more importantly, to recognize the importance of viewing their activities in relationship to the whole system. It means moving away from the mind-set that quality is a departmental activity to a philosophy of developing highly efficient and effective systems and techniques to ensure customer satisfaction and the success of the organization.

Changing the culture is usually a slow process in mature environments, but the internal audit program can be a catalyst for change. In fact, my own mental model of the internal audit moved slowly from last-minute to progressive, including increased confidence in the ability to introduce change because it could be reinforced through the audit. When the marketplace is collapsing around you, the sudden and dramatic change suggested by business process reengineering may be the only hope. However, it is not a sound practice in successful organizations trying to address specific identified needs. That is because of risk. A significant change has a high level of risk because your process measures may not be sensitive enough to identify a failure lurking ahead.

Changing the culture to a greater focus on quality through the internal audit was subtle and took time. In some ways, I didn't realize it was happening until it started to appear. Implementing the program got the immediate attention of the managers because of the high-level visibility of the program; the entire management team was watching the progress. They were reacting to the audit activity, preparing for the audit by reviewing their processes and holding department sessions to train key personnel. They learned about the systems but it took repeated audits over a couple years for the culture to start changing, meaning more employees understood and took ownership of their responsibilities for the quality system.

The internal audit as presented in this book consists of two stages. In the initial phase you introduce the program and develop the necessary tools and personnel in preparation for implementing the audit program; key in this is development of the audit scoring guide and checklists. Once completed, you then move into the second stage, where the progressive audit process is followed (discussed in detail in Chapter 14).

In the old days of auditing, it was more an activity that preceded the ISO audit. Now, the audit is a process that follows a cycle. By this I mean it recognizes an audit season where the major processes or departments are audited according to the audit schedule. After completion, there is a postseason period where the results are reviewed and strategic planning occurs to improve the quality system as well as the audit process. There is also a preseason where updates and training are performed, based on the formulated strategies, in preparation for the new audit schedule.

This chapter introduces the steps (Figure 9.1) in preparing for the audit as well as our first experience with the new audit process. It then goes on to present value-adding

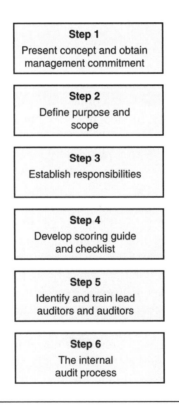

Figure 9.1   Progressive audit steps.

benefits. Subsequent chapters will describe the steps in more detail, including the strategies for management involvement, developing the scoring guide and checklists, and auditor selection and training that are important to implementing a successful internal audit program. Starting in Chapter 14, the audit process will be detailed, discussing concepts of the audit schedule, conducting the audit, audit of the internal audit, and pre- and postseason activities.

STEP 1: PRESENT CONCEPT AND OBTAIN MANAGEMENT COMMITMENT

Key concepts of the audit program must be presented to the management team to gain commitment and support. Commitment from the plant and department managers is critical for a number of reasons: committing time for the audits, dedicating personnel as team members, supporting the teams by respecting the auditors even though some will have limited experience, and taking ownership of the program. In addition, since the internal audit will be expanded to investigate matters in more detail, they must be willing to change their methods based on the audit results.

To demonstrate how our organization could have effective audits with teams from various backgrounds outside of quality, I circulated copies of the supplier survey because the scoring guide presented in this book had not yet been developed. The survey offered a format that could be revised into a scoring guide and easily followed. It provided credibility to the program because the survey was based on an established corporate system, defined, and in a well-organized format. A complete scoring guide is available in Appendix A of this book.

The internal audit was a requirement of the ISO standard and we were getting by with our traditional internal audits. This new approach provided the added benefit of getting more people involved in the audit from the various manufacturing and nonmanufacturing areas. Through using audit teams, far more employees in the organization would be questioned about their understanding of the system, including expansion to all shifts. The scoring guide would address all the specific requirements of the ISO standard as well as the quality management system in an understandable format. Since we would select individuals for the teams from various areas in the plant to expand well beyond the quality department, they would be trained on the requirements in the quality manual and the scoring guide would provide a reference on what they should ask.

The buy-in was unanimous. The plant manager was a huge supporter of the team concept and felt that this would be a good opportunity for employees to get involved. The managers liked the idea that it would get more personnel in their department understanding the system and felt that more detailed information would help them identify opportunities in their area. The audit was accepted as an opportunity that could have a positive influence on the facility in terms of quality.

STEP 2: DEFINE PURPOSE AND SCOPE

The main purpose of the internal audit is to ensure an effective and timely evaluation of quality activities against what is defined in the quality manual. Since my resources were limited based on last-minute audit results, it also meant developing the team concept to have more parties involved to carry out this activity (no more last-minute audits). Finally, it must also raise the level of understanding of the quality system in the workforce.

The audit scope must ensure that we cover all the requirements of the standard. In addition, it must also address all the important requirements of our quality system for the specific area being audited. Since the purpose is also to raise the level of understanding, the audit must involve all the managers in their respective departments, including their frontline supervision, technical personnel, setups, and operators.

STEP 3: ESTABLISH RESPONSIBILITIES

I wanted to remove myself from performing the internal audit so that I would no longer be directly involved. My role as quality manager would be in supporting the program through overseeing development and implementation. To me, this meant ensuring it meets its purpose and scope, obtaining the necessary resources, and providing some authority should issues arise. The supplier quality engineer would be the lead auditor because of prior auditing experience. This meant training auditors and heading up the audit team. It would be a plant activity, reporting to the plant management team, and each of the major manufacturing areas would be audited to the same standard once each year.

STEP 4: DEVELOP SCORING GUIDE AND CHECKLIST

The only checklist available was the one used for the last-minute audit. It was basically the ISO 9001 20-element requirements, including terminology, rewritten in a question format to ensure that all elements were addressed. Using it for the new program would require an enormous amount of time to train everyone on the standard and it still would be difficult for most members of the team. There was a clear need for some sort of audit guide that the team could use that both addressed the ISO standard in commonly used terms and, more importantly, addressed specific quality systems requirements of our organization. This would require an extensive revision to the existing ISO checklist so I enlisted the new lead auditor to help.

Since he was so familiar with auditing suppliers, the suggestion was made to treat each internal manufacturing area as a supplier organization and use the supplier quality systems survey for the internal audit, with necessary modifications. The supplier survey followed an entirely different concept than the checklist, requiring results to be quantified through scores, with a final overall rating. This would allow each area to compare themselves to previous years and judge improvement efforts. In addition, each question was enhanced with bullet points to ensure proper understanding of its intent. The supplier survey was revised to address our internal quality systems and ensure coverage of the elements of the standard (1994 version). In the first year of the audit program we only used the scoring guide.

STEP 5: IDENTIFY AND TRAIN LEAD AUDITORS AND AUDITORS

As a group, we decided that the first department audited would be a support department for engine assembly because the assembly area had hundreds of employees and we didn't want to start with an area that large. Where in the past there was reluctance of managers to volunteer as part of the audit, this time we openly discussed the importance of getting the right mix on the first audit team. It was decided that two assembly operators would be involved since they were the customers of machining, the department to be audited. To keep the team independent, we added a receiving inspector and one of the managers who had prior experience as a buyer on the supplier systems survey team.

The assembly manager found two operators to volunteer, both considered good workers with positive attitudes. I established training guidelines to ensure that all important areas of the quality manual were covered and the lead auditor developed and conducted the actual training (since he had previous experience, lead auditor training was minimal). The training session took a half day, discussing key sections of the quality manual and how they related to the audit questions.

The auditors learned standard audit practice, questioning techniques, and how to use the scoring guide. We stressed the importance of taking good notes during the audit since that information would be needed for writing up the results. They also discussed ethics to emphasize the fact that the purpose was to honestly report what they found while assuring confidentiality of comments made by employees. We had concerns that if names were given for specific comments made rather than overall impressions, future audits could be jeopardized because people on the shop floor wouldn't trust us.

STEP 6: THE INTERNAL AUDIT PROCESS

The first audit scheduled was a component-manufacturing department. This was communicated weeks ahead to the department manager so preparation could be made. Specific times for interviews of key personnel were developed to ensure availability of resources, including rooms and times for the tour. Additional departments were not scheduled until the first audit was completed to test the concept and allow modifications if necessary. None were needed so the remaining manufacturing departments were scheduled and completed that first audit year.

The scheduled day arrived and the audit began with the opening meeting, conducted by the lead auditor and team. A sign-in sheet was passed around to document the activity.

In attendance were the plant manager, department managers, supervisors, and myself as the quality manager. They had reviewed previously sent scheduled times for various activities and requirements for personnel available to assist on the tour, so everyone was clear on the agenda. They also laid out the audit format using the scoring guide and explained all of the areas in the department that would be covered. At this point, the opening meeting was concluded and all parties left except for the manager of the department.

The lead auditor began with the interview of the manager using questions directly from the scoring guide. It had been developed based on the quality manual requirements and the flow of the audit to make it easy to follow. Since the manager was responsible for the department, they were the owner of the various systems in the department, including the informal activities necessary for its success. This included performance goals, customer satisfaction determinants, continuous improvement strategies, and the methods for communicating this information to the employees.

The results of this phase of the audit, which lasted approximately two hours, determined the manager's understanding of the defined systems. It also established the undocumented systems so we could determine their effectiveness during the subsequent questioning of supervisors, setup personnel, and operators during the tour. With this methodology, we could report on knowledge of and compliance to procedures and also effectiveness of the overall systems based on the initial structure laid out by the manager.

After completing the manager's portion of the audit, the next phase was the supervisor interviews. In the audit program, managers have the option to be present during the supervisor interviews. It is here that most of the same questions asked of the manager are asked again of the supervisors. Some managers prefer hearing the responses directly during the interview, although they may have an influence that will affect the supervisor's comments. The preference is to have the supervisor alone with the team to determine if the intended message is consistent.

The main purpose of the manager and supervisor interviews is to identify how well that particular department is managed. The underlying intent is to raise the level of understanding and subsequently raise the bar on the quality culture. In the organizational structure, the manager provides direction and should closely monitor results, while the supervisor has more direct responsibilities for carrying out strategies, including the direct reporting of most of the department personnel on that shift.

It is through determining the effectiveness of the communication between the manager and supervisor, their understanding of the necessary systems, and the results of the various measures used that the lead auditor can establish the effectiveness of the organization. In addition, since the supervisor has direct responsibility for most of the department personnel, any additional systems they have established that are necessary to the functioning of the department must also be understood.

After the supervisor interview was concluded, we scheduled time for the team to meet privately and discuss what they had heard and noted through a working lunch. The team discussed responses to the questions on the scoring guide and came to a consensus on the management of the organization. This was important because in the afternoon, the team would divide up, so they could cover all the machining lines and off-line processes, and we wanted to ensure consistency as they questioned department personnel.

The afternoon session consisted of the shop tour where the audit team observed operations and questioned many of the employees about their quality activities. This was defined in the scoring guide, including areas that addressed the level and effectiveness of the communication. Each audit team observed employees performing inspection activities, entering information into the statistical software, interpreting the data, and reacting to the results. Per the scoring guide, they questioned personnel regarding training, such as how they knew what to inspect, how to set up equipment, and their reaction plan for any nonconformity. The auditors noted various gage numbers to verify that they were in the calibration system, verified product identification, material control systems, preventive maintenance activities, and noted document numbers to verify control, all per the scoring guide.

After the tour, the team gathered privately in a room to discuss the notes and observations. This was a team effort, although the lead auditor had final say if disagreement arose. The lead auditor systematically led the team through all the various sections in the scoring guide, which ensured that they covered all necessary elements of the standard pertaining to the department, gained consensus on the evidence of meeting the requirement, and agreed on a final score. Notes were taken for each section explaining the reasons and specifics for the result.

Through this audit methodology, the scoring guide format helped the team through the final report, generating any necessary discussions based on their notes and gaining consensus for the audit. Once the audit was scored, with the supporting information noted, the team identified the positive aspects found during the audit and any opportunities for improvement. Any corrective action required would be noted at that time. The training guidelines, audit ethics, scoring guide, results, and corrective action system (we called ours a system audit response or SAR) were developed in an MS Access database available to all personnel.

The plant manager, quality manager, and key department personnel were called back for the closing meeting. After getting signatures for documentation, the lead auditor discussed the overall audit process and thanked everyone for their participation. Each section was then reviewed, explaining the scores and specifics for the scoring decision based on the team notes. Any issues were raised at this time so there was discussion between the team and department personnel.

The final score with a corresponding overall rating was given followed by positives, opportunities for improvement, and any corrective actions noted with agreed-upon due dates. The lead auditor was responsible for publishing a written audit report within a week after the audit. I also decided to have a summary presented a few days after the audit by the audit team. This was presented in one of the regular morning meetings of the management team.

These audit reviews went well that year, the first one being the most memorable. The room was filled with managers, support personnel, and the audit team. This was the first time with the new team concept and although I thought the audit went well, I didn't know what the management team would think. The lead auditor began by giving an overview of the process. He said overall it went very well and each member provided good input into the process. A summary was given and as each operator-auditor reviewed their section, you could tell they were nervous. The lead auditor then wrapped it up with the rating, positives, and opportunities for improvement.

The plant manager asked the operators what they thought of the process. I didn't know what to expect. After a moment, they said it was a lot different from what they expected and a good experience. One auditor went on to say she never realized there was so much to our quality system and that she would start telling others in her area how thorough the system was. The other said she developed a new appreciation for all that the machining department went through to provide parts to her assembly line and others in her area needed to understand that wasn't as easy as they thought. The area manager said he was surprised at how thorough the audit was and that he got a lot of value out of hearing how his department understood the messages he sent. He said there were some good ideas raised on how to improve the systems. I realized the new methodology was a success.

KEY VALUE-ADDING CONCEPTS

Over that first audit season, I began to see far more value in the audit process than I had originally thought. When we first developed the team concept using the scoring guide, my thoughts were mainly focused on getting more coverage in the audits. In other words, I could ensure that we had a realistic audit schedule throughout the year, cover all manufacturing areas, and I didn't have to do it alone. In addition, the old audit checklist was based solely on the ISO standard and did not necessarily fit our work environment so it was awkward to use. The progressive audit was designed around the flow of the major processes and easy to follow by the teams. It was also expandable.

In the second audit season, since production in many areas ran 24 hours, we expanded the audit to cover the major processes on all shifts. I could have never accomplished this activity with the last-minute audit. In addition, one of the lead auditors developed an audit checklist that covered all areas of the scoring guide but with easier-to-understand questions. This became the working document on the shop floor and the scoring guide was the final summary report format.

In the third audit season, I became the divisional quality manager. The position meant overall quality responsibility for three manufacturing plants and my intent was to expand the audit program to cover the three facilities across two states. A proposal was made to add a quality engineer position to develop, facilitate, and support the internal audit program throughout the division, in addition to performing other quality engineering responsibilities. Gaining approval for this position not only showed a commitment to quality by upper management but also a realization of the value internal audits would add to our division, based on the previous successes.

I hired a quality engineer, who previously worked for me as a supplier quality engineer. He was charged with modifying the scoring guide and related checklists to reflect the ISO 9001:2000 upgrade while I provided input and approval of the final draft. The quality engineer was an important position divisionally because it provided oversight of the program across the three manufacturing facilities in addition to a focus on the audit itself that would result in significant improvements.

A more mature progressive audit methodology was presented to the management team at each facility, and although all three management teams supported the program, it was not without some skepticism. One of the plant managers openly discussed his reservations with me about time commitments and value because of concerns about pulling away important resources needed for his improvement strategies. I was able to gain his support that first audit season and later in the year, in the management review, he openly stated that it was a good program and became a strong supporter of the methodology.

There are important concepts about the progressive audit that add much benefit to the organization. Although most organizations have an audit program, many struggle with obtaining value from this activity. It does not have to be this way. I believe this methodology can add tremendous value to any organization, based on the following key concepts.

Team-Based Auditing

The team concept was critical to the success of the program. When I was performing the last-minute audits, everyone thought that I owned the program. I could get other managers, including the plant manager, to assist me in the annual audit, but the common perception was that it was a requirement and it was my responsibility. When you introduce it as a team-based audit, the perceptions change dramatically. The audit is now looked at as a plant activity and although quality facilitates it, the ownership is spread out among the management team. Once the plant manager felt he was an owner of the process, he took greater interest in ensuring its success.

This paradigm shift was subtle and gradually started to surface over that first audit season, until it eventually became part of the quality culture in the facility. I look at this as a milestone that must be achieved for a successful program. The mental model of the audit changes from a necessary evil that identifies incorrect procedures to an annual analysis of their area. The manager sees it as an important tool that provides a summary of how their organization, which is the department or major process, is functioning in relationship to the various systems and processes that they have defined.

Team-based auditing is also an important model for the employees. That is because they become active participants rather than passive observers in quality system improvements. Tremendous value is added to the audit process when you have members from various backgrounds in the organization on the audit team. A team member from the human resources area will add greater understanding to audited sections on training, communication, and employee involvement because of their background. However, they also can bring new clarity to understanding about areas they are not familiar with because they will ask questions others may not think to ask.

Audit teams are also important for the quality manager that is too involved in the internal audits. When performing last-minute audits, I realized that time became the critical factor. As we came closer to the ISO audit, I felt more pressure to get the job done. Rather than a valuable activity to be managed, it became a task to complete in a short period of time.

Team-based auditing allowed me to step back and manage the program rather than perform it. The quality manager from the Poplar Bluff facility pointed out that even though he was independent of most areas in the plant, he was still close to the processes because he owned the quality manual. He also was closely involved in the quality activities in the various areas. The quality manager is too close to the system to be the auditor.

Understanding of Systems and Processes

Another important role of the progressive audit is to help people understand the concept of systems and processes, and why they are important. To do this, the audit must have a broad scope and offer a learning opportunity. The reason I suggest a broad scope is because very focused audits provide detail but do not necessarily force discussions of overall systems. To promote system and process thinking in the various departments of the organization, the audit must be asking general open-ended questions about how each area is managed and how department activities are affected by the various systems (accounting system, information system, and so on).

These questions must lead to the identification of the relationship between a process and its related activities, inputs, outputs, and measures. The audit is broad through probing for understanding of high-level processes such as the planning process or communication process. It then becomes more focused through investigative activities focused on uncovering logical relationships of specific activities and tasks to these broader processes. This provides a learning opportunity for both auditor and auditee in determining if the defined relationships do exist and add value to the organization.

The audit scope is also broad in that, per progressive audit methodology, all areas or departments are audited to the same or similar format and technique. In our case, production areas fall under the manufacturing process. This encourages discussion between the managers over similar operational sequences and efficiency measures, providing opportunity to benchmark the better approaches that successfully accomplish a specific task. Even in the management reviews, we promote overall awareness of strengths and weaknesses in the organization because of this commonality.

More specifically, since we audit all major manufacturing areas each audit season, each manager regularly hears and discusses the key points of the quality system in the morning meeting when results are presented. Certain common themes like control and planning issues begin to appear that lead the management team to make decisions to improve specific systems and processes, which is formalized in the management review. Since the audit also requires discussion with many employees within the department, overall understanding of the various systems within the department increases.

The audit also creates an understanding of the importance of relationships in a systemic sense. This is a key point for movement toward creating a sound quality culture. Audits are about systems. In fact, the audit is a systematic activity, which means it is a system itself "characterized by order and planning."[1] By nature of the format of the audit program and scoring guide, it identifies the various systems and processes as part of its structure because it is organized around them.

To plant personnel, certain systems seem obvious, especially when they directly affect the employee, such as the attendance system. Yet people don't always think of attendance as a system but rather in terms of various activities or rewards and punishments for following it. In other words, they see the term "attendance system" as a generalization for a group of activities or rules. The quality system also falls into this category. Employees may have specific tasks related to quality, but the term is viewed to mean activities everyone should do so the product has good or excellent quality. If we look to the dictionary, the term *system* has two distinctly different meanings[2]:

1. A set of objects or phenomena grouped together for classification or analysis

2. A group of interacting, interrelated, or interdependent elements forming a complex whole

In the first definition, the term *system* becomes a means of grouping activities. If you work in the quality department, you are part of the quality system. If you are performing inspection, you are doing an activity that is also part of the quality system, even if you don't belong to that department. If engineering and quality make a decision to release product that has some identified problem, the cry from the workforce is "where is our quality system?", although they don't realize that testing and product deviations may also be part of the system. In the same regard, I have heard claims that we cannot deviate because of ISO, almost as a battle cry for compliance to some lofty value. The thought process here is clearly that system means categorizing some common activities.

There is a significant difference in the second definition because the word *relationship* becomes a factor. In this case, the various activities are viewed in light of their interaction and interdependency. The term *system* no longer means merely to group activities but rather a planned relationship of key activities and tasks to accomplish a common objective or strategy. These relationships occur not only within a specific department or discipline but also between other departments or disciplines. As the definition states, it views the organization as a complex whole.

To achieve success in an organization, systems must be viewed in terms of relationships. The challenge is thinking of systems in this light rather than merely as a grouping of common activities. The ISO 9001:2000 standard, in its emphasis on processes and interfaces, has moved us significantly in this direction. The upgrade raised the mental model of an organization toward interrelated systems by defining them as processes. Comparing definitions, we have the following:

- System: a group of interacting, interrelated, or interdependent elements forming a complex whole

- Process: a set of interrelated or interacting activities, which transforms inputs into outputs

In process thinking, we have expanded the concept of the systems definition by also defining inputs and outputs for the system. In process thinking, we also need to think about an owner, a supplier, and a customer. There should be objectives, measures, and goals, not as a requirement for all processes, but present for most key processes. Where systems thinking can become somewhat theoretical and nebulous, process thinking brings systems to life since they have a beginning and an end, and can be measured.

Although beneficial, this movement toward processes, relationships, and interfaces has presented a significant challenge to business because of its complexity. The process map may look simple, but it can be deceiving. We can no longer have systems stand by themselves, but we must identify how they contribute to the success of other systems and measure their effectiveness as it contributes to the organization as a whole. To do this we must break them down further into their various processes.

ISO has moved organizations toward process maps that simplify previously cumbersome procedures into logical flows and sequences. It has made the quality management system easier to understand because in defining our various processes, we develop the pieces to the puzzle called the system. Then we relate the various systems to define the organization and it becomes a visual presentation of the whole organization at the highest levels.

Although process maps make the quality system easier to understand, there is a significantly more important benefit to them. Each map is a piece of the puzzle and is not only important in itself but must fit properly within the whole. The objective tells you why it is important, the measure is a monitoring tool, and the goal establishes a target that aligns it with the organizational strategy. In process thinking, a system is in fact a collection of interrelated processes.

The internal audit and its broad scope question and probe for this understanding. Initially, the level is somewhat basic, but as the level of understanding within the audit team and management grows, the organization will develop greater sophistication and detail in its processes through continuous improvement efforts. One must create widespread understanding of the current systems and processes in order to improve them.

Continuous Improvement

To repeat what was previously stated, the internal audit program should create an appreciation and understanding of systems and processes. Auditing processes requires investigation of key interfaces and relationships. This is necessary to verify effectiveness since suppliers and customers of a process play a pivotal role. It begins with auditing the basics but as the knowledge base grows, the systems and processes will change and become more efficient and effective; in other words, you will have continuous improvement.

On the supplier side, this leads to auditing upstream in the organization to improve the quality of output of higher-level processes, and horizontally to improve the interfaces. On the customer side, it leads to auditing downstream to ensure that the correct objectives, measures, and goals have been identified. This is both a tremendous challenge and a tremendous opportunity for improvement within the organization. Let's explore an opportunity for improvement that is both an input and output of many processes in an organization, namely information.

Since processes and interfaces are not always well defined or understood, management spends a large part of their day sorting out massive amounts of information to assure themselves that the jobs are getting done. They have some clearly defined objectives and measures but also many less-defined responsibilities, not to mention substantial amounts of supporting documentation and opinion. This information relates to various areas of responsibility but much of it is on the perimeter dealing with a multitude of issues. The perception of managers is that there are systems in place, but their role is one of a creative energy source, reacting to their changing environment and directing the energies of the staff as necessary to accomplish what they perceive are their departmental goals.

One huge source of information is e-mail, which has opened up new opportunities to give people a greater purpose, which is to inform everyone. Organizations encourage managers to see all of this potentially important information so that much of their productive time is spent unproductively opening, looking over, and deleting electronic correspondence and reports. This requires identifying what information must be acted upon, what may be needed in the future, what should be filed for reference, or what can be ignored. Much time is spent reading useless information in order to get to the small percentage that is useful. The underlying result is that this inefficient activity encourages waste in the organization.

This also means managing all of the meetings that occur. Everything we do now seems to require meetings. If we add up the productive time unproductively reading e-mail and include the time attending unproductive meetings, management seems to have moved the productive time to after work hours. In other words, we work longer hours because we have to stay after the unproductive people go home so we can accomplish something.

Finally, there are the phone calls. Managers call other managers and their subordinates because the electronic information leads to more questions that can only be resolved through direct dialog. At times it is an informal decision-making process or brainstorming session. Sometimes there is an immediate need to "get on this one" that must be personally conveyed. Formal meetings that are supposed to resolve issues raise other issues that produce countless other conversations until they are resolved.

A constant complaint heard in many organizations is the fact that there are so many meetings and so much information to read; it generates the feeling that it is nearly impossible to get anything accomplished. This is a symptom of a serious issue and that is that the organization has inefficient processes. There are many reasons to call, send e-mail, or have meetings. Some are legitimate, but much of information overload is due to the following:

- Employees use the chain of command for information flow, which produces a constant stream of questions and subsequent answers that are initially inadequate so that the cycle runs again until the right answer is heard or other pressing issues take precedence.

- Critical information necessary to ensure that processes are running correctly is not well defined or understood.

- Employees do not understand their processes so either tasks are missed or they perform additional and unnecessary activities to ensure that all bases are covered.

- Employees do not believe that others understand their respective processes so they question results, duplicate activities, or hold additional meetings to ensure that everyone's informed.

- Management doesn't recognize the processes as effective so lead times are cut short, sending the message that procedures are made to be circumvented to get the job done.

To better understand, let's explore the topic of how managers manage. Business writers differ in their opinions about successful management styles, ranging from doers and controllers to leaders. Henry Mintzberg analyzed the role and thought process of a manager and concluded that they manage on three levels: an action level, a people level, and an information level.[3] He said there are commonly held myths that managers are systematic planners, that senior management needs a formal information system, and that management is quickly becoming a science and a profession. Instead, he cited research that suggests that much of the role is still based on dialog and memory and has not changed in the last hundred years:

- No study has found patterns in the way time is scheduled; managers seem to jump from issue to issue based on the needs of the moment.

- In two British studies, managers spent 66 percent and 80 percent of their time in verbal communication.

- Mintzberg studied five chief executives and found mail processing a burden. He noted that one came in on Saturday to process 142 pieces of mail in three hours to "get rid of all the stuff."

- An analysis of the mail received found that only 13 percent was of immediate or specific use, leading to the conclusion that little mail provides current information.

According to a recent *Wall Street Journal* article, since 1999 the number of daily e-mails has tripled in North America to an amazing 11.9 billion. Regarding the users of this information, 48 percent of office workers spend one to two hours per day reading through their e-mail. It went on to say that 10 percent of workers spend over half of their day reading e-mail.[4]

Mintzberg found that managers seem to cherish "soft" information, especially gossip and hearsay because of its timeliness; today's gossip might be tomorrow's fact. Rather than write it down, they preferred to store this information in their brains. Because of this, inefficiencies can prosper. There is also a reluctance to delegate critical responsibilities since knowledge of specific issues is not widely available because the processes are not well defined. Just as there are subsystems in existence on the shop floor, they also flourish in the management ranks.

In looking at Mintzberg's three levels of managing, there is a relationship to one's level of influence. I look at this as how much you can maximize your effectiveness. The action level means you are a "doer."[5] Since upper-level managers don't necessarily do anything, according to the research, at this level you are managing specific projects and activities to ensure they are getting done. You are one step removed from those performing the actions, but close enough to know the details and ensure that they are accomplished. You can also be described as the champion for change in your unit, where you are both managing it and an active member of the team.

Moving outward to a larger sphere of influence, you operate on the people level. This is where the leaders live. Much research and energy has gone into this activity because it is crucial to an organization. At this level, a manager can lead on an individual, group, or unit level. Managers are concerned with developing the culture of leaders since they can stay a step removed from the action level and still have confidence that the appropriate activities are occurring. It appears that most of a manager's time is spent in these two levels, which is supported by research. However, I believe the most effective manager, while actively working at both action and people levels, operates on the informational level. I also believe this is the area most underutilized in organizations.

At this level, you are two steps away from the purpose of managerial work.[6] It is at this level where a manager processes information to generate action by other people. The manager is the "nerve center" of the unit where they have access to a wide variety of information. Everyone else in the unit is a specialist, knowing more of the details than the manager. The manager's role is as more of a controller, using information to direct activities in the following ways: developing systems, designing structures, and imposing directives.

The reason I feel this is the most effective level is because it provides structure; in other words, you are defining processes. It also establishes efficient activities that can live on after the manager has left. One can champion a new technology or be a charismatic leader of an organization, but when one leaves, a hole is left in the organization. Managing at the information level offers a manager broad influence because well-structured systems promote a common language with understanding of the necessary activities and controls to ensure that the objectives are properly met.

Efficient and effective processes must be the goal of any organization because they promote widespread understanding and educate others who will replace the managers that leave. They also create confidence rather than chaos because the data clearly identify where you must put your resources. To achieve this you must have accurate and useful information. You must also have processes that are well defined, efficient, and effective. When this occurs, there is less need to spend significant time publishing or reading peripheral information because all you need to see are the measures.

To ensure that efficient and effective systems and processes are in place, all levels of management need to be active proponents of internal systems audit programs. This is obviously not the case in general. There is one explanation for this; management does not obtain value from the audit program. The reason is that management does not understand the benefits of an audit program because it has been ineffective in the past.

If we look at the growing global acceptance of the ISO 9001:2000 standard, there is some perceived lack of value and also confusion in its interpretation. John E. "Jack" West provides a key insight. He said that one key factor that influenced the delays in registration to the upgrade was the relative maturity of the quality management system.[7] According to West, organizations with immature systems faced four difficult issues in the new standard:

- Continual improvement, because it was not linked to the quality system and they haven't made efforts to measure their results.

- Customer focus through measurement of customer satisfaction.

- Top management's role through more involvement in determining if they are carrying out their required role.

- Processes versus procedures, which he felt was the most important aspect of the standard.

West's four issues relate to performance or understanding the customer's requirements and measuring continuous improvement. The older 20-element system (ISO 9000:1994) ensured that you had documented procedures and were following them, but didn't necessarily ensure that those procedures contributed to a satisfied customer nor to the success of the business. He argued that a mature quality management system developed effective systems and processes because it established appropriate measures to verify that they are effective (one of the underlying quality principles of ISO is decisions based on facts and data).

Might an immature quality system also explain increased workloads and confusion for the quality manager? If the system were mature, customers would have fewer issues because the performance measures would have resulted in continually improving the processes; in other words, customer satisfaction. Mature systems would also mean that many are involved in their implementation so there is less need for the close oversight of a quality manager. Rather than direct involvement in each area to develop processes and measures, those responsible would be developing them.

We must also remember history because there was a vast learning curve in coming to the point of a global quality management system standard. Up until the release of ISO 9000:1987, there was no international standard. This monumental effort moved the global quality community toward a best-practice approach to continual improvement of the quality management system. It raised the bar at the time of the 1987 release and again with the upgrades of 1994 and 2000. This also argues well the point that upgrading to the new standard ensures growth in the quality system, especially since you must now measure it. As pointed out by West, immature systems do not have adequate measures so they are slow to upgrade (change).

Continuous improvement is not necessarily a quick process, especially in regard to understanding and improving processes from a system perspective. It is improvement based on a cycle of uncovering issues, deciding on the best course of action, implementing it, and auditing the next season to determine effectiveness. It is a slower process because it usually focuses on pieces of the whole that must be improved because the findings usually relate to only certain aspects of a process. It is also gradual because it requires changing patterns of behavior and thought processes of people.

Changing the Quality Culture

Management uses the quality management system to affect the quality culture of the organization through their commitment and support of the various aspects of that system. As management's understanding and belief in the important quality principles increases, greater purpose and commitment will be evident in subsequent quality initiatives and changes. It is a cycle of continuous improvement that raises the level of awareness and discipline in the organization.

Three key elements must be present for this to occur. First, there must be a means of stimulating awareness in management of the direction the organization must take to improve. This is important because if no such stimulation occurs, the quality management system will become stagnant. One obvious method of raising awareness of issues is through measures and related organizational goals.

When numbers are not being met, there needs to be action taken to improve. One purpose of the audit is to provide feedback on compliance to defined activities, so the audit results provide opportunities for improvement. The internal audit season also stimulates awareness of issues simply through greater understanding of the system by repeated exposure and discussion. It also forces people to reevaluate the quality system, why they do certain things, and why they are important.

Second, there must be a means of incorporating this new direction from management into the organization. This is always a dilemma because the methodology is typically focused on training programs with periodic follow-up when implementing a new system. However, a well-developed audit program allows management to have an established means of verifying that change is both implemented and understood as part of normal business practice.

There is an important distinction in these approaches. Typically, when implementing a new system there is a champion and team heading up the training programs and implementation of the change. There are obvious interests at stake so follow-up can be biased, shedding a positive light when in fact there may be serious issues. Also, since this is a nonnormal process, extra focus is on these activities and unintentional efforts can occur to distort reality. The internal audit program is team-based and an entity in itself and, by nature, an unbiased analysis of the various systems and processes. In this regard, management receives honest feedback on initiatives.

Finally, there must be a means of maintaining and monitoring effectiveness so adjustments can be made if necessary. In the typical process of implementing a new system, follow-up occurs for a finite period of time until it is deemed successful. Afterward, a measure may be implemented to monitor the change but many times it just becomes part of the overall system. Over time, employees adapt it to what they find to be the most efficient means of achieving the desired end so it changes. Management believes it to be as implemented while the reality is something different, sometimes significantly.

The internal audit is a reoccurring activity, the purpose of which is to verify that systems and processes are implemented as intended and to identify variations so management can determine whether they should be incorporated or corrected. It is an important feedback mechanism on those systems and processes that management has deemed important to the ultimate success of the business. Employees' understanding and degree of implementation are affected by their attitude and commitment to quality, or the quality culture. Raising the culture is a slow process that requires consistent and sustained effort and high visibility, all products of a progressive audit methodology.

Measurable Results

The scoring guide was a document originally structured around the various elements of the older ISO standard. In the third audit season, it was upgraded to reflect the new standard. Each section has a number of questions with bullet points defining specific activities or documents that must be found in order to receive full credit. Each question is worth two points maximum if all requirements are met, one point if partially met, and no points if little evidence is found. This is covered in detail later in the book, as well as completed scoring guides and checklists in the appendixes.

The first sections relate to how the organization is run, which means probing into customer satisfaction, quality policy, goal setting, communication, training, and continuous improvement. The next sections address management of the process such as advanced quality planning, defining requirements, controlling the process, material control, gauging, and inspection. It finishes up with control of nonconforming product and corrective action.

This scoring guide provides a format for the auditors to follow with specific questions to ask. It also provides a framework for training since the team spends much of the time discussing the questions in relationship to the organization and the requirements of the manual, which leads to an understanding of the processes and systems. Because it is organized around the manufacturing process, it is a complete document that the team needs to cover as its goal for completing the audit (there are separate scoring guides for other areas such as quality, purchasing, and so on). It is very specific to the task yet applicable to any manufacturing or assembly process, provides quantitative results so the feedback is relative, and is written in terminology suitable for our environment.

I believe in quantitative results because they force a reaction. Each section has a score; the overall audit results in an overall score and rating of excellent, very good, good, conditional, or unacceptable. The department and plant manager can see the scores for each section of the audit report and identify areas for improvement in addition to the specific audit findings. As a quality manager, I wanted to have a report for each major process/department, broken down into specific systems or subprocesses, so I could review and easily identify strengths and weaknesses, which this provided.

Scoring an audit also presents challenges. Managers are told that it is a "snapshot" in time, so the scores could vary by a few points depending on the team yet overall ratings would be consistent. As we expanded to more audit teams, new teams tended to be more lenient because of inexperience so scores were somewhat higher.

One consideration for a standard format audit document is revision and change; we revised the audit annually because we found sections that needed to be improved so the scores would be based on different or in some cases, tougher questions. However, the audit is relative to that period of time and the score reflects that. The department improved its systems, and we kept raising the bar, but you could still use it as a comparative tool to make judgments and identify opportunities against previous audit results.

Improvement to the Bottom Line

The audit team should investigate whether the various process measures accurately reflect the process and if they are sensitive enough that actions can affect the measures. For example, Briggs & Stratton Corporation uses *economic value added* (EVA) as a financial measure for each facility, major manufacturing process and department, as well as to justify significant equipment upgrades. In this case, a manager can affect their EVA value based on controlling specific drivers, but if that control were out of their hands, it would not be an effective measure.[8]

It is appropriate here to discuss an interpretation of the intent of the ISO standard. Although it is a quality management system standard, the philosophy taken here is not purely a quality-related one. When developing the process maps and objectives, the decision could be made to include financial as well as productivity objectives and measures. This, in effect, elevates the quality management system to a "business management system" since it includes other organizational measures.

Taking this approach is meaningful because customer satisfaction and product quality have an impact on organizational profitability and performance. On the other hand, the quality management system and the ISO quality system standard are moving organizations toward verifying the reliability and effectiveness of the process measures. Through introducing productivity and profitability measures into the quality management system, organizations can use the internal audit and management review process to analyze on a regular basis the appropriateness of organizational initiatives against those metrics. This also brings quality into the boardroom because of its relationship to performance measures.

In an article by Ittner and Larcker, the authors found through field research that only a few companies realized the benefits of nonfinancial measures on their profitability.[9] The companies that did show a significant return on assets and equity over a five-year period had established cause-and-effect links between financial and nonfinancial measures. They found that the less successful companies were measuring aspects of performance that did not matter. The root cause was a failure to determine which measures have the most powerful effects on economic performance. For example, companies in the restaurant industry devoted financial resources to reducing employee turnover, when further analysis found profitability related to turnover among supervisors and not the lower-level workers.[10]

Improved Feedback on the Quality System

When I was touring the facility as the quality manager with the plant manager, how openly did operators respond to our questions? This same issue existed in the past, when the audit was performed in our organization by a divisional quality manager and prior to that, a corporate vice president of quality. This may be effective for auditing the management team but I question the reliability of the responses from employees on the shop floor who do not know who these individuals are, let alone what they are asking because of terminology. Responses are far more open when the people asking the questions sit in the same lunchroom as opposed to an outsider who doesn't seem to fit the "culture."

Builds Credibility for the Quality Program

If the internal audit program is well organized and professional, it promotes new emphasis on and respect for the quality system. This promotes confidence in the quality system in achieving stated objectives because people have a better understanding of the systems and consistently practice what is required due to this understanding, and it also promotes the idea of continuous improvement because they understand how the system works. This also allows you to put more detail in your procedures without fear that they will be difficult to implement. A common avoidance practice is to word procedures vaguely (to ensure that an ISO auditor won't stumble on a nonconformance) rather than define an activity in a way that provides benefit.

The audit provides valuable information to the management team through understanding of how all shifts are operating, including identification of differences. It provides feedback to management that what they are communicating is also understood, uncovers employee issues related to the systems and culture, and identifies areas needing more training or guidance. Since it is in a standard format, it offers opportunities to identify high-performing areas that can be modeled elsewhere in the organization. Because of this value it provides credibility for the quality system.

Expandable

The progressive audit is not an entirely new concept. It is a means of adding much value to existing methods. Like any method or technique, you can implement it to varying degrees. Initially it was a procedure for analyzing the major manufacturing and support process within a facility but was expanded to include all shifts in each area. These same methods were expanded to programs for three different manufacturing facilities within a division and the potential exists for the program to be corporatewide should that be the strategy of the organization.

It also provides an opportunity to implement the same quality management system throughout a division, creating an internal "best practices" quality system, and offering common understanding between facilities. It allows you to utilize the audit teams to expand into focused audits on such activities as major product introduction projects or analyzing specific incidents for greater insight.

Increased Focus on Quality

I have found that the progressive audit simply gets people talking a lot more about quality, not just product quality, but about the whole quality system. When people see teams of four to six auditors meeting with managers in a room with papers strewn on the table, they start asking questions. They see teams touring the workplace on a regular basis and hear results in their department meetings. Much discussion and review of the system occurs when the audit schedule shows their area is coming up because they want to be prepared.

Auditors from other areas, such as human resources, will discuss the audit and quality system with their manager and peers prior to when they are scheduled to be on one of the teams. Just the fact that they are an audit team member and have increased understanding of the quality system will bring more discussion into their normal workday. In fact, in an opening meeting for our ISO audit, one management team discussed the value of the internal audits and how much it has helped raise the awareness in the workforce. Because there is a lot more activity with a progressive audit methodology, it gets others not directly involved asking questions and discussing quality.

I believe the internal audit process at Briggs & Stratton has grown from a required and somewhat useful annual activity to a part of the organizational culture. It has been widely accepted as an important provider of information on our quality-related activities and a means of raising the level of understanding in the workplace. This has occurred because of the key concepts and benefits described above.

I have been an active driver of the progressive audit methodology over the last four years and should I remove myself from the picture, I believe this activity will not only carry on but flourish and grow. That is because both management and participating employees see value in this process, both at the plant and divisional level. If recommendations were made to eliminate this activity, there would be nothing to take its place and I believe managers would resist.

It is not always a pleasant activity because the lead auditors and teams have gotten very good at auditing and post challenging questions to the management team. Managers and supervisors have grown accustomed to defending their actions and decisions, relating the responses back to the defined quality systems, and because of this process, the knowledge base has grown.

In preparation for their upcoming audits, I still see areas busy getting their "documents" in order and refreshing their personnel on the important processes and tasks. But even in this preparation, things have changed. Where in the past, they would be seeking guidance and advice from the quality manager in their preparation, the manufacturing team now conducts these activities. That is because they understand the quality management system and responsibilities. This means the ownership of the quality system has shifted.

ENDNOTES

1. Webster's Revised Unabridged Dictionary (Los Angeles: MICRA, 1998).
2. www.dictionary.com (Lexico Publishing Group, 2003).
3. Henry Mintzberg, "The Manager's Job," in Joyce S. Osland, David A. Kolb, and Irwin M. Rubin, *The Organizational Behavior Reader,* Seventh ed., (Upper Saddle River, NJ: Prentice Hall, 2001).
4. Marlon A. Walker, "The Day the E-Mail Dies," *The Wall Street Journal* (August 26, 2004).
5. Mintzberg, "The Manager's Job."
6. Ibid.
7. John E. (Jack) West, "Is There Time?" *Quality Progress* (March 2003).
8. Joel M. Stern, John S. Shiely, with Irwin Ross, *The EVA Challenge* (New York: John Wiley and Sons, 2001): 48–49.
9. Christopher D. Ittner and David F. Larcker, "Coming Up Short on Nonfinancial Performance Measurement," *Harvard Business Review* (November 2003).
10. Ibid., 91.

10

Implementing the Progressive Audit

Implementing the progressive audit rests on one important premise: you must want it to add value to the organization. Otherwise, it is just another activity that satisfies some requirement. In fact, since this methodology expands on the internal audit program through team-based auditing and specific scoring guides for the various areas of the organization, it will require more work than traditional or last-minute audits. It also requires very good planning.

OBTAINING COMMITMENT

To begin, this methodology first needs the commitment from quality (Figure 10.1). The quality manager will personally need to give up ownership of the audit. By this I mean your initial role will be that of a champion and then one who manages it by providing support and resources. This means you don't perform the audits. In my case, this was an easy task because I did not believe I was gaining much benefit from the activity. The last-minute audit was not going to change the quality culture since too few people were directly involved in the process.

Some quality managers believe strongly in personally performing the internal audits. I have heard the argument that "if I do it then I know it will be done right." This creates an audit program that may be effective, at least in that quality manager's eyes, but ends when the individual moves on. Since they are performing the audits and running the program, it is their program so there is not much interest from outsiders except when they are audited. There is misunderstanding on the part of quality managers in the idea that they are the only ones capable of performing this activity properly.

Other quality managers will find the extra work implementing the progressive audit too demanding because of the resources necessary to organize a structured program like this. They may also raise concerns about support by management. Maybe they have a designated person that performs all the audits so they are efficient and do not demand a commitment of teams of employees. They may even prefer to be directly involved because it keeps them close to the system and processes. I would still argue the case that it promotes

Figure 10.1   Progressive audit Step 1.

a quality management system owned by quality rather than the management team because that quality manager is too close to the quality system to effectively audit it.

Quality managers have a lot of responsibility in an organization, which is one of the reasons for last-minute audits. A 2003 survey of quality professionals revealed that of those working more than 40 hours per week (91 percent), a quarter of the respondents added at least 10 hours to their workweek as a result of the standard.[1] Although nine out of 10 were at least moderately satisfied with their job, quality managers said that work was more demanding and felt that time constraint was the number one problem affecting their job. In fact, almost 20 percent of them said the demands were so high that some of the work didn't even get done.[2] The reasons given:

- Increased workload with fewer employees

- More work, responsibilities, and expectations

- Customer demands for greater responsibility in relationship

- Program goals not getting completed

- Work can't be done on time

- Transition to the new system

The solution remains changing the belief system of key management personnel in the organization so they take an ownership in the audit process. Quality management provides oversight of the program to ensure that it addresses all the necessary requirements. Teams require personnel from various areas in the organization, not just the quality department. Since resources are typically lean, other managers must see the potential value of this process and allow personnel from their areas to participate. In other words, they must make a commitment to quality, which means in this case providing resources to better analyze their activities.

So the first step of implementing the progressive audit is presenting the audit philosophy and program to the management team and getting commitment. This only makes sense since the audit is a team-based activity, not just a team that works for management and audits the various areas. It requires the management team itself to oversee and support the program, accept the results, and commit to the improvement efforts. The quality management system by definition is a management system and responsibility for its success should fall on management's shoulders.

Although the benefits of this methodology were discussed previously, the important aspects of the progressive audit philosophy can be broken down into the following three key components:

1. *Management commitment and support.* Management owns the quality management system and accepts the responsibility of analyzing and verifying its effectiveness through the internal audit program, supporting it through a commitment of oversight, resources, and responding appropriately to the results.

2. *Team-based activity.* Employees also own the quality management system and are encouraged to participate in its analysis and improvement as an audit team member, where they will learn all of its important quality concepts, develop the skills necessary to judge the system, and will commit their time and energy to its success.

3. *Continuous improvement.* The organization will commit to aggressively analyzing the quality management system and related activities, take necessary actions based on the results of the audit, and continuously improve the effectiveness of the audit process. Expanding the scope of the audit into more processes, improving the scoring guides through updating their questions, and improving auditor skills through training and experience during the audit season will accomplish this. This will affect the organization in three ways:

   a. Expand management philosophy and understanding of quality management systems and tools.

   b. Raise the level of awareness, expertise, and understanding of the workforce (quality culture).

   c. Improve the implementation and effectiveness of the quality management system.

Management commitment is important to ensure the success of the program, which is stated often in quality publications. How you get there is another story. It is naïve to believe that there should be a commitment because the program is labeled quality. They should commit because they see potential value in the activity. That means presenting the audit methodology as an opportunity to improve the organization. In many cases, this must also raise the level of understanding of management.

This leads us to the next key concept, team-based auditing. Management should be concerned about the quality culture of the organization. Employees need to understand the quality system, and although much time and effort can be put into training programs, follow-up to solidify basic understanding is difficult. This is where team-based auditing provides a valuable means to promote greater understanding and involvement.

It allows employees to participate in the audit. This requires in-depth training in the system, followed by interviewing, observation, and analysis of data, which bring the theoretical into practical reality. They are given the opportunity to understand it well enough to make decisions on its adequacy and effectiveness. In addition, the scope of the audit is expanded so more employees are interviewed by the team and from varying perspectives, based on the background of the auditors. This will solidify the understanding of the workforce through questioning for understanding.

The third concept is continuous improvement, an important and often-explored process in the ISO audits. In a sense, to continually improve suggests a continual focus on something; otherwise, how can you continually improve? You might get by performing last-minute audits, suggesting that your continual improvement cycle is annual. In addition, there are probably certain areas of the quality management system that are in the sights of management due to some specific issues. But ultimately, the only method I know of to regularly focus on the quality system itself, except for a rewrite of the quality manual, is the audit.

The progressive audit methodology has an audit season, which means there are regular audits going on throughout this period of time. Teams are seen on the shop floor and in the offices and results are reported and discussed regularly in management and department meetings. There is a continual focus on the quality management system because of the consistency of the audits. Even in the "off season," management is planning its strategy for the next audit season, as discussed later in this book. This elevates the concept of quality beyond product issues and their related tools and procedures to performance of the quality management system, specifically its defined processes.

Common themes arise through opportunities for improvement, and analysis occurs to develop a means to resolve the issues and ultimately improve the system. In many cases, the audit creates some confusion and conflict regarding interpretation of intent. This is extremely beneficial since it requires serious discussion on philosophy and value to the organization and results in greater understanding of the management system. In some cases, it will force management to investigate new concepts, possibly benchmarking other companies, so a significant improvement can be implemented. The internal audit acts as a catalyst for improvement. It increases the understanding of management on quality methods and tools, raises the bar of the quality culture, and improves the overall effectiveness of the quality management system.

PURPOSE OF THE AUDIT

Once the program has been presented to management and approved, the next step is determining the audit purpose and scope (Figure 10.2). This is important because it sets the direction you must take for developing the scoring guides, teams, and audit schedules. There can be a number of purposes for the internal audit. In some of the literature these are called types of audits. It depends on how much you want to break down the activity into its details. You can have system audits, product audits, process audits, management audits, conformance or compliance audits, project audits, and regulatory audits. Ultimately, internal audits come down to three purposes, two of which are verification and identification. The progressive audit philosophy also recognizes increasing knowledge as a purpose of the audit.

Verification

One purpose of the audit is to verify. When you implement a corrective action, at some point in time you must verify that it was effective to close it out. In the same way, when you implement a quality system, you must verify that it is meeting its intent. There are several aspects to this verification activity. You must audit the quality management systems manual to verify that it complies with the standard to which you are registered,

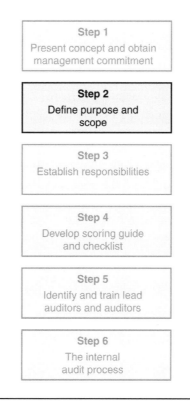

Figure 10.2 Progressive audit Step 2.

assuming you are registered to a standard. Otherwise, changes may have been made that no longer meet the requirements of the standard, not to mention the stress created when the registrar finds a quality manual that has somehow drifted away from the standard. This also encourages a good review of the standard itself.

You must verify that the quality management system is suitable for the organization. Another often-used term in ISO and one purpose for management reviews, *suitability* means that something is appropriate for a purpose or objective and proper for situations or circumstances.[3] Management establishes organizational strategies and those should fall within the overall commitments of the quality policy. The quality management system must support the policy or it is not suitable. Whether or not you use the terminology, the fact remains that the system must meet the needs of the organization.

The audit must verify that the quality management system is effective. This means that it gets results. In one sense, this means that management has developed a specific method for accomplishing a necessary task, and based on investigation and observation, the audit has verified that it is being carried out according to plan. The internal audit is effective when it understands the system and takes into consideration its intent. The audit is ineffective when it investigates the minute details of the defined activities, verifying that they are or are not occurring, but misses the big picture of whether the system is accomplishing the purpose for which it was designed.

In another sense, to get results there must be some quantifiable measure. This is auditing the effectiveness of the performance aspect of the quality management system. In a typical process, you should have a measure and stated goal. The owner of the process monitors the measure against the goal to determine if they are meeting their strategy and the process is running properly. The audit, in verifying effectiveness, investigates whether the measure is in fact looked at and reacted to, and has a goal. But is that measure an accurate predictor of the process itself?

In the move to developing the process approach, there is a learning curve to truly understand the various defined processes. There probably are quantifiable measures and nicely developed charts for tracking, with goal lines established. In my own experience, I have assisted in defining some of these measures only to realize later during the audit that those measures were an input into the process rather than a measure of the process itself. The results looked great but the process was struggling. We thought we were doing fine, based on those results, but we really weren't measuring the process correctly. In this case, the audit found an opportunity for improvement because the process measure for performance was not effectively measuring the process.

Identification

This leads us to the second purpose of the audit, identification. This is an extremely important conclusion of the verification activity. The audit will show that the team has either verified that everything is acceptable, including positive aspects worth noting, or there will be corrective actions and opportunities for improvement. Since the audit performs verification for suitability and effectiveness, it will subsequently identify issues that will provide improvement to the organization.

For example, the audit looks for gaps between the processes as defined versus as implemented and identifies specific areas where these differences exist. A discrepancy can be either the activity not performed according to plan, or the plan not accurately defining the activities performed. It is here where you would be identifying the subsystems discussed earlier in this book, which represent the methods and activities that are unknown or unrecognized by management. This may be a documented process or one defined by training. In either case, the gap is an identified inconsistency that needs to be resolved.

There can also be performance gaps, such as the one stated, where the measure did not accurately predict the performance of the process because the results identified a need to establish better measures. In other cases, a process may not be performing as planned but the improvement activity is ineffective because it doesn't drive actions to resolve the issues. As an example, a continuous improvement process tracks customer parts per million defects but no improvement trends are evident.

It is clear that identification of issues is an important purpose of the audit. I would suggest that one measure of the effectiveness of the audit process is the generation of opportunities for improvement by the audit teams. These documented conclusions provide decision points for the management team to evaluate and then implement genuine improvement to the organization, including potential strategies for the future. Identification of sound improvement opportunities generates the perception in the management ranks, including upper management, that the audit adds value to the organization.

Increasing Knowledge

The value of these opportunities for improvement depends on the knowledge base of the audit team, the third purpose of the progressive audit. Knowledge will be defined here as developing a thorough understanding of the quality management system and its various processes, including the various quality tools. This is another key aspect of the audit process that will generate the perception of the audit as a value-adding activity.

Developing a thorough understanding of quality systems and methods occurs through periodic exposure to all aspects of the system over an extended period of time. There is much logic to the quality system structure but it is complicated due to the many relationships of the various processes. One can study systems and learn about them, but it is only through repeated interaction with the various aspects of the system that understanding occurs. Team-based auditing provides a tremendous opportunity in this regard, especially in three key areas: effectiveness of the audit team, effectiveness of the management team, and developing select individuals.

Increasing the knowledge and experience of the audit team is paramount to deriving value from the process. Auditors need to understand the system to identify improvement opportunities. This occurs through the auditor training program, auditing with more experienced individuals, and through interactions within the audit process. In many discussions with less experienced auditors, I will hear them talk about it being a learning experience though they do not get the "big picture." Their understanding is more at a base level, meaning they see the specifics of the various activities but do not understand the relationships between them.

However, less-experienced auditors bring fresh perspectives to the audit. Because of their limited understanding of some of the areas they are auditing, they will ask the obvious questions that result in a finding that the obvious has not been addressed. In other words, they are far enough away from the process that preconceived ideas don't get in the way. It is important to add new auditors for this very reason.

The audit raises the level of understanding of the management team through the repeated focus on the management system throughout the audit season. You want to have the management team involved in reviews of the various audits because common themes emerge and it generates discussion and new ideas. In some ways, this can be compared to marketing. The purpose of advertising campaigns is to get a particular product in the minds of the consumer in a positive light. Catchy ads can affect market share just as no exposure to the product will result in the consumer losing interest.

Management systems are a part of the daily activities of an organization. Without regular exposure to the organization's method of defining these systems, they become activities that are performed rather than a bigger picture of relationships of processes. I have seen cases where management perception of the system was that it was ineffective when in fact very good practices were defined but no one knew they were there. We tend to see the system by what we do rather than going back to verify whether we have drifted from its original intent. The internal audit encourages good habits of thoroughness.

The last point is identifying and developing skills in certain select individuals as a purpose of the audit. The audit allows management to offer opportunities for growth to certain individuals by encouraging them to participate on the audit teams. Supplier quality personnel are lead auditors. Their position requires a high skill level in assessing organization's systems through supplier surveys. As lead auditors, they can hone their skills through the internal audits, which is especially valuable for new supplier quality personnel. This also keeps them close to our manufacturing operations, so they can better support them when working with the supplier base.

Purchasing personnel are also part of the audit team. Engineers, product designers, and manufacturing engineers are auditors and, in some cases, lead auditors. Human resources and administrative personnel are on audit teams. This creates knowledge and understanding far beyond what any training program could hope to attain. In addition, certain individuals may have potential within the organization. What better way to offer understanding of the organization's systems than to have them become an auditor.

To summarize, the progressive audit program must address three purposes: verification, identification, and increasing the knowledge of the workforce. With these aspects addressed, the next item is the audit scope.

SCOPE OF THE AUDIT

The scope of the internal audit program should include all major processes within the facility. It should address the high-level plant processes as well as the major processes or departments including support functions. Since the ISO 9001 standard requires an internal audit of all requirements of the standard affecting the organization, the scope must address this requirement as well.

This means in its purest sense that all processes must be audited as well as their related procedures as defined by the quality management system. Practically speaking, this may not be reasonable. Organizations could have many detailed processes so that to audit each one could be quite time-consuming. To satisfy the requirement of auditing all processes, we should audit the higher-level or major processes so the key activities of the organization are addressed. The major processes will also have relationships with lower-level processes and procedures, which may drill down even further to another level of detail. If the measures accurately reflect the successful performance of the major process, there should be no need to drill down further into every defined process of the organization if it is meeting its goals. If not, that will give the audit team reason to analyze at a more detailed level.

There is a practical side to auditing in that you want to obtain value from this activity. I do not believe that teams of auditors should be spending their time dissecting every detail of the organization on a regular basis. I have seen this type of audit performed and the auditee is left with numerous corrective actions in such detail that it becomes difficult to develop an action plan. The end result is frustration and dread for the next round of audits.

The audit scope should be at a level in the organization such that all the important activities necessary for successful operations are addressed. This means the high-level processes should be audited to verify that measures and goals accurately represent operations at a management level and yet are sensitive enough so that any trends will indicate a need for action. In a sense, the auditee would be top management of the facility, such as the plant manager, since this addresses the plant system. This auditing strategy should ensure that:

1. All important management activities are defined by the organization.

2. Interfaces are analyzed to ensure that they are properly aligned and meaningful.

3. High-level measures and goals effectively identify performance issues.

4. Management insight is at a systems level rather than bogged down by reports cluttered with details.

5. Planning is effectively turning strategies into improvement outcomes.

The audit scope must also include the next level, which addresses the major plant processes. Each major process will be audited so the organization can determine if the process is properly defined, its relationships are meaningful, and the measures accurately reflect whether the process is performing as planned. The auditees would be each area manager. This auditing strategy should ensure that:

1. All important activities are addressed within the process as if the process is a business.

2. Vertical (both up and down) and horizontal interfaces are audited to ensure that they are properly aligned and meaningful.

3. Measures and goals are sensitive in identifying process performance issues.

4. Management receives insight at a systems level rather than through reports cluttered with details.

The scope should also include all the support processes within the facility. In some cases, this may require auditing outside the facility if management resides elsewhere, such as divisional or even corporate ownership. These processes or functions have such an impact on the organization that they should be audited separately. In Figure 10.3, the relationships of the scoring guide to the major process are depicted. In addition, the various scoring guides are shown for the specific processes or functions. If the sales function is within the organization, a scoring guide would be recommended.

The specific scoring guides for processes outside of manufacturing are not included nor discussed in this book. It is my recommendation to modify or expand on the manufacturing scoring guide to address these processes or functions, referencing the ISO 9001:2000 standard and the organization's quality management system.

If the relationships are meaningful and performing as planned, there should be no need to go to the lower-level detail since you have concluded that the processes are properly defined, implemented, and effective. Should the team uncover an issue, they can then drill down further to uncover the cause of the problem.

There are some assumptions made in this strategy. Since I do not know your organization, you may need to go one level deeper, depending on how your processes are defined, to adequately audit your organization. The second- or third-level processes may simply not define the activities in enough detail to perform a thorough audit. On the other hand, your high level may define certain activities to the extent that you may not need to go further. However, generally speaking, this level of auditing provides a solid audit scope from which the scoring guides and audit plan are developed.

The internal audit is a dynamic process. In my experience, each year we have expanded the internal audit based on what we learned from the previous audit season. This was not my decision as the quality manager but rather motivated by suggestions from the audit team and management. As the audit results reveal highly successful processes and suspect ones, audit strategy would suggest that strong processes receive high-level audits and weak ones more detailed audits. In addition, as the lead auditors and teams develop expertise through experience, more detailed audits can be performed focusing on specific processes, interfaces, and sequences.

A logical initial approach is to establish the scope at the level suggested above, making sure to review it against the requirements of the standard. Since you are also trying to establish the audit teams, obtain buy-in from management, and improve the organization, this strategy focuses on the goal of establishing a sound internal audit program. This strategy addresses the three key elements of the progressive audit methodology:

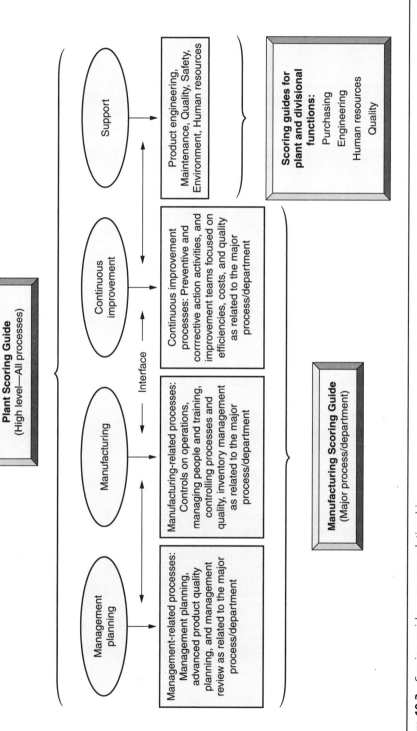

Figure 10.3 Scoring guide—process relationship.

1. Management commitment and support

2. Team-based activity

3. Continuous improvement

In reality, the first audit season is focused more on establishing the progressive audit methodology, and continuous improvement is addressed by the fact that you now will have educated more employee team members on the management system, brought quality systems into the regular spotlight through results updates, and expanded the overall management commitment through support of the teams. In subsequent audit seasons, it can be expanded to multiple shifts. Once you have established the scope of the audit, the next phase is determining responsibilities.

ESTABLISH RESPONSIBILITIES

Establishing responsibilities (Figure 10.4) at this point in the process means determining who is going to manage the audit program and develop the scoring guides. In my situation, I initially assigned the task of managing the program to the supplier quality

Figure 10.4   Progressive audit Step 3.

engineer. This was a mutual agreement because he considered it an opportunity to learn the internal operations. This proved mutually beneficial because within two years, he accepted the position of quality manager at one of our regional facilities. I believe his experience in the internal audit program was an asset in the interviews because it gave him greater understanding of operations and systems.

Managing the Audit Program

The decision of who will manage the program is important. It can't be simply a matter of sending someone off to lead auditor training and declaring them the manager of the program. There must be some credibility established by the individual within the organization prior to assigning them to this task. In our case, that individual had considerable respect because of the way he managed the supplier base. A big plus was the fact that he also had several years' experience auditing suppliers. It was a fairly easy sell to management.

This individual must also have good communication skills, both verbal and written, since they will be presenting results to management, selecting and training the auditors, developing the checklists, and facilitating the post-audit planning sessions. The audit program manager should also have experience as a lead auditor, which means they must know the quality management system and have experience in the audit process.

They must understand systems because he or she will be responsible for training the auditors. Some of this understanding is gained during the process of developing the scoring guide because they will also need to understand the standard. Much of this will come with experience as the program is implemented and maintained.

Although I stated that the audit program is better served if the quality manager supports but not owns the program, they will be actively involved in developing the necessary documents because of their knowledge of systems. The person selected must have an aptitude for systems thinking so they can appropriately interpret the standard in relation to the quality management system. Eventually, the management team will see the program through the audit program manager so it is important that they have credibility within the organization.

Once the internal audit program matures, you should have assembled a team of experienced auditors. Responsibilities will shift so that the lead auditors will establish schedules and conduct the audits with little involvement from the audit manager. They will also perform the training for new auditors and provide mentoring. At this point, it is important for the audit manager to serve more as a source of knowledge of the quality system and provide seasonal direction.

As a case in point, I recently took over managing the program as the divisional quality manager due to a personnel change. We had over a dozen lead auditors between the three facilities so I conducted the preseason training. Rather than simply reviewing the audit process and some minor document changes, the lead auditors requested more in-depth discussion on the processes and measures for consistency of interpretation. During the training, I was able to go into considerable depth on the manufacturing processes, with numerous questions asked by the team. It not only improved their understanding but mine as well since I was receiving insight on understanding from the three different facilities.

I was also able to provide direction on the scope of the audit. Having previously reviewed this direction with the management team, we changed the focus to less interviewing time and more emphasis on reports, trends, and projects for improvement. Since I was directly involved in setting this strategy, it was easy to convey because I had close knowledge of the subject.

The point is that to continuously improve the quality system and the internal audit, there may need to be a change in the audit manager position. It is important to maintain some independence from conducting the audits so they can be managed, but the key factor in mature audit programs is having someone experienced and knowledgeable managing it to provide the depth of understanding to facilitate improvements.

ENDNOTES

1. Larry Adams, "More Work, More Pay," *Quality* (July 2003).
2. Ibid.
3. Charles A. Cianfrani, Joseph J. Tsiakals, and John E. (Jack) West, *The ASQ ISO 9000:2000 Handbook* (Milwaukee: ASQ Quality Press, 2002): 162.

11

The Internal Audit
Scoring Guide

The scoring guide is the document that defines all the necessary activities and documentation that must be reviewed or observed during the audit of a process. It identifies the related ISO and quality management system requirements in an organized and logical order to make the audit process as efficient and effective as possible. Developing a good scoring guide (Figure 11.1) is critical to the success of the program. It requires much planning and study of the organization's quality system and of the standard to which you are registered.

Once the scoring guide is developed, the lead auditors will then develop the audit checklist, discussed in the next chapter. The purpose of the checklist is to put the requirements from the scoring guide into an easy-to-understand format that each team member will use during the audit. It is a list of questions with space for comments and observations to be noted during the audit, including lists of items and quantities that must be reviewed. These include gages, audit documents, SPC charts, and work instructions to ensure that document or gage numbers are noted so the currency of the revision or calibration can be noted. The audit results are then reviewed from the checklist and summarized on the scoring guide.

In a sense, the audit scoring guide is the road map of the audit. To illustrate its importance, if I am planning a trip I will look at a map to learn how to get where I'm going. If I have a detailed roadmap, I can drive anywhere in the United States, including Alaska. I did this in 1970, driving an old $65 Plymouth from Milwaukee, Wisconsin, with my friend. The accuracy of the map was critical because if it was wrong, we could have ended up in the wilds of Florida instead of a campground in Fairbanks.

Now we could have asked directions along the way rather than use a map, which is what we did sometimes. The problem with that approach is that you are relying on your own sense of direction, general knowledge of where you are going, and opinions of others, including assumptions of their expertise. You do not have the big picture of where you are going nor do you have much of a plan to follow. Asking directions for an entire trip may be exciting to some but ultimately of high risk.

The scoring guide should be viewed in the same regard. If it is not accurate and complete, your audit teams could end up in the wilderness. No matter how good the

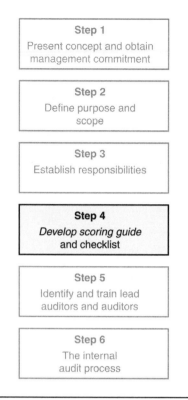

Figure 11.1 Progressive audit Step 4.

training program, the quality management system is too complex for someone to understand without much experience or a good map. The scoring guide becomes a map that they depend on in preparation for the journey of the audit season. Just as I would pull out the map at a crossroad in the middle of the Yukon to determine where we were and where we needed to go, the audit team will use the scoring guide to make decisions about the process and suggest a future direction for that process to stay on course.

The scoring guide is an auditor's toolkit that contains all the specifics of what must be addressed during the audit. One scoring guide isn't used for every major process because it would be quite extensive. Instead, they are somewhat unique to the processes and areas audited. For example, we have scoring guides for processes such as manufacturing, engineering, human resources, quality, purchasing, and the high-level facility processes (plant manager). The manufacturing scoring guide is used for a number of different major processes within the facilities but will not be sufficient for a unique process such as engineering, although there are similarities.

WORKING PAPERS—INTERNAL AUDIT DOCUMENTS

Published books and papers sometimes refer to this document, along with our checklist, as *working papers*. The definition is "documents required for an effective and orderly execution of the audit plan. By format and content they describe the scope and approach of the audit assignment and its operational elements."[1] There are various opinions regarding how these are to be developed. Some authors suggest that the lead auditor and audit team develop this document as part of the audit planning process. The auditors will have information from prior audits, so it becomes a matter of pulling the necessary statements and questions together that are important for the area to be audited. Each audit is considered unique so new working papers are developed each time.

Another technique is to take the ISO standard and simply rewrite the clauses into a checklist, which was the method I used for the last-minute audit. The advantage is that you are ensured of covering all of the requirements of the standard. The disadvantage is that you need auditors knowledgeable on the intent of the clauses. Unless you know the standard, the questions asked may elicit blank stares in the auditee because you can't put them in common terminology.

Both of the above techniques require experienced auditors. In the first case, the auditor must develop the questions prior to the audit. This means the scope must be developed and understood prior to each audit so the necessary requirements are adequately covered. The value and thoroughness of the audit depends on the auditor. This can lead to inconsistencies between audits of major processes depending on the auditor's experience. It also increases the time commitment of resources for each audit in developing a checklist.

To elaborate: We have a manager over each major manufacturing process. Since there are similarities in these processes and their related quality activities, the managers will expect consistency between the audits. If each audit team develops their checklist prior to the audit rather than using a manufacturing process scoring guide, there will be some differences in the way areas are audited. This is especially noticeable during results reporting to the management team.

In the second scenario of developing an audit checklist by rewriting the ISO standard, the intent of the audit is focused on meeting the standard, not the quality management system of the organization. There is value here but it is limited to the experience of the auditor's interpretation of the various requirements. Also, since the standard is generalized to suit many industries, it limits the ability to address specific activities considered important to your organization. Finally, it makes it extremely difficult to have an effective team-based auditing approach since the auditors will need a thorough knowledge of the standard. This risks becoming a last-minute audit.

I believe this is an often-repeated scenario. The previous auditor gets a different job so the organization needs someone to conduct the internal audits. To ensure that the new person is properly trained, they send the individual off to lead auditor training prior to the annual audit. After a week of training, and with certification in hand, they now have a new auditor. This person pulls together their working documents from the class, basically rewriting the standard in a question format, and nervously performs the annual audit with a different version and focus than the previous audit. This is a "certified" last-minute audit.

The progressive audit philosophy always looks at ways of adding value to the audit process. It is truly a continuous improvement program. Since we want to promote team-based auditing because it adds value through educating many on the system and brings fresh ideas to the process, we must have a consistent format. We don't want to add variation by the teams creating unique scoring guides and checklists during the season. Rather, we develop a complete scoring guide that can be used by many teams throughout the audit season. When I became a divisional quality manager, we modified the manufacturing process scoring guide I used at one facility so it could be used at three different facilities. We then used that guide throughout the audit season.

SCORING GUIDE RATIONALE

To understand the rationale behind a standardized scoring guide, you need to look at the management focus of the above-mentioned scenarios. Auditor training and an ISO-based checklist assume that once a person is trained, they have the skills to successfully perform an audit. They may have learned technique and some tools, but do they really gain knowledge in such a short time? This person must understand the various systems and processes of the organization to make a decision on compliance. However, we discussed earlier that our intent is to go beyond compliance and add value through continuous improvement suggestions. Do we really think this approach will meet that additional goal?

In the other scenario, suggested by some publications, the lead auditors develop the working documents prior to the audit. The assumption here is of knowledgeable auditors that also understand the quality system. Both approaches are dependent on the knowledge and skills of the auditor, which could change with each audit season. It is difficult to measure the effectiveness of this type of audit process. The format is not necessarily consistent year after year so there is no measurement by comparison. You can rely on the input of the auditees but responses will typically be "good," "OK," or "not as good as last year." The ultimate measure is completion of the task and whether it produces any recommendations for improvement or corrective actions.

From a management perspective, there is an assumption that if you base the audit on the standard or you have an experienced auditor, you will have a good audit format. But how do you know that the questions represent the strategies of the organization, are correctly asked, and the receiver understands them, except by feedback from the auditees? I believe that the above scenarios reveal a somewhat "hands-off" philosophy by management to the internal audit. Assign the task to someone and train him or her if necessary, but just make sure it gets done for this year; next year is too far off to concern us.

In many cases, the auditor is the quality manager, where you have someone knowledgeable of the standard and the quality system because they probably developed the manual. They also know the operations of the facility, especially the areas producing defects. I would also think that they know auditing techniques because they have performed audits to verify corrective actions.

In this situation, the quality manager would have a tendency to rely on their knowledge and expectations of what they believe the manual states, which may be different than the perceptions of those working in the areas. In other words, he or she is so close to the quality system that they would bring in the aspect of bias. "What do you mean it's vague, it says it right here" becomes the answer to any noncompliance. The other problem is that they know exactly where many of the issues are, so they either avoid them or spend the majority of their time investigating and writing them up. This also raises the concern that no one else learns the techniques and system.

In the progressive audit methodology, the scoring guide is critical to the process. Its format and content are consistent throughout the audit season by design. Management reviews the various scoring guides prior to the audit season and deems them appropriate and acceptable. The focus is then on the quality of the audit season, ensuring that all major processes are audited and the team has both experienced and newly trained members. One basic tenet of the philosophy is that there is a consistent focus on the quality management system throughout the audit season, ultimately supporting the initiative that the organization desires to know itself, not reinvent the format each year or prior to each audit.

The scoring guide adds value also by assuring the continuous improvement of the audit process itself. During each audit season, suggestions to improve the audit arise through the auditors. This may be in the form of a revised interpretation or improving a specific subsection of the scoring guide. Since we have a consistent scoring guide throughout our three facilities, a team of lead auditors can improve the scoring guide for the next audit season. By standardizing the audit, we allow ourselves the ability to continually improve the audit process by improving the scoring guide. In fact, this analysis and revision is built into the audit process. Called postseason planning, it is discussed later in this book.

Finally, the scoring guide adds value because it requires a review of the quality management system against the ISO 9001 standard. To develop the manufacturing scoring guide, we reviewed all the requirements in the standard per the specific process for which the scoring guide was intended. As discussed in detail in this book, all the areas related to manufacturing were noted on a spreadsheet. We then identified all the quality system specifics as they were defined in the quality manual and created questions and bullets for each statement, checking them off on the spreadsheet to ensure that all areas of the standard were covered.

The end result was a group of scoring guides that addressed the ISO 9001 standard and also the specific methodologies used to meet the pertinent clauses of ISO and our quality management system. Equally important, they also addressed the need to audit all the major processes within the organization. Following this approach, we were able to identify some areas in the quality manual that were not well defined or clear, which became evident during the process of developing the guide.

THE MANUFACTURING PROCESS SCORING GUIDE

This book will discuss the manufacturing process scoring guide in detail.[*] The other scoring guides follow the same format and approach, so once the methodology is understood, these can be easily developed to focus on the specific major processes and needs of the organization. The manufacturing process scoring guide prints out as an eight-page document and is maintained in our document control system. It is a controlled document with a revision level, with any changes requiring approval by the vice president, plant managers, quality managers, divisional quality engineer, and myself. This review and approval occurs during a post-season planning meeting.

This scoring guide serves as the highest-level document defining the requirements of the audit, from which checklists are developed. It defines the scoring method, the questions to be answered, necessary documents that must be reviewed, and also basic audit guidelines for the teams. Once the audit is completed, the scoring guide also documents the results of the audit including final score, comments on findings for each section, recommendations for improvement, and any corrective actions.

The manufacturing process scoring guide is broken down into three disciplines: management of the organization, management of the process, and nonconforming product and corrective actions. (Since engineering, quality, human resources, and purchasing have their own scoring guides, these functions are not addressed in great detail when auditing the manufacturing process except as they directly pertain to that process.) Each of the three disciplines is worth a specific number of points, dependent on the number of questions contained within the section, with total points summed at the bottom of the scoring guide. There is an overall rating scale of excellent, very good, good, conditional, and unacceptable for the quality system, found by dividing total scored points by total available points multiplied by 10. This was done so we could have an easy-to-understand rating scale of 1 through 10, carried out to one decimal point.

The scoring guide cover page also documents the lead auditor, team members, management personnel audited, date, and specific process audited (aluminum machining, assembly, and so on). To some extent, it acts like a scorecard for the process. When someone looks at the audit results, the first thing they will see is a quick overview that will provide knowledge and level of implementation of the quality management system. A sample cover page is shown in Figure 11.2.

When printing out a scoring guide in preparation for an audit, the second printed page discusses general audit guidelines and specifics on scoring. This page serves a number of purposes. One is for teams to have a reference in their hands that can be reviewed with the auditee should issues arise. It also is used as an overview during auditor training. And it is a tool used by the lead auditor to review audit practices with new team members during pre-audit planning. We have this defined as a process in the quality manual as well but considering that we have many audit teams, it is important to put a frame of reference for this activity in their hands prior to and during each audit. Following are the general audit guidelines.

Audit Guidelines

The internal audit will be conducted by an audit team consisting of representatives from various areas of the plant. The team should be independent of the area, meaning no member should currently be assigned to that area during normal operations. Team members should receive training in general auditing concepts and techniques by the lead auditor, facilitated by the quality assurance department. Each team will have a lead

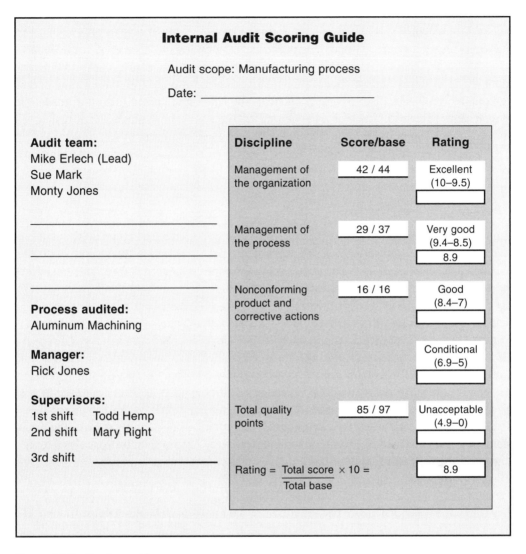

Figure 11.2 Scoring guide cover page.

auditor chosen by the plant manager and quality manager and report their findings to the plant management team, which will request, monitor, and verify necessary corrective actions.

Prior to the audit, the team should familiarize themselves with the quality management system in regard to procedures and processes related to the areas being audited. It is good auditing practice to make copies of important procedures, process maps, and work instructions to have readily available during the internal audit. It is also recommended that the team print out the operation sequence (flowchart) for the particular line(s) being audited, if available.

The internal audit is a detailed review of department operations at a particular point in time. Personnel being audited (the auditees) should be given ample opportunity to respond to questions and if unclear, it is the auditor's responsibility to ensure that the questions are clearly understood. The purpose of the audit is to determine if the department is in compliance with quality procedures and related work instructions and determine if the systems and methods are effective for the area. Any items found not in compliance should be discussed at the time of the finding to ensure that all information was properly reviewed. The area must demonstrate compliance through proper responses and current documentation to verify that activities have occurred.

Finally, the audit was not developed to classify nor rate departments but to provide a means to benchmark operations and establish goals for continually improving them.

Audit Scoring Guidelines

A questionnaire is used to help guide the audit team when evaluating the quality system (see Appendixes B through G). Each numbered element is worth two points, with the exception of housekeeping. The general housekeeping score is subjective, based on the team's overall impression at the time of the audit. The auditor should note certain details during the audit for documentation purposes, such as document numbers or dates that were reviewed and control numbers of gages that were verified for calibration. Comments are encouraged in each area to detail the auditor's findings.

Note: Each section has a letter question (A, B, C, and so on) followed by additional questions designed to expand on the original question. To award full points, the area personnel must have responded appropriately to all questions. In many cases, this will also require documentation to verify that activity has occurred.

Scoring the audit is a simplified process to provide consistency between the audit teams and to some extent, between audit seasons for each major process. It is represented by the following requirements:

- 2 points—All requirements met; satisfactory responses/activities

- 1 point—Requirements partially met; some question details not fully addressed

- 0 points—Little evidence of activity in area of questioning

This methodology was developed during a research project in 1991. The supplier quality system survey of our corporation was revised for this project with a goal of providing more consistency in results between all the supplier quality personnel. The research concluded that reducing the scale to 0–2 points as opposed to 0–4 or some other scale provided more consistency. This was incorporated into the supplier survey and has served our organization for a dozen years.

Audit Question Format

Each particular question is defined by at least one bullet point noting the necessary requirement that must be considered. In other words, based on the question and bullet points, requirements can be determined by the auditors because sufficient information is available at the point of decision making. When you consider that the manufacturing process internal audit consists of 97 total points or approximately 46 questions (five points are awarded for housekeeping), each one broken down by at least one defining bullet point, this simplified scoring method becomes quite accurate and repeatable among the different teams and facilities. Following is a sample question related to statistical process control (SPC). We have an online SPC system and use control charts with calculated control limits in all our facilities. The question refers to technical personnel that enter and interpret the information:

C. Do they understand out-of-control and take appropriate action to correct?

- Are they reacting to out-of-control processes?
- Is there evidence of appropriate responses?
- Can setups analyze historical data to investigate issues?

This question would have a total possible score of two points. To receive the full score, the auditors need to receive satisfactory responses from all personnel interviewed in that area. They must understand out-of-control, properly react to it through investigation of the root cause, and take appropriate action to correct and isolate inventory if necessary (based on procedures and training of personnel). In addition, the auditor needs to see evidence of notes in the system briefly describing conclusions and action taken for the out-of-control point. Finally, technical personnel need to demonstrate that they can analyze historical data by manipulating the software to view potential trends.

If the auditors find someone that does not react properly, they award partial credit and note additional information based on the interviews, such as "personnel not properly trained." If minimal understanding and use of the charts are found, no points are awarded. In addition, depending on the nature of the product and quality requirements, a corrective action may be written.

When an audit team has finished their interviews and observations, they meet privately to discuss results and score the questions. Notes made during the audit on the checklist are an important aid to discussion, so as the team works their way through the scoring guide, they use simple logic per the comments on the checklist and their observations: did the auditee(s) cover all the bullet points? did they only address some of the points? or were they weak in that area?

In this example, the scoring guide has a number of questions exploring various aspects of statistical analysis of the process, so the end result is a thorough analysis of that aspect of the quality management system. Keep in mind, this audit not only addresses the ISO standard but also the quality management system as defined by the organization.

Scoring Guide Flow

We have reviewed the scoring and question format and will now move to the format and rationale of the guide. Audits should never be random activities with auditors walking around asking numerous detailed questions. Audits are not about taking a bunch of maps and procedures into various areas of an organization and expecting auditees to say the right answers and do the right things. If this happens, employees probably have been coached in their responses. It is my belief that the audit should be organized around a sequence of activities and events that follow the flow of the process or procedure audited. The audit process must have a logical arrangement of investigative activities that allows understanding to build upon itself. The rationale behind the scoring guide is to arrange the questions around this logical order of investigative activities. During the internal audit, your initial investigations should focus on gaining a basic understanding of the structure. This structure is defined both by the quality manual and the managers and supervisors of a process. Then, utilizing this knowledge, you can audit the related activities so a conclusion can be drawn whether practices reflect management directives.

Processes and procedures are about logical relationships and sequences of thoughts and activities that result in a desirable output. It is the goal of the auditors to uncover this logic and conclude that there is compliance and it still makes sense. A certain amount of this information is already available by reviewing process maps and related procedures. However, these may not accurately reflect the intent of the organization. Management may have changed the strategy, the employees may not understand or be able to carry out the directives, both groups may have differing versions of what is defined, or the organization may have learned more about itself through the audits and now has a deeper understanding of its processes.

The remainder of this information is only available through uncovering the intent of management and the message received from the recipient. One point to make for clarification is that the manufacturing process internal audit may address more than one process. In our organization, it actually addresses a number of processes affecting a specific area, as defined by our quality management system. The scoring guide is designed around the high-level manufacturing process, which is further defined by specific process maps for manufacturing, continuous improvement, communication, corrective action, preventive action, advanced product quality planning, and interfaces with production planning, shipping, maintenance, safety, and training.

In the following sections, I will display the questions grouped in the scoring guide format, separated by the key subsections, and then review some key aspects for each question. I will suggest certain tasks or explanations the auditors will be looking for as well as some discussions on auditing techniques. I will also try to tie the line of questioning back to the ISO 9001:2000 standard to explain how we cover the standard in our audits. The scoring guide example is very similar to the one actually used, but certain questions have been revised because some terminology is specific to our organization.

MANAGEMENT OF THE ORGANIZATION

The Management of the Organization section is designed so that the auditors and management personnel spend the necessary time understanding and defining how the high-level and related processes are planned, managed, and improved. The audit views the manager as the owner of his or her own business, which is the sum of the various processes and activities making up the department. In the scoring guide, Management of the Organization is broken down into four subsections:

1. Process Overview

2. Commitment to Improvement

3. Communication

4. Advanced Product Quality Planning

The audit determines compliance to the defined quality management system. As described under Purpose of the Audit, it also identifies nonconformances and opportunities for improvement. Since the scoring guide is also designed to audit to the ISO 9000:2000 standard, it states in Section 4, General Requirements, that management shall:

- Define its processes, interactions, and sequences, and how they relate to the organization as a whole.

- Determine criteria to show they are effective.

- Ensure that resources and information are available.

- Demonstrate that there is a means to monitor, measure, and analyze.

- Demonstrate that there are planned results and actions to accomplish them.

With these audit objectives in mind, the first activity of the audit team after the review of the related process maps and procedures is to meet with the manager for the process overview. The audit team must determine the manager's level of understanding of the quality management system as it relates to managing his or her area of responsibility, including how they manage customer satisfaction.

Management of the Organization also addresses most of Section 5 of the ISO standard, Management responsibility. This is broken down into the following areas:

- 5.1 Management commitment

- 5.2 Customer focus

- 5.3 Quality policy

- 5.4 Planning

- 5.5 Responsibility, authority, and communication

- 5.6 Management review

As a point of reference, "top management" in our organization is recognized as the plant manager of the manufacturing facility, the highest level at the facility, which has worked well for the ISO audits. Although there is much input and direction from upper management, including establishment of the quality policy and higher-level objectives, the plant manager is a decision-making authority and provides direction and establishes controls for each separate facility.

Process Overview

The first subsection in Management of the Organization is Process Overview (Figure 11.3).

The first question is "Is there an understanding of the manufacturing process (map) as it relates to your area?" To answer this, the team will be looking for an explanation of the major process affecting the manager's area of responsibility, as defined by the quality management system. The manager should be able to describe the manufacturing process and how it interfaces with the related high-level and major processes. This means he or she should be able to present the relationship of their area of responsibility to the facility as a whole, which will include the various inputs, outputs, and measures.

It is helpful, especially in the first couple of audits, to have process maps on the table because there must be agreement between the documentation in the quality management

---

Management of the Organization

1. Process Overview

A. Is there an understanding of the manufacturing process (map) as it relates to your area?   _____

  • Is there a consistent understanding of process, inputs, and outputs?

  • Are the interfaces of the other key processes understood?

B. Is there an understanding of the process objectives and measures?   _____

  • How do you analyze your measures?

C. Have goals been established for each measure?   _____

  • Are the goals documented?

  • Do plans exist for improvement based on this information?

D. Is customer satisfaction managed?   _____

  • Is the customer known? (Internal and external)

  • Are there measures in place to gauge and track customer satisfaction?

  • Are the measures tracking favorably?

  • Have actions been taken to improve customer satisfaction?

E. Is there a general awareness of the quality policy?   _____

  • Can the area personnel show how they are meeting their commitment to the quality policy?

Figure 11.3 Scoring guide—Process Overview.

system and the manager's explanation. Typically, the manager will use the related maps during the discussion as a reference. In addition, the manager will need to define other related processes affecting their area of responsibility.

For example, Figure 11.4 is an illustration of the earlier discussion on auditing scope with the four high-level processes as continuous improvement, management, manufacturing, and support. The shaded ovals in dark gray represent the particular manufacturing process being audited. There are also ovals that represent related processes that impact the manufacturing process being audited. The dotted arrows indicate relationships between processes within that high-level process.

The high-level manufacturing process not only encompasses the specific major manufacturing process map (dark orb) including the levels down, but also has an interface to major processes such as purchasing, quality, production planning, shipping, management planning, and the continuous improvement teams. Those processes may have different process owners. The continuous improvement team process will also be owned by the manager and will be addressed later in the scoring guide. There is a definite relationship important to the success of the manufacturing process, indicated by the horizontal arrows. You will see scoring guide questions addressing those interfaces because the intent is to address the major process as if it was a business entity.

What explanation should be expected from a manager of a manufacturing area? You may not get detailed descriptions of interfaces, especially in the first audit, but there should be a good description of how the manager manages the organization in relation to the other key processes (or departments). Manufacturing has a strong relationship to the management process through planning, so there should be a formalized method for determining how to meet capacity needs, cost reduction goals, quality improvement initiatives, and productivity improvement initiatives. Management planning is addressed in the manufacturing scoring guide through long-range plans, advanced product quality planning, and allocation of human and capital resources.

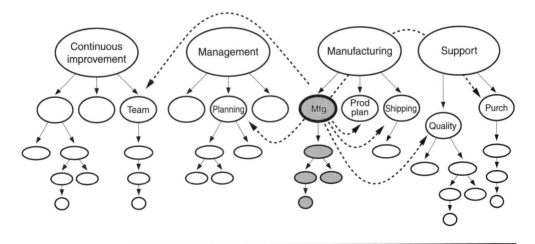

Figure 11.4 Process levels relationship.

There also should be management commitment as part of the management process, which the scoring guide addresses through understanding of the quality policy, establishing objectives/measures/goals, communicating these to the staff, and evaluating effectiveness in the management review (management review is specifically addressed in the quality management process scoring guide).

There is a relationship between manufacturing and the continuous improvement process, identified here as problem-solving team activities. This occurs when management utilizes teams to analyze the numbers representing results of the manufacturing process and then develops strategies and actions to meet improvement goals and initiatives. There is also a relationship to the support processes such as quality, engineering, purchasing, and human resources.

Considering the various audit methodologies available, one could develop very specific audits focused on each process, as suggested in some publications I have read. In many ways, I feel this thinking reflects the older standard and its element approach. The organization is a system of many processes and when they work together successfully, you will have an efficient and productive business. From the management perspective, major decisions are made based upon high-level measurement results that encompass the various processes within the organization. No activity really exists by itself.

The challenge in auditing, and for that matter successfully running a business, is finding the right strategy to break the organization down into logical and manageable relationships that can be accurately controlled, analyzed, and improved. Asking every manager about the various processes and interfaces forces clarification through the effort of the manager trying to define it, improving their understanding, which results in improved processes.

Should weaknesses be found, opportunities for improvement include training sessions for the management team of the area. They may also include a review of the process map if inaccuracies are found. Corrective actions are issued if there are significant or numerous inaccuracies in the maps versus the process.

Returning to the process overview, the second question "Is there an understanding of the process objectives and measures?" leads into discussion of the specific objectives of the process and the related measures; it then looks for established goals. Management must have objectives for the processes in the form of profitability, product quality, customer satisfaction, controlling inventory, and productivity. With those objectives, there should be logical measures that accurately provide insight as to whether the process is functioning properly. The objectives provide a rationale for the subsequent measures and the measures with their respective goals will tell you the story of the effectiveness of that process.

There must be a sound methodology for establishing objectives and measures. This assumes an interface with the management process or management planning. Results of previous years should be analyzed to establish the latest improvement goals as well as future strategies so there is great importance in the accuracy and sensitivity of the measures of a process.

Although in quality we can't always guarantee the bottom-line financial return of our decisions, it must still relate to our strategies and methods. Unprofitable organizations will be destroyed by the competition, whether in this country or abroad. Organizations must have a means of analyzing and verifying that objectives and related measures are effective in identifying activities that have a positive as well as negative impact on business performance. Opportunities for improvement should be issued if defined measures are not clearly part of department strategy or correctly used to track performance. Corrective action should be issued if measures are defined but not used because the relationships must be clarified.

Measures by themselves provide value but do not necessarily generate action. That is the purpose of the goal (question C, "Have goals been established for each objective?"). The auditor must find that management has established realistic goals for each measure. When a manager appropriately responds to the questions and can display documents verifying that actions have occurred to achieves goals, a number of activities have been verified. It demonstrates that management planning is effective since the processes, sequences, and interfaces have been defined. It is effective if the measures reflect the objectives of the process, and realistic goals have been met.

In reference to the standard (ISO Section 8.2.3 Monitoring and measurement of processes) the organization must apply suitable methods for monitoring the processes. It goes on to state that these methods must also demonstrate that the process can achieve planned results, and if they are not achieved, corrective action must occur. By exploring the objective and related measure, the auditors can determine if there is a logical relationship of the measure to the process. The goal demonstrates the decision that specific results are to be achieved and the numbers versus the goal ultimately demonstrate the overall success of the plan, the process, and the manager or process owner.

Typically the audit team will look for line charts consisting of monthly data points showing trends. We also use color-coded scorecards making it easy to identify acceptable versus negative points. The audit team also expects to see a goal line or numerical value.

The reason for this is not only to document the goal as a reference point upon which decisions are based, but it is also management's responsibility to communicate this target within their department. It is important that staff understand the measures and goals because these should influence their efforts to provide suggestions for improvement. They also define what management considers being successful.

Finally, it is important that concrete plans are in place in case goals are not being met or there is a negative trend. There should also be a solid explanation for a drop in one period. This indicates the commitment of management to its planning and improvement processes. This also indicates an effective measure because actions have been taken; otherwise, it is just a number needed to pass an audit but has no real meaning in normal operations.

If measures and goals are not well-integrated into daily operations, an opportunity for improvement could be written, especially in the early going. A corrective action should be written if negative trends are present with no corresponding action plan to resolve them or good documentation explaining the reason for the trends.

Section 5.2 of the ISO standard, Customer focus, states that management must determine customer requirements for satisfaction and ensure that they are met. Question

D ("Is customer satisfaction managed?") ensures discussion of this requirement. All manufacturing processes will have a customer, and the manager must be able to identify who it is, their requirements, and the related measure for customer satisfaction. In many cases this will not only be an internal customer but also the end user of the product. There must be evidence of the validity of the measure chosen and also evidence of actions taken for improvement.

Regarding specifics of what the team is looking for, formal tracking of customer satisfaction in a major manufacturing process may not be found other than possibly in minutes from meetings or conference calls. The audit team will be expecting to find good feedback measures such as ppm's or scrap and rework reports specific to their area. Complaints will be handled in Commitment to Improvement and Section 3, Nonconforming Product and Corrective Actions. Remember, the ISO standard looks at three specific aspects of addressing customer needs in the manufacturing process. There are also expectations of strategies related to product development (engineering, sales, marketing) and capacity planning for future needs not addressed here:

- *Satisfaction.* Customer perceptions about a product or service such as a formal survey with appropriate measures that can be tracked.

- *Feedback.* Quantitative measures such as defect report summaries.

- *Complaints.* This is the formal and informal documented corrective action system.

The last question, "Is there a general awareness of the quality policy?" explores the understanding of the policy among employees. Many organizations invent policy and mission statements that become slogans to hang on a wall. The audit should determine if this is the case and force the organization to recognize the quality policy as a driving force behind planning activities and important decision making. Since the quality policy should have an impact on the processes, it is appropriate to question a manager on how they are meeting the intent of the policy.

In ISO Section 5.4.1, Quality objectives, those objectives should be measurable and consistent with the quality policy. By definition, the standard calls an objective "something sought or to be aimed for, related to quality" (Section 3.2.5, Fundamentals and vocabulary). The auditors will be looking for a statement of the policy from the manager and an explanation of how it relates to their objectives, measures, and goals. Opportunities for improvement will be related to better integration of policy into planning and establishing objectives. A corrective action will be written if no integration of policy into operations is present.

Commitment to Improvement

The next subsection in the scoring guide is Commitment to Improvement (Figure 11.5).

Section 8.5.1, Continual improvement, in the ISO standard states that an organization must continually improve the effectiveness of the quality management system through policy, objectives, audits, analysis of data, and corrective and preventive action.

---

2. Commitment to Improvement

A. What is the process for continuous improvement? _____

- What are the objectives, measures, and goals?

- Have actions been taken to achieve the goals?

- Have improvement initiatives been addressed in long-range plans?

B. Is there evidence of improvement in the area? _____

- Were improvements made as a result of process measures?

- Is there evidence of improvement projects in the capital budget?

- Have goals been met?

C. Does management involve the employee in decision making? _____

- Are team and board meetings held on a regular basis?

- Is there recognition of the employee?

D. How does the area obtain knowledge in the latest technologies? _____

- Are employees encouraged to attended seminars and best-practices meetings?

Figure 11.5 Scoring guide—Commitment to Improvement.

In most sections in the scoring guide where the teams are looking at data or results, the auditors will expect to see efforts made to improve the process.

Within the ISO standard, the product realization process develops the manufacturing process as specific product planning and product production activities, including verification of requirements met. In other words, all the necessary activities that relate to producing the product. The ISO standard develops a measurement, analysis, and improvement process to demonstrate not only product conformity through use of product measures but also continuous improvement of the quality management system. In our organization, we have three high-level processes to address these requirements: planning is part of the management process, production and measurement is part of the manufacturing process, and analysis/improvement is part of the continuous improvement process.

Some organizations have taken the "flow" of the standard and wrapped their manual around it, which was common with the older 20-element version. That's the approach we used in the past because it made it easy for the audits and process wasn't an issue. However, you tend to adapt and manipulate your quality system if you do this with the 2000 version because the standard was developed to define the needs of many types of organizations. It won't tell you how a process should flow because that is unique to each organization.

Where in the past we could pull the manual during the ISO audit and the clauses would match, including the numbering sequences, we now have a separate ISO reference document that relates the new process maps and procedures to the requirements of the standard. This is not a requirement but it was developed because it eliminated some confusion during the ISO audits. The point is that our quality system was revised to meet the new requirements based on the needs of the organization and not on the organization of the standard.

Manufacturing and continuous improvement teams are separate major processes with their own maps in our organization, and fall within their respective higher-level processes—manufacturing and continuous improvement. Try as we might to come up with more creative names, the reality is that we have top-level and second-level process maps with similar names because they define core processes, just at different degrees of detail.

The manufacturing process map addresses casting, stamping, machining, and assembly operations, which enabled us to develop one manufacturing scoring guide for all those operations. Rather than a separate map for each group, we were able to identify the key sequences and process measures to appropriately define them in one map. This encourages commonality between operations because there are certain basics that all must do for a quality system. In other words, we specify what must be done to ensure a quality process.

For example, the measures for all the processes are somewhat common; productivity, staffing, product quality in the form of process capability indices summaries, and schedule compliance, including controlling inventory levels. Even the operation sequences are similar in that you receive raw materials or components (receiving inspection is a separate department), perform operations to produce a finished product, monitor the process parameters, perform inspection on the product, and move it to the next department. Within those operations, we define decision points for secondary operations such as trim, but there is enough detail to address all the key operational areas.

In the manufacturing process map, management and employees are focused on meeting production demands, which also encompass quality of product, correct staffing levels, efficient utilization of equipment, and maintaining proper inventory so assembly is not shut down. Everyone is wearing a production "hat" and although I refer to it as the manufacturing process, it could also be called a production process.

When they put on their continuous improvement "hat," management steps away from the manufacturing process to look at the trends, analyze the details against the goals, and plan for improvements. Rather than focusing on meeting daily numbers, as in production mode, the team is studying machine uptime, tooling life, inventory, direct and indirect labor, and other measures to find ways of squeezing efficiencies and meeting the productivity targets. Although both processes may include the same people, the mind-set is different because one is focused on meeting the numbers (manufacturing) while the other is focused on results of the previous weeks and months through summary reports comparing actual numbers to the goals (continuous improvement).

In Briggs & Stratton Corporation, team concepts have existed for many years as a formal entity. Initially they were modeled after "quality circles" in our Milwaukee operations and met regularly to work on problems. When the regional plants began production, the concept of business improvement teams (BITs) became the norm. In more recent years, greater emphasis has been placed on financial as well as equipment improvements, including quarterly EVA reviews with upper management.[2] Team members worked in various areas of engineering, manufacturing engineering, quality, production control, maintenance, accounting, and safety. This provided a broad concept of improvement focused beyond the product to overall department improvement opportunities, which also satisfies the ISO standard. Given this background, we can explore the questions of the subsection Commitment to Improvement.

When the audit team moves to this section, they are looking for an explanation of the continuous improvement process from the manager (question A, "What is the process for continuous improvement?"). The initial discussion is focused on the improvement process management has developed, objectives, measures, goals, actions taken to achieve them, and the actual strategies for improvement. These actions should have a relationship tied back to long-range planning activities since it is there that strategies and goals are developed and documented. Planning, whether it is for product or process improvement, must be deliberate and have a purpose.

Once the process structure, plans, and goals for improvement have been defined, question B ("Is there evidence of improvement in the area?") asks the manager if, in fact, improvement has occurred. It is one thing to plan these activities but another to carry them out. There are measures and goals for the process but have actions been successful or are the trends ignored? The manager may have planned for equipment upgrades in the long-range plan but the audit looks for implementation, either on the shop floor or documented in the capital budget.

ISO Section 5.1, Management commitment, states that top management shall demonstrate their commitment through providing the necessary resources to ensure continuous improvement. If you find nothing in the capital budget, it is difficult to argue that there is top management support. It is also difficult to argue that you have a focus on continuous improvement. It is one thing to commit to quality in the policy statement and quite another to put capital resources into a process for the purpose of improvement.

The internal audit provides an opportunity to identify these issues to upper management since they review the results through reporting and in the management review. Organizations all try to run lean, and product or process improvement initiatives may be rejected if no efficiency gains are realized that improve the bottom line. This would be considered a corrective action unless other activities have demonstrated improvement in the area. In that case, documented findings from the audit become opportunities in management review to discuss initiatives that get shot down yet are also necessary for improvement. Patterns of organizational behavior may emerge that must be addressed; either upper management must start approving quality improvement initiatives to demonstrate support for the quality policy or improvement planning must also incorporate operational efficiencies.

Question C relates to employee involvement in the improvement process ("Does management involve the employee in decision making?"). Teams are important to the success of an organization. Although the ISO standard does not specifically address team-based activities, it is an important concept in raising the quality culture in the organization. Organizations need to involve the employees because they are closest to the process and can offer valuable insight into quality issues and process inefficiencies.

In addition to capital budget items, the audit team will look for documented improvement projects. These can be in the form of meeting minutes of the various improvement teams but it also should be expected that use of the corrective action and preventive action systems is present. There must be clearly defined projects, based on the analysis results of the process measures, that include time frames for implementation and verification activities showing their effectiveness. If this isn't present, there is an opportunity for training on use of relevant quality tools (corrective action, cause-and-effect analysis). If those tools are not well developed, there is an opportunity to do so. A corrective action may be written if the approach is informal and not effective. This leads into the next question.

Question D addresses the issues of employee skills and education ("How does the area obtain knowledge in the latest technologies?"). ISO Section 6.2.1 states that employees affecting quality in their work must have the appropriate skills, education, and experience. In this case, the organization should promote upgrading of technical expertise through seminars and organizational best practices. There should not be an inability of the workforce to learn new technologies because of inadequate training or skill level. The next subsection is Communication (Figure 11.6).

Communication

In the ISO 9001:2000 standard, communication is specifically addressed in three areas under Section 5, Management responsibility:

- Management commitment (5.1). Management is responsible for communicating the importance of customer, statutory, and regulatory requirements.

- Quality policy (5.3). Management must ensure the policy is communicated and understood within the organization.

- Responsibility, authority and communication (5.5). Management must define and communicate the responsibilities and authorities in the quality management system, and must establish a communication process so the effectiveness of the quality management system is communicated.

In this third subsection of Management of the Organization, the audit team investigates the manager's communication process within his or her business. By this point in the audit, the audit team and the manager have reviewed the relevant processes, measures, goals, and improvement strategies, and their relationship to the quality policy. The auditors have made notes of these discussions in their audit checklist. This provides the key information used to run the business. The manager now must explain how information is shared, at what levels, and explain the various means for disseminating it. This also provides insight into what the auditors should expect to find when they begin their interviews of the supervisors and other area employees.

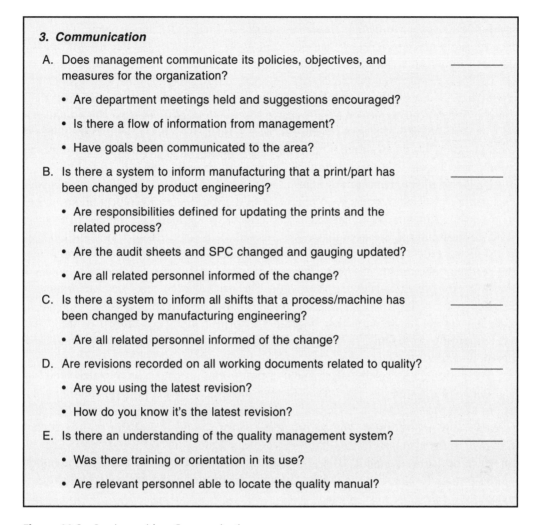

Figure 11.6 Scoring guide—Communication.

Question A ("Does management communicate its policies, objectives, and measures for the organization?") explores how management informs employees about overall business objectives, how they are measured, and the business goals. It seems logical that managers would share this information with their employees but this is not always the case. There may be a situation where the manager does not believe in the process as defined so although it is documented, the system isn't effective because it is not practiced. Evidence of this would be lack of communication to the supervisory staff and include the possibility that the measures do not reflect the operations. The opportunity for improvement here may be educating the manager on the process.

Another situation is where a manager is somewhat autocratic and directs operations rather than promoting a team concept. In this case, the objectives and measures may be valid but only have value to the manager. He or she directs all operations but the staff has limited knowledge of the strategies and goals. The audit finding would indicate a lack of communication of key measures and goals throughout the department. In this case, the opportunity for improvement would be more effective use of teams based on the continuous improvement process. Any other action probably lies with upper management if they want to enforce emphasis on teams; if the manager is effective, there may be little follow-up action. A corrective action could be issued but the directive to do so must be clearly written in a procedure or defined by management. Since communication addresses the personal traits or styles of managers, opportunities may require a more prudent approach than demanding action from the audit team.

Questions B ("Is there a system to inform manufacturing that a print/part has been changed by product engineering?") and C ("Is there a system to inform all shifts that a process/machine has been changed by manufacturing engineering?") relate to product-specific information and how it is disseminated to the shop floor. Question D ("Are revisions recorded on all working documents related to quality?") requires review of the pertinent documents to ensure they are properly maintained and current, which is typically discovered during the floor tour. The organization may have a formal and detailed process for updating specifications in the engineering system yet have an informal system for moving that information to the employees closest to the actual manufacturing operations. In my experience, getting information to the shop floor is the more difficult task.

The reason for this is that mechanical or design engineering is an organized and logical discipline. Engineers are trained to take meticulous notes because this historical information provides important clues should product designs need to be modified, as a reference for new designs, and to provide history should a problem with a current design arise. It also documents that the necessary testing has occurred and the results on which decisions are made. Blueprints and specifications communicate all the important information related to the design and must be accurate and controlled so errors or inadvertent changes do not occur.

Manufacturing engineering and operations tend to be more practical and focused on meeting production requirements. Equipment is not necessarily made specific to a product so modifications must occur to meet requirements. They are always "tweaking" something. Although documentation of changes to equipment is critical, the priorities of getting equipment running sometimes result in less effort being devoted to documenting all necessary details. Even when it is done, experience is invaluable for keeping machines running and much of that is in the mind rather than on paper.

Because of this culture, change management may be less formal and passed along through a simple review of a document, e-mail, or, in some cases, by word of mouth. This can breed a culture where there is less control of the process than desired. The questions lead the auditors to discuss change management to determine if the organization has established a formal or informal process, or opportunities for improvement if it doesn't reflect an effective system.

Question E ("Is there an understanding of the quality management system?") asks if there is a general understanding of the quality management system, including the use of the process approach as well as the location of the manual. The purpose of this question is to develop some confidence that the manager did not simply print out the necessary process maps to prepare the management team for the audit yet not have a practical understanding of their contents. It also asks if there was training on the quality manual's content and use.

We have now covered the first three subsections of the manufacturing scoring guide, which relate to management of the organization. By this point in the audit, the audit team has developed a good understanding of the manager's knowledge of the organization in relation to the process approach, the customer, and continuous improvement. The manager has explained those important processes, the key measures and goals including important strategies, and how this relates to the staff in successfully running the business. In many ways, these sections provide the "big picture" of the business but only from the manager's perspective. What remains is the last subsection, Advanced Product Quality Planning (Figure 11.7).

Advanced Product Quality Planning

An organization, business, or department cannot be properly managed unless there is adequate planning and control over new products and processes, as well as changes to existing ones. This is essential in business because you will have to address it one way or another. Either a product is properly introduced or all the mistakes will be cleaned up later, at a much larger cost to the company. In the ISO 9001:2000 standard, this is

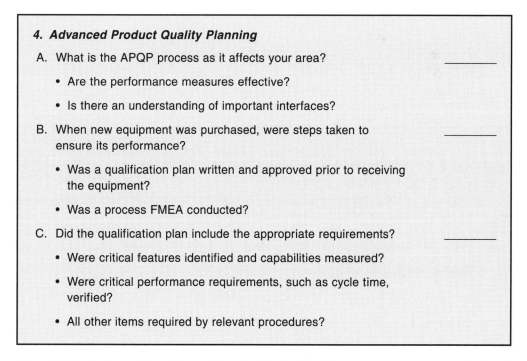

4. *Advanced Product Quality Planning*

A. What is the APQP process as it affects your area? _____

  • Are the performance measures effective?

  • Is there an understanding of important interfaces?

B. When new equipment was purchased, were steps taken to ensure its performance? _____

  • Was a qualification plan written and approved prior to receiving the equipment?

  • Was a process FMEA conducted?

C. Did the qualification plan include the appropriate requirements? _____

  • Were critical features identified and capabilities measured?

  • Were critical performance requirements, such as cycle time, verified?

  • All other items required by relevant procedures?

Figure 11.7 Scoring guide—Advanced Product Quality Planning.   *Continued*

Continued

D. Are advanced product quality planning techniques being used for _____
   current projects and improvements?

   • For current projects, is APQP being conducted?
     (See capital budget, APQP map.)

   • Are certified operations current?

   • Are all production processes defined in the system?

E. Are setup instructions established and available for use? _____

   • Are the instructions current?

   • Has training occurred on the procedures?

   • Do they contain key process variables?

   • Have process parameters been established?

F. Are there written operator instructions for each process? _____

   • Do they adequately describe the operation performed?

   • Are they available at the workstation and understood by
     the operators?

G. Are FMEAs being used to prevent possible defects? _____

   • Were FMEAs completed for all major process and product
     changes?

   • Is there a system or plan to review previous FMEAs to verify
     effectiveness and completion?

H. Are there provisions for first-piece inspection at setup, process _____
   change, die change, or shift change?

addressed in the Product realization Sections 7.1, Planning for product realization, and Section 7.5, Product and service provision.

In Section 7.1 Planning for product realization, the organization shall perform the following:

• Plan and develop the processes necessary to make the product.

• Develop the quality objectives for the product.

• Establish processes, provide necessary documents, and dedicate resources.

• Provide the necessary verification, validation, monitoring, measuring, and tests.

• Provide the necessary evidence that this has occurred.

According to Section 7.5.1, Control of product and service provision, the organization shall plan and manufacture product under controlled conditions, meaning the following:

- Product characteristics information must be available.

- There must be work instructions.

- The equipment must be suitable for the work required.

- Monitoring and measuring devices are available and implemented.

- There is a method for release, delivery, and post-delivery.

Note: service is not addressed in the manufacturing scoring guide, which also includes a post-delivery requirement.

Question A ("What is the APQP process as it affects your area?") addresses the process of advanced product quality planning, which is different than continuous improvement. This process addresses new product as well as new equipment introductions in the organization, as related to the major process audited. The manager must explain the process, including interfaces with management planning, product engineering, and potentially the functions of sales and marketing, and possibly meetings with the customer as well. This process follows recognized methodologies but flow and interfaces may vary with the organization.

Question B ("When new equipment was purchased, were steps taken to insure its performance?") addresses new production equipment purchased by the manager. The focus is on developing technologies that are effective for manufacturing the product. It asks if required steps were taken using a qualification plan prior to taking receipt of the equipment. In addition, was a process FMEA performed? Although the questions do not define the activity, equipment qualification should be a very specific and detailed procedure to ensure that proper planning occurs and the equipment meets requirements for performance and quality.

The qualification plan should require a project time line defining all the necessary activities and responsibilities that must occur prior to accepting delivery. This might include a detailed standards document defining all the product and process requirements, including process capability for specific product and process features. This would include process requirements such as cycle times, equipment reliability, guidelines for components, and performance criteria that must be met during the equipment runoff (running product at the equipment builder to ensure that it meets predetermined criteria). The manager should present this documentation, including all required approvals, during the audit interview as verification that the activity has occurred.

If no formal qualification occurred, a corrective action should be written since this would not comply with ensuring quality in the process. Opportunities for improvement could be written for missing dates due to unforeseen issues not identified in planning, equipment not meeting measures defined in the plan, or personnel needing additional training on the process.

Following are questions C ("Are advanced product quality planning techniques being used for current projects and improvements?"), D ("Are setup instructions established and available for use?"), E ("Are there written operator instructions for each process?"), and G ("Are there provisions for first-piece inspection at setup, process change, die change, or shift change?"). These refer to internal operations once the equipment is installed for production. Since this is a manufacturing scoring guide, the emphasis is on operations such as the work cells, including each individual station within that cell, to ensure that the final product is consistently correct. It is during this process that control plans are developed for each operation, defining the measures and methods necessary to ensure quality of process and product.

Once the control plans have been developed, supporting documents such as setup instructions, operator instructions, audit sheets, and visual standards are written. Process verification activities are performed for processing parameters, gage measurement analysis (GR&R), and statistical capability for producing the various product features. Implementing sound processing parameters is as important as developing sound product parameters that are monitored. Often much effort is put into establishing measures of product features based on their tolerances, but if the process itself is not well-defined and controlled, for example, there is variation in the speed of a machining spindle, it is arguable that true control of the process is not achieved.

In some cases, especially with older equipment, establishing parameters is difficult. Auditors must understand operations so corrective actions are not written when parameters can't be clearly defined. It may be better to use opportunities for improvement to identify a need for the management team to investigate.

Question F ("Are FMEAs being used to prevent possible defects?") refers to the process FMEA (PFMEA), which plays an integral part in developing control plans since it defines why a check should occur (failure mode, effect and cause). The PFMEA also recommends the method for doing the check (detection and actions taken) and preventing the recommended method from failing.

Understanding and documenting why a measurement activity should occur is important to organizations. This prevents certain detection activities from being discontinued because no one remembers why they were put in place. This is only valid if the PFMEA is dynamic and regularly updated when new issues arise or there are changes to the process.

The PFMEA is a concise historical record that provides a logical analysis of the process, including conclusions, in a simple format for the purpose of assuring quality. The internal audit verifies that this management planning activity has occurred during the manager interviews. Verifying that it is implemented and effective occurs during the floor tour. This can be explored further in publications on the FMEA process such as the AIAG manual.

This completes discussion of Management of the Organization, the first of three major sections in the manufacturing process scoring guide. Up to this point, the audit team has spent a significant amount of time with the manager of that department. In the audit methodology, the team would move on through the remaining two sections of the scoring guide.

MANAGEMENT OF THE PROCESS

Management of the Process was developed separately from Management of the Organization to move into manufacturing-specific activities directly related to controlling equipment performance, employee responsibilities, and ultimately manufacturing the product. It provides a transition point for the team from management strategies, directives, and reporting in the first section to discussions of the necessary details and daily activities that result in a successful operation.

The audit team is still working with the manager, answering questions related to the scoring guide. This section provides interesting discussions because there is a tendency to delegate responsibilities because the line of questioning is getting closer to the manufacturing processes. Managers are supposed to manage and for this reason their understanding of the details may differ from what actually occurs in the areas. Where in the first section we expected to find the vast amount of knowledge held by the manager (management of the organization), in this section the details are probably known more by the employees working closest to the operations. However, the manager still must have a sound understanding of the processes and procedures since he or she has overall responsibility. This section is broken down into the following subsections:

- Statistical Process Control

- Product and Process Audits

- Job Performance

- Material Status

- Preventive Maintenance

- General Housekeeping

Statistical Process Control

Figure 11.8 shows the first subsection of Management of the Process, Statistical Process Control, from the scoring guide.

The ISO 9001:2000 standard specifically mentions statistical techniques only in Section 8.1, General requirements for measurement, analysis and improvement. It refers to organizations demonstrating conformity of product, conformity of the quality management system, and continuously improving the effectiveness of the quality management system. Although the 1994 edition had a specific clause (4.20) for statistical techniques, there was no requirement that the need for their use is established but only that it is identified. Many organizations simply chose to state that they were not needed.

The 2000 edition substantiates many of its clauses by stating that a suitable means of measurement and monitoring must be in place. Basically, you must demonstrate results quantitatively. This is difficult to do without use of various statistical techniques. In regard to manufacturing processes related to machining and assembly, process control charts (or process behavior charts) are necessary to verify control in order to validate the

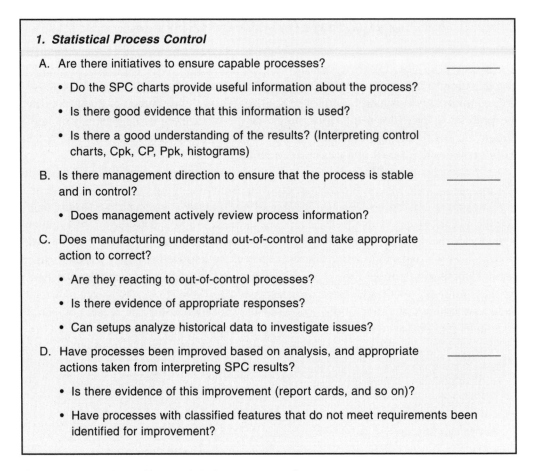

1. Statistical Process Control

A. Are there initiatives to ensure capable processes? _____

   • Do the SPC charts provide useful information about the process?

   • Is there good evidence that this information is used?

   • Is there a good understanding of the results? (Interpreting control charts, Cpk, CP, Ppk, histograms)

B. Is there management direction to ensure that the process is stable and in control? _____

   • Does management actively review process information?

C. Does manufacturing understand out-of-control and take appropriate action to correct? _____

   • Are they reacting to out-of-control processes?

   • Is there evidence of appropriate responses?

   • Can setups analyze historical data to investigate issues?

D. Have processes been improved based on analysis, and appropriate actions taken from interpreting SPC results? _____

   • Is there evidence of this improvement (report cards, and so on)?

   • Have processes with classified features that do not meet requirements been identified for improvement?

Figure 11.8 Scoring guide—Statistical Process Control.

process capability indices. An exception might be when there is automatic 100 percent measurement built into the process or manufacturing methods that prevents nonconforming product. In my experience, you still need statistical verification.

In high-volume engine production, with millions of engines manufactured at each facility annually, process control charts are necessary to ensure the quality of the components and assemblies. In the small engine division, SPC has been a management directive and is now fully implemented throughout the facilities, utilizing online control charts throughout the operations on the floor. This required much training in the facilities so personnel would have a sound understanding of its use and interpretation. This section explores its effectiveness.

To audit this section, the team will also audit the output of the planning activity in the Management of the Organization section. As part of APQP, management must define all the manufacturing processes in their area of responsibility. The result is a flowchart of each machining cell depicting the sequence of operations and subsequent controls to ensure quality (control plan). In addition, there should be quantitative measures such as capability indices for the various operations. The team will have this documentation available as both a reference and requirement to audit the various processes in the area and to determine if they are accurate and current.

Question A ("Are there initiatives to ensure capable processes?") asks if the specific control methods are appropriate for the process and if actions have been taken based on the results. Some organizations are required to implement SPC by the customer and as a tool it simply provides verification that the requirement is met. Someone enters the data into the system and that's the end of it. Other organizations have implemented it as a result of a management directive to maintain certain technologies. The end result still may be less than planned in that it is still just a directive; some managers will believe in it and others won't. Regardless of the motive for implementing SPC, the end result should be to measure and control the process and not just be a showpiece for management or a customer.

If the purpose of its implementation is not for the right reasons, the control charts will not be appropriate for the process. The answer to the bullet "Do the SPC charts provide useful information about the process?" will be "no" because it simply is electronic documentation of a check. This could be cause for a corrective action or opportunity for improvement, depending on the importance of the feature and the capability of the process. The charts are appropriate if they reflect the process through the measurement of a specific product feature at an appropriate frequency and the information is useful for the user.

For example, you shouldn't have an attribute chart when variables measurement is required. Attribute checks have their place but will not reveal subtle process variation on critical product features, rather only if they are acceptable or not. Another concern would be too much information displayed as a single measurement point. One chart shouldn't include multiple process variables, such as more than one machining spindle or multiple tools, that can't be broken down and analyzed. You could not answer "yes" to "is there good evidence that this information is used?" because the chart would not separate out the variation in the process. Finally, the last bullet addresses certain features that are classified on prints because of their importance to the functionality of the product and the requirement that they must be controlled.

Finally, does management understand the reporting? Various indices are used such as Cpk and Ppk in various formats to display the performance of the operations. There must be a proper understanding of these data summaries so appropriate action can be taken.

Question B ("Is there management direction to ensure that the process is stable and in control?") investigates the involvement of management in the effective use of SPC. This again addresses the purpose of its implementation; is it a directive or is it to control and improve processes? Does management even understand the use and interpretation of a control chart? This gets back to my earlier comments about a lack of understanding of the purpose of SPC on the shop floor.

In the reality of manufacturing, setups and operators only have so much control over the processes. They can adjust the mean and in most cases address out-of-control points if the process has historically demonstrated control, but processes that are not capable require management involvement. If the equipment has too much inherent variation, it will need replacement or upgrading that requires commitment of resources and understanding of the statistical method. Finally, the bullet point under question B asks if management reviews the information. A telling sign is if a manager cannot find the chart on his or her computer, let alone interpret the results.

Writing opportunities versus corrective actions may support an initiative or kill it. Developing a culture that focuses on process performance as opposed to just meeting specifications will take time to develop. Firing off a corrective action will identify a problem but it may be more beneficial to identify needs through an opportunity. On the other hand, if SPC has been around for a while and there is a directive to utilize it, a corrective action will properly identify an issue of not meeting requirements.

Although previous questions reveal an understanding of the methods by the users, question C ("Does manufacturing understand out-of-control and take appropriate action to correct?") specifically explores this topic. Managers must be able to explain their methods for ensuring proper interpretation and reaction to a measurement that is out of control. They must understand what that means, including the various ways a process will not be considered in control. Observing and interviewing those entering the information as well as those interpreting the information will reinforce the answer to the question. For SPC to be effective, there must be an appropriate response to points that are out.

Most SPC software allows for a note to be added to an out-of-control point that identifies the cause and resultant action so the team may look for this information as verification. In addition, when on the shop floor, the auditors will ask the setup to go back historically on the chart to determine if appropriate actions have been taken previously and break down information to show their understanding of the software. This also allows the team to identify repeat issues that have not been addressed. One must note that out-of-control also refers to trends above, below, and crossing the centerline. These rules should be taught in training classes.

Finally, question D ("Have processes been improved based on analysis, and appropriate actions taken from interpreting SPC results?") asks for results showing that processes have been improved through analysis of the charts and indices. The first bullet references a "report card," which is a summary report of the processes in an area that is regularly sent to management in our organization. From this information, management can identify specific operations that need resources dedicated for improvement, especially those with classified characteristics. To prevent SPC from becoming an exercise in documenting checks, there must be strong management involvement. Employees will react appropriately to the charts if they know that management understands the methods and dedicates resources for improvement so that there are solid, positive results. The next subsection is Product and Process Audits (Figure 11.9).

Product and Process Audits

Product and process audits also relate to APQP in that appropriate methods and techniques for quality planning have been defined, and this section documents that they have been implemented. Although much of the product information may be monitored

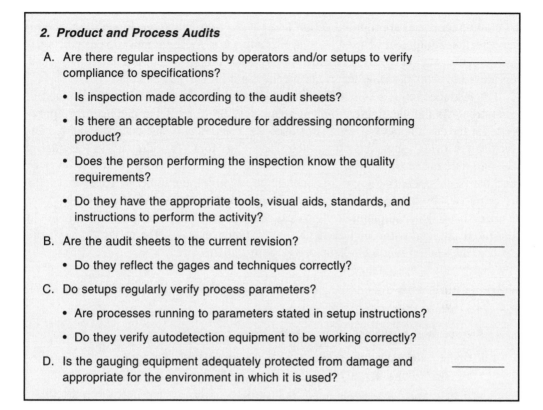

Figure 11.9 Scoring guide—Product and Process Audits.

through SPC, there are also various inspections and tests that are not monitored statistically. Question A ("Are there regular inspections by operators and/or setups to verify compliance to specifications?") relates to visual and attribute inspections by operators and setups. This information is defined in an audit sheet as well as operator instructions displayed near the station.

Related to this is the importance of understanding how quality is defined through the audit sheets, visual aids, and available standards. Management must ensure that it is communicated correctly and employees performing this inspection must understand the quality requirements defined in the documents, have them readily available, and also understand their significance. In addition, there must be a clear understanding of the procedure for addressing nonconforming product, including isolating any suspect inventory. Question B ("Are the audit sheets to the current revision?") ensures that the documents are current, accurate, and provide sufficient detail so the employee understands the requirement.

Question C ("Do setups regularly verify process parameters?") addresses the process parameters. Since APQP also requires that important process variables must be defined, this question verifies that this information is used to set up and run the equipment. There should some type of manufacturing audit to verify that the parameters are adjusted per the requirements and appropriate action taken if they are incorrect. In addition, should autodetection equipment be used to control product quality, there must be periodic verification with a standard or other method to ensure its proper function. There can be little confidence in error-proofing if the equipment is not properly maintained.

The last question requires the auditors to verify that the gage is appropriate and in calibration ("Is the gauging equipment adequately protected from damage and appropriate for the environment in which it is used?"). There is only one question in the manufacturing scoring guide related to metrology. This topic is addressed in the quality scoring guide because manufacturing doesn't own metrology. However, the shop floor checklist (see Appendix G) requires auditors to identify the number of gages that must be verified as being in the calibration system and correct. Management should also have an understanding of the calibration process. Should there be an issue, a finding should be written up against the quality department, which manages the calibration system. The next subsection is Job Performance (Figure 11.10).

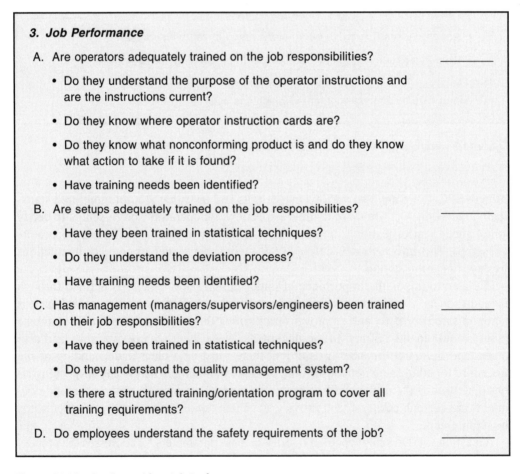

3. Job Performance

A. Are operators adequately trained on the job responsibilities?   _____

  • Do they understand the purpose of the operator instructions and are the instructions current?

  • Do they know where operator instruction cards are?

  • Do they know what nonconforming product is and do they know what action to take if it is found?

  • Have training needs been identified?

B. Are setups adequately trained on the job responsibilities?   _____

  • Have they been trained in statistical techniques?

  • Do they understand the deviation process?

  • Have training needs been identified?

C. Has management (managers/supervisors/engineers) been trained on their job responsibilities?   _____

  • Have they been trained in statistical techniques?

  • Do they understand the quality management system?

  • Is there a structured training/orientation program to cover all training requirements?

D. Do employees understand the safety requirements of the job?   _____

Figure 11.10 Scoring guide—Job Performance.

Job Performance

The Product and Process audit section addresses employee understanding of the quality requirements. Subsection 3, Job Performance, emphasizes employee understanding and proper training. In some cases, an employee may be the last person to inspect a product prior to it getting into the hands of the customer. It is critical that they have been properly trained on their job, which is the focus of question A ("Are operators adequately trained on the job responsibilities?").

An important point to mention is that formal training programs are developed through the human resources department, which has its own scoring guide. Although the human resources department is asked to demonstrate the effectiveness of the programs, the manufacturing audit provides important information about the training process and competency of the employees since they are required to demonstrate their skills to the auditor. In addition, management has the responsibility to determine specific on-the-job requirements and training programs, which are audited in this section.

Operator instructions detail task and inspection requirements, including verification of basic safety practices (explored in question D, "Do employees understand the safety requirements of the job?"). The manager will explain employee responsibility in more general terms. Through observations and questions, the auditors can assess if these instructions are commonly used. If an employee has an explanation of their job responsibility different from what is described in the instruction, either the instruction is incorrect or the employee has not been properly trained. This results in an opportunity for improvement or a corrective action if no training has been performed. The auditors expect to find that the operator has a good understanding of the operator instruction cards, can easily locate them, and has had adequate training that is appropriate to the difficulty of the job they are performing.

Employees must clearly understand the quality requirements of the various jobs they must perform. The job instructions identify specific inspection tasks, whether visual or by gauge, and also what potential defects to look for. Training is important because the auditors look for a clear explanation of the quality checks, including identifying the features on the product by the operator. Should gauging be involved, they must have good technique and confidence in their ability. The last bullet prompts the auditor to conclude, after discussions with the various operators, that all the training needs have been identified. This many times is based on concerns raised by the operators during the audit.

Question B ("Are setups adequately trained on the job responsibilities?") investigates the understanding of the setup personnel responsible for the operation of all the machines and equipment. This also includes ensuring that operators have the parts, equipment, and understanding necessary to perform their jobs. There are formal and extensive training programs that must be completed since their skills are critical to keeping the operations running. The audit does not explore the technical skills (addressed by the human resources scoring guide) but more the performance of the system requirements necessary to ensure quality and efficient operations.

The manager must explain what the requirements are; the setup must explain and demonstrate the required inspection audits and show documentation for all equipment under their responsibility related to quality, equipment parameters, preventive maintenance, and proper station setup for the operator. This will include understanding of the setup instructions, quality audit sheets, SPC charts, and operator tasks since they have overall responsibility as well.

The setup must have good understanding of the statistical software because they will need to manipulate the data to analyze any process changes. They must also be able to interpret the control charts for the auditors. Since the manager and/or supervisor will be present during the audit, determination is made as to their understanding of the quality management system, statistical techniques, and their organization of a sound training program for their area of responsibility. The final three subsections are Material Status, Preventive Maintenance, and General Housekeeping (Figure 11.11).

Material Status, Preventive Maintenance, and General Housekeeping

Subsections 4, 5, and 6 complete the Management of the Process section in the scoring guide, addressing product identification, preventive maintenance, and general housekeeping. The manager is asked for explanations of the methods employed to ensure that these are organized and controlled activities. During the shop floor tour, the auditors are looking at the product in various stages of completion, whether in containers, on racks, or on overhead conveyors. Inventory is minimized, but product needs to be suitably identified according to procedure. This is addressed in the ISO standard Section 7.5.3, Identification and traceability, which states that where appropriate it should be identified, including quality status.

Preventive maintenance is necessary to ensure that equipment is reliable and operating efficiently. The ISO standard does not contain any specific clause addressing maintenance requirements but the organization must ensure that the equipment is "suitable" for production.[3] Section 6.3 of the ISO standard, Infrastructure, does state that the organization shall "determine, provide, and maintain" the process equipment so product conformity can be attained. Whether specifically prescribed or not, there is an obvious need to properly maintain the equipment.

In subsection 5 of the scoring guide, question A ("Have PM programs been established for new equipment?") places emphasis on APQP in regard to developing the maintenance plans. Since earlier efforts of the auditors were spent investigating equipment qualification (management of the organization—advanced product quality planning), this provides follow-up to ensure that the planning becomes reality on the shop floor.

Question B ("Is there an established PM program for the existing equipment?") addresses maintenance plans for existing equipment, which also have a relationship to APQP because operations should have a certification process requiring a review of equipment efficiencies. There is a strong relationship to the continuous improvement process (management of the organization). Auditors should look for evidence that

---

4. Material Status

A. Is material clearly identified per procedure?   _____

   • If not on overhead, is product identified by WIP or completed tickets?

B. Is nonconforming material clearly identified to ensure that it cannot   _____
   be mixed with acceptable product (reject, hold, and so on)?

5. Preventive Maintenance

A. Have PM programs been established for new equipment?   _____

   • Is the PM schedule an output of APQP?

B. Is there an established PM program for the existing equipment?   _____

   • Does it identify the required activities and are they performed?

   • Was it established based on an analysis of defects or downtime?

   • Does it identify responsibilities for PMs?

C. Is there a PM program for the tooling?   _____

   • Is there a satisfactory tracking system?

   • Is the tooling corrected when parts do not meet quality requirements and are these corrections verified through a layout inspection report or first-piece inspection?

6. General Housekeeping

A. Are all areas neat and orderly? (Scale 0–5)   _____

   • Are the floors clean relative to the process?

   • Is there management direction regarding a housekeeping policy?

Figure 11.11 Scoring guide—Material Status, Preventive Maintenance, and Housekeeping.

maintenance plans were modified based on defect and downtime analysis, resulting in improved efficiencies.

This is a good example of a closed-loop process that can be recognized as the plan–do–check–act cycle developed by Shewhart and later made famous by Deming. Management plans the necessary activities for efficient operations (APQP), implements those activities (certification of operations), checks or analyzes the result (continuous improvement process teams), and acts by updates to the plans (revising APQP documents, PFMEA, control plans, preventive maintenance). The audit process follows this same flow through following the checklist (and scoring guide), resulting in good coverage of the entire process.

Question C ("Is there a PM program for the tooling?") addresses tooling, verifying that there is appropriate action taken to ensure it is properly maintained and changes verified. The last subsection, General Housekeeping, is added to the scoring guide to rate the working environment. This completes the Management of the Process section of the scoring guide.

NONCONFORMING PRODUCT AND CORRECTIVE ACTION

This is the last section of the manufacturing scoring guide but a very important one. The audit team has reviewed all aspects of the operations. Measures for the processes have been reviewed in light of the operations, including discussions of inefficiencies, defects, and negative trends.

At this point, the discussion turns to analysis, correction, and prevention of non-conforming product. One important reason for this section being last is to determine effectiveness of the quality management system. If the auditors find a lot of activity in this last section, it is arguable that the previous two sections were not effective. In other words, organizations that have sound planning processes, thoroughly implemented, should have few if any major issues in their corrective action program.

If the auditors have found weak areas resulting in negative trends in the process measures, there should be much activity to correct the problems, including focused efforts on prevention activities. Consequently, minimal corrective action activity would indicate underlying issues related to management philosophy, both within the manufacturing area and the organization as a whole because they are not focused on correcting problems. This last section tells much about management commitment and discipline.

Nonconforming Product

Subsection 1 addresses the control, analysis, and elimination of nonconforming product (Figure 11.12) and the response to its impact on the customer. I would argue that the amount of attention paid toward nonconforming product is relative to the customer, the scrap/rework cost, and the organizational culture. I would define culture here as the commitment toward maintaining a certain level of quality in the product and the perception of what that acceptable level is.

There are obvious issues here. If the customer is angry, a lot of attention should be given to raising the level of quality because of the potential impact on future business and the heightened interest of upper management. If costs are high, especially in conjunction with angry customers, you are probably looking at some sort of organizational change demanded by upper management. Customer and cost will have an immediate impact through a focus on process improvements, as well as long term by raising the bar of the quality culture.

Nonconforming Product and Corrective Actions

1. Analysis of Nonconforming Product

A. Is there a system for reviewing nonconforming product and determining its disposition? _____

  - What is the procedure when stock is rejected?

  - Who is responsible for disposition of product?

B. Does nonconforming product require engineering or quality approval prior to release to production? _____

  - Are formal deviations or written approval required?

  - When this occurs, are corrective actions issued to ensure that the problem does not repeat?

C. Is there a system for reworking nonconforming product? _____

  - Do rework operations require reinspection?

  - Are rework instructions written, available, and in the document control system?

D. Are steps taken to reduce the number of defects produced? _____

  - Is there evidence of an initiative to reduce defects?

  - Is root cause identified for top defects?

  - Is permanent corrective action implemented?

  - Is data from monthly summaries, scrap reports, and significant internal quality complaints used to drive improvement?

E. Are QA daily reports used to monitor performance on a regular basis? _____

  - Is this information reacted to in a timely manner?

  - Are corrective actions issued/implemented for reoccurring issues?

F. Are customer (OEM) complaints and returns analyzed and corrective action and feedback given in a timely manner? _____
Note: (For parts relative to the area.)

  - Do the setups receive this complaint information and are they involved in corrective action activities?

  - Is this a customer feedback measure?

Figure 11.12 Scoring guide—Nonconforming Product.

Less obvious is that at some point the customer and cost measures, which should be part of the management system, reach a level that is considered unacceptable by management, yet improvement initiatives can be buried in teams so they are off everyone's radar. This is also the territory where arguments are made that the costs to improve outweigh the benefits. There may be few corrective action initiatives because there are "teams working on it." The trend line may even look good for the measure but only because some issues are excluded for various reasons.

It is here that the challenge arises for the audit team to report the facts and for the organization to react to the findings. The team has reviewed the management measures and discussed all the related processes. This last section has them focused on the acceptable level of quality as determined by management. Is there a strong focus on detail and improvement or is there complacency with the status quo?

Question A ("Is there a system for reviewing nonconforming product and determining its disposition?") is focused on defining and understanding the system for dealing with nonconforming product. In the ISO standard, clause 8.3, Control of nonconforming product, states that the organization shall identify and control so it does not inadvertently get delivered to the customer. The organization has the options to eliminate it, get permission from the customer to ship, or prevent it from occurring. There also must be reverification of the product if the defect is corrected.

The questions may state the obvious in that formal systems are defined in the quality manual. However, the progressive audit methodology is also intent on educating the auditors and auditees by asking the obvious. In addition, there are levels of implementation depending on the culture that the audit attempts to define. This question is addressed to management, technical personnel, and frontline operators to determine consistency of application.

Question B ("Does nonconforming product require engineering or quality approval prior to release to production?") addresses the authority to make decisions on disposition. It is important that appropriate personnel are involved, especially when decisions may affect the final product. This is to ensure that proper testing and analysis occurs so a correct decision is made and documented (formal deviation) and that a corrective action is issued to prevent future issues.

One point to note here is questions in the related checklists ask if appropriate approval from the customer as well as engineering and quality is needed if product is used "as is." This is a requirement in the standard as well as in our organization but the format requires a question, which is important to clarify with the auditors.

Reworking product presents a significant challenge to any organization because of the risk of poor quality getting to the customer, whether it is recognized or not. The product is typically reworked out of the normal stream of production so it does not go through the same process of checks to ensure it is correct. If an organization is running near capacity, employees "volunteer" for rework on off-shift hours, so you may have people doing the rework that are unfamiliar with the job. There is nothing more uncomfortable than explaining to a customer why a component was missing from a recent shipment of product because you "missed it" during the rework operation. When product is reworked, question C ("Is there a system for reworking nonconforming product?")

asks if there is a defined system that ensures appropriate methods with instructions are developed. Also, the resulting product quality should be verified, part of the ISO clause 8.3. There should be a disciplined and systematic approach to rework.

Questions D ("Are steps taken to reduce the number of defects produced?"), E ("Are daily reports used to monitor performance on a regular basis?"), and F ("Are customer complaints and returns analyzed and corrective action and feedback given in a timely manner?") relate to the continuous improvement efforts and the culture. During the audit of the continuous improvement process, trend charts and data summaries were reviewed to determine if improvement efforts were active and effective. In this section, the auditors will focus on the corrective actions taken to eliminate the issues. There should be a formal program to define defects, establish improvement programs, develop root causes, and eliminate their occurrence. This should be understood and driven by the manager.

The daily reports represent a system in which issues are identified during the normal operations through e-mails that provide some useful details and history. Organizations may or may not have a formal system to document, but there are opportunities buried in these daily reports. This usually does not merit a formal corrective action but if repeated, identifies a potential issue that should be corrected.

Customer complaints may deal with the outside customer or the internal customer. Component manufacturing departments may have few issues related to the end user or external customer, unlike a final assembly department. The internal inspection, detection, and audit systems within the department will identify nonconforming product. In addition, the assembly inspection, detection, and audit systems will also identify nonconforming product. If defective components ultimately reach the end user, there has been a system breakdown leaving an opportunity for improvement in the design of the product, process, or inspection/detection system.

Whether or not internal corrective actions are issued to component departments depends on the management philosophy. This may be left to the continuous improvement teams working on improving the measures, with a formalized complaint issued only for more serious issues. If there are internal defects, they must be addressed one way or the other and question F along with question D really speaks to the culture, the perception about quality levels, and the commitment to improve it.

Corrective Actions

Subsection 2, Corrective Actions, is about closure and continuous improvement (Figure 11.13). At some point in the future, there must be verification that the actions implemented were effective. This suggests there is some type of measure of the defect so it can be positively determined that the defect has been eliminated or at least prevented from occurring at any noticeable rate. If this isn't the case, repeat issues will surface, preventing the organization from achieving genuine improvement. Even if automatic detection or error-proofing has been implemented, there still should be a subsequent verification of effectiveness. It is an awkward situation to explain to a customer that although 100 percent detection is in place, it was inadvertently turned off because it was not working properly.

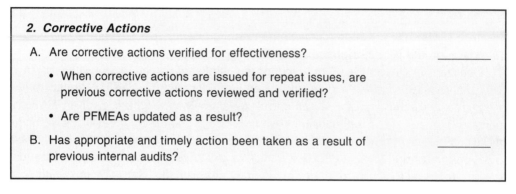

Figure 11.13 Scoring guide—Corrective Actions.

Finally, it is appropriate to address any outstanding issues or opportunities related to previous internal audits. This necessitates a review of previous findings for an area, whether a corrective action for nonconformity was written, or an opportunity for improvement was suggested. Many suggestions were made within the context of explaining each subsection. Internal audit findings, especially corrective actions, are discussed during the management review. Open issues should be verified and closed, but during the internal audit an additional review is performed to ensure that the action was thorough and permanently resolved the particular issue. As stated, it is about closure.

ENDNOTES

1. Charles A. Mills, *The Quality Audit* (Milwaukee: ASQ Quality Press, 1989): 121.
2. Joel M. Stern, John S. Shiely, with Irwin Ross, *The EVA Challenge* (New York: John Wiley & Sons, 2001): 66.
3. Charles A. Cianfrani, Joseph J. Tsiakals, and John E. (Jack) West, *The ASQ ISO 9000:2000 Handbook* (Milwaukee: ASQ Quality Press, 2002): 206.

12

The Audit Checklists

Why do you need an audit checklist (see Figure 12.1)? The auditors have a detailed scoring guide with bullet points that documents all the criteria for the audit. The questions are direct and easily understood. It would seem that a checklist just adds the work of maintaining another document when all the information needed is already there in the scoring guide.

Figure 12.1   Progressive audit Step 4.

The checklist was not part of the initial concept of the progressive audit methodology. The concept was introduced two audit seasons later by one of our lead auditors, as a result of suggestions to improve the effectiveness of the audit process. Teams initially used the scoring guide, but it seemed to encourage auditors to immediately score a section rather than take notes. It resulted in important information not being available during the team discussion because auditors relied on memory.

During the audit, many questions referred to more than one area of responsibility. Auditors became confused in certain subsections of the guide because they didn't understand who should be asked what question. For example, they would question the manager about goals and neglect to ask employees on the shop floor, so you couldn't verify the communication process. During the audit scoring phase, reviewing information was difficult because it was hard to separate out the manager's response from those of supervisor, the setup, the manufacturing engineer, or the operator.

The point to make is that although the early results of the internal audits were excellent with many suggestions for improvement, there were still opportunities to improve the process. The lead auditors had experience and played a key role in ensuring the success of the program. However, issues like scoring too early in the process and misunderstood questions put additional responsibility on the lead auditor. Although the training was thorough it did not compensate for inexperience. The questions needed to be broken down and organized better to ensure that all auditors were successful.

In a sense, the scoring guide becomes the internal standard from which the working documents are derived. Last-minute audits rewrite the ISO standard into questions; progressive audits develop a standard specific to the organization. Much up-front work goes into scoring guide development to ensure that it meets the requirements of both the ISO standard and the organization's quality management system. There is a point to make here in that the quality manual must be reviewed to verify that it meets the requirements of the standard and also when any changes occur. Developing and maintaining the scoring guide promotes a thorough review.

Once the guide is verified to be complete and accurate, the next step is to copy or rewrite it into specific focused checklists to ensure that all the necessary details and positions are audited. In other words, we've added another level of detail to the audit process to ensure that it is thorough and effective. To do this, the audit program manager and lead auditors copy each question and related bullets from the scoring guide into the checklist. However, questions are revised to make them easy to understand and only questions pertinent to the auditee's area of responsibility are noted.

FOUR KEY POINTS

To better understand the concept of the checklist, its importance can be summarized in four key points:

- Specific checklists are defined by job responsibility.

- Questions are easy to interpret and ask.

- Note taking is encouraged.

- Scoring is accurate, consistent, and based on fact.

The first point to make, checklists are specific by responsibility, means there are multiple checklists. In our organization, there are seven specific to the manufacturing scoring guide: manager, supervisor, manufacturing engineering, setup, operator, and the shop floor. The checklist for the manager has all the questions from the scoring guide that are specific to the manager, which is basically everything in the scoring guide. When the audit team is in the manager interview, they will have this document in hand and not the scoring guide.

Table 12.1 identifies the relationships of the specific scoring guide sections and the various manufacturing checklists, based on responsibility.

Because the manager is the business process owner, it is expected that he or she will have the most in-depth understanding of the overall organization. There is much detail asked for in the checklist regarding the Management of the Organization section, but they also must explain how they manage the process and deal with customer complaints. The supervisor is also expected to know much of this information but where the manager is the ultimate planner, the supervisor carries things out. We would expect their knowledge to be related to interpretation and implementation rather than the reasons behind the strategies that the manager should know.

The manufacturing engineer should also understand the overall objectives but their focus is more technical. Where the overall process objectives and measures should be understood, we would expect the engineer to have specific knowledge about equipment qualification, process improvement, and maintenance activities. Finally, setups and operators should also have a basic understanding of the process objectives and measures, but the focus in this area will be on specific job responsibilities, training, and communication from the management team. In addition, this checklist will ask for specific documents to be audited and requires revision levels and identification numbers.

The questions follow the same order and intent as the scoring guide since that is the new standard, but our second point says they should be rewritten to make them easier for an inexperienced auditor to understand and ask. Where the scoring guide may have bullet points to further define what is needed to meet the requirement, the checklist may have specific questions for each bullet or additional notes so the auditor can better interpret its intent. The format is such that it is easy to follow so auditors will know exactly where they are during the audit process.

The third key point is that note taking is encouraged. The checklist is written in a format such that a question has adequate space for notes, including all the related bullet points. This ensures that all the stated requirements in the scoring guide are addressed. There is no mention of rating. This encourages auditors to write specific comments from the auditee. It is important for all of the auditors to note comments and observations made during the audit because of different possible interpretations. In addition, one auditor may catch a comment made or see something in a document that the others missed that may be pertinent to meeting the requirement.

Table 12.1 Scoring guide—checklist by position matrix.

Scoring guide	Manager checklist	Supervisor checklist	Manufacturing engineer checklist	Setup checklist	Operator checklist
Management of the Organization					
1a	X	X	X		
1b	X	X	X	X	X
1c	X	X	X	X	X
1d	X	X	X	X	X
1e	X	X	X	X	X
2a	X	X	X		
2b	X	X	X		
2c	X	X	X	X	X
2d	X	X	X	X	X
3a	X	X	X	X	X
3b	X	X	X	X	X
3c	X	X	X	X	X
3d	X	X	X	X	
3e	X	X	X	X	X
4a	X	X	X		
4b	X	X	X		
4c	X		X		
4d	X	X	X	X	X
4e	X	X	X		
4f	X	X		X	X
4g	X	X	X		
4h	X	X	X	X	
Management of the Process					
1a	X	X	X	X	
1b	X	X	X	X	
1c	X	X		X	
1d	X	X	X		
2a	X	X	X	X	
2b	X	X	X		
2c	X	X	X	X	
2d	X	X		X	
3a	X	X		X	X
3b	X	X		X	
3c	X	X	X		
3d	X	X	X	X	X
4a	X	X		X	X
4b	X	X		X	X
5a	X		X		
5b	X	X	X	X	X
5c	X	X	X	X	
6a	X	X	X	X	X
Nonconforming Product and Corrective Action					
1a	X	X		X	X
1b	X	X		X	
1c	X	X		X	
1d	X	X	X	X	X
1e	X				
1f	X			X	X
2a	X				
2b	X				

The final point is accurate and consistent scoring. The argument I hear against scoring from those outside the organization is that managers will find inconsistencies between various departments or when comparing year to year, which takes away from the intent of the audit. Basically, the argument is that they will focus on the score rather than the findings. The underlying problem is lack of confidence in the scoring method because it becomes difficult for the lead auditor and team to achieve consistent results so it comes across as pure guesswork.

With the use of the checklist, there is more detail in the notes that provides more factual information during the team analysis and scoring session. If all auditors have similar notes and findings, it becomes fairly easy to determine if a department fully met, partially met, or did not meet a requirement. When you consider that the various positions are broken apart through individual checklists, the audit team has a large amount of information to review and determine compliance.

Consistency year after year in scoring the same department and consistency between various departments and audit teams is less of a challenge because of the detail of the scoring guide and multiple checklists. An important point is that all internal manufacturing audits are asking the same questions to the same positions in the organization. Rather than rely on interpretations from various audit teams or lead auditors as to what they want to ask and to whom they will ask it, it instead is specifically determined based on the working documents. This doesn't mean actual scores will compare because the team may not interview the same employees every year nor will they see the same documentation between departments. The auditees may respond differently from year to year. What it does mean is that there will be consistency in the overall level of rating, which means it should not be excellent one year and only good the next unless something has changed in the department.

The progressive audit methodology is successful because much planning and detailed work goes into the process prior to the first audit question being asked. It takes the concept of advanced product quality planning that all quality and business professionals should believe in and relates it to the internal audit process. You simply must do the homework up front to avoid a substandard product during and after the execution of the process.

METHODOLOGY OF THE CHECKLIST

To better understand the methodology of the checklist, I will show a section of the scoring guide and related checklists to illustrate the format and compare content.[*] Specifically, to provide a good understanding of their relationship to each other and the audit process, I will focus on the overall management of the organization in the Process Overview section. Although the scoring guide and checklists are somewhat unique to our quality system and organization, I believe focusing on a more general discussion of systems and processes will allow me to illustrate the format of the checklist.

Management of the organization addresses the overall structure and understanding of the processes that define operations, customer satisfaction, communication, and planning. As a reminder, the process overview (Figure 12.2) looks at the high-level department processes and related measures, customer satisfaction, and the quality policy.

The format of the guide only allows space for notes at the end of the section. By design, it only has space for a numerical value for compliance to the specific question and a summary statement of how those values were determined at the end of each subsection. When completed, the cover page becomes a summary of audit findings that by nature of the rating provides a quick understanding of the strengths and weaknesses in that department. Should the user of the document want more information, they can go to

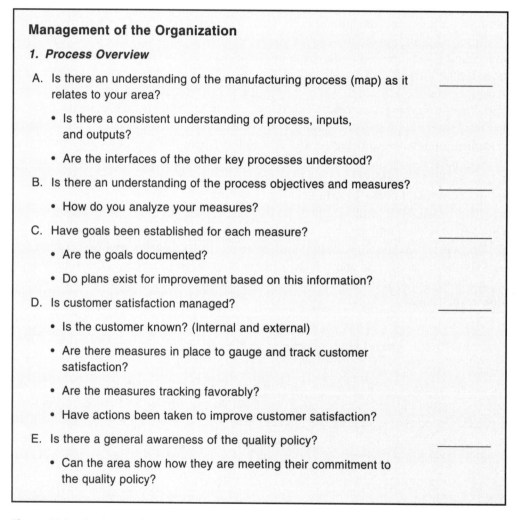

Figure 12.2 Scoring guide—Process Overview.

the specific subsection to see the scoring for the specific questions and read the summary information. The guide is a historical document that provides a quantitative analysis in addition to information summarizing the decision for each subsection.

In practice, once all the interviews and shop floor tour have occurred, the team meets to review the results. During that team discussion and scoring session, agreement will be reached and the score for each question will be noted. The lead auditor will write comments pertaining to any issues found that lowered the score, in addition to any positive findings in the area. The documents the auditors will be looking at to make this decision will be the checklists and their notes based on the employee responses and auditor observations. It becomes far more factual rather than subjective and based on memory.

Manager Checklist

The manager checklist is shown (Figure 12.3) in the format of the document.

Manager Checklist

Date: _____ Name: _____

Process: _____

Management of the Organization

1. Process Overview

A. How does the manufacturing process (map) affect your area?

- Describe the process, including the inputs and outputs.
- What are the important interfaces (relationships) with other processes?

_____

_____

_____

_____

B. How do you track the performance of your process?

- Are the measures reviewed?

_____

_____

_____

_____

Figure 12.3 Manager checklist.   *Continued*

Continued

*Identify documents reviewed and key measures for tracking.

_____

_____

_____

_____

C. What are the goals for your process?

  • Where are they documented?

  • Plans for improvement? (Auditor note: should have action plans if negative results)

_____

_____

_____

D. How do you ensure the satisfaction of your customer?

  • Are measures in place? (Need to see chart)

  • What actions have been taken to improve customer satisfaction? (Discuss both internal and external customers, if applicable)

_____

_____

_____

_____

E. Describe the quality policy.

  • What role does it play in your area?

  • Are you meeting your commitment to the policy? (Should see measures)

_____

_____

_____

_____

One noticeable difference is that unlike the scoring guide, the checklist has more space for notes below each question. In a sense, since there is a sizeable area defined for notes, it tends to encourage auditors to write comments and observations. There is no suggestion of any rating, so it gets the mind of the auditor focused on the question and response rather than trying to summarize the results in a numerical value.

Another focus the document creates is that of the task at hand, meaning all the questions in the document must be addressed before moving on to another area. This is why the flow of the questions should relate to the logical flow of the audit. Since the manager is the owner of the process, he or she defines the processes and policies for the area. There is obviously an overriding system defined by senior management, but that manager has played a key role in defining the methods used within the quality management system.

Although this was discussed earlier in describing the progressive audit methodology, it is important enough to review again. In the flow of the audit, it is important that the team first gets an understanding of how that manager's organization is structured, defined, and run. It tells you if the manager understands his or her own systems and is in control, which is very important. This control can be through empowered teams or more autocratic, but that person is responsible for the performance of their area so they should be able to convey a clear understanding of their methods to the team.

The manager cannot be in the plant on every shift to ensure that all the necessary audits, preventive maintenance, and important activities occur, although some think they can. In reality, they must rely on their staff and systems to ensure that operations are running efficiently. This means their measures should be well understood and of great importance because they tell the manager at any point in time if they are succeeding or not.

There are many approaches to management. Some managers manage by direct involvement, working on equipment and having a significant presence on all shifts. They are doers and have an enormous amount of detailed knowledge of their organization. Other managers manage through well-developed systems and methods, having key people in place but insisting that everyone understands what is expected. Some managers are less knowledgeable and performance is more influenced by talented employees within the department.

There are various approaches to management just as there are varying degrees of success, and the audit team must understand how a manager manages prior to interviewing other members of the staff or touring the shop floor. Just as the scoring guide is a further definition of the quality management system, the manager interview sets the standard upon which the comments of the supervisors, manufacturing engineers, setups, and operators are evaluated. Even if teams run the department, the manager is the leader. It is very important information that must be understood up front and subsequently built upon because this will determine the effectiveness of the quality management system.

In the manager section 1, Process Overview, following the format of the scoring guide, the questions are:

1. What is your process and the important interfaces?

2. How do you track performance?

3. What are your goals?

4. What do you do to ensure customer satisfaction?

5. How do you address the quality policy?

The auditors are looking for the manager to define how he or she manages their organization. The team will note the details or obtain copies of documents of specific measures and goals for later reference in the subsequent interviews and in the team scoring session. Within the context of each question, the audit team is also looking for an understanding of the quality management system. The following thoughts should be occurring in the mind of the auditor for process overview:

- What is the depth of his or her understanding of the process as defined?

  - Does this manager understand the process approach and quality management system?

  - Is it a well-structured organization or is it loosely run?

    o According to the manager, is it a team environment or is it management directed (more authoritarian)?

  - Should I expect to find well-organized and defined activities or experienced personnel and a strong training program (less documentation)?

- Are the objectives and measures well thought out and accurate?

  - Are the measures "real" or just there because of the quality system?

  - Do they have good measures that are just not defined or do they not have specific data showing how the department is running?

- Do the measures indicate the level of performance?

  - Does the manager refer to something other than defined measures to gauge performance (that questions the understanding, accuracy, and buy-in to the system)?

- Were realistic goals set based on analysis of the process?

  - Does the manager have a strategy for performance?

  - Is there a negative trend that no one's reacting to, indicating lack of understanding, accuracy, or buy-in?

- Does the manager understand the customer and make an effort to define customer requirements?

  – Is there legitimate concern for the customer shown by good measures and improvement or is the focus more on getting product out the door?

  – Can he or she describe efforts made to improve satisfaction that are documented and evident in the measures?

- Does the quality policy really mean something to the manager?

  – Can they define specific activities related to meeting it or is their response just a reiteration of the policy?

There are other important aspects related to understanding the organization not addressed in this discussion on the checklists, namely continuous improvement and communication. The audit team must understand the improvement process to understand how overall improvement is achieved. The questions in Process Overview do not go into any detail on this. In addition, it is also important to understand the communication vehicles to determine how information is moved through the various levels within the department in addition to what information is conveyed. This is all covered in the scoring guide and checklists but not addressed in this discussion.

Supervisor Checklist

Once the manager interview is completed (all questions on the manager checklist addressed), proceed to the next level of management, the supervisor. In our organization, large departments have more than one supervisor on the shift, in addition to supervisors that manage the second and third shifts. Typically, only one supervisor checklist is used although more than one supervisor may be audited. Additional checklists could be used if necessary and would be meaningful for different shifts, but one should be concerned with creating excessive documentation to be reviewed during the scoring sessions. Regarding rating a department based on the comments of three different shifts, the team will rate based on the weakest shift and note that in the results. It is not an overall average.

With the notes in hand from the interview with the manager, the audit team asks many of the same questions of the supervisor that were asked of the manager, per the supervisor checklist. Since the manager has defined the quality management system per the questions in the three major sections, the supervisors will now explain from their perspective how the organization is managed and communicated. It is not expected that they would have the same depth of understanding as the manager because their information would be more product specific. However, the supervisor has direct reports that run the day-to-day operations so an understanding of the key processes, goals, customer satisfaction issues, and communication methods is critical.

If the supervisor doesn't know or understand this information, the effectiveness of management of the organization is in question. As discussed earlier, it is possible that the manager successfully operates under a "need to know" basis and only provides limited information because of this management style. This can be confirmed by the supervisor interview and you typically find a quality system that is not understood, with measures not effectively representing the process. It is a quality system that is not bought into by the management team because they have accepted it without challenge rather than ensure that it is correct. If issues were found, the manager didn't understand them or the communication with the staff was ineffective.

Organizations truly focused on improvement accept any identification of issues as an opportunity. Such has been my experience since using the progressive audit methodology in our organization. The management teams may not have all areas completely addressed but positive attitudes and enthusiasm for improvement have been commonplace. Using straightforward, "obvious" questions may reveal a lack of understanding or a procedure not implemented, but it should not be taken as a personal attack on an individual. If that reaction occurs, there is a lack of understanding of the purpose of the audit or fear of recrimination by management.

The supervisor checklist for process overview is shown in Figure 12.4. Note that in the subsequent checklists, I will only show the pertinent questions to save space since all checklists follow the same format with a lined area to encourage note taking.

The supervisor section Process Overview also follows the format of the scoring guide and in general the questions are the same:

1. What are your processes?

2. How do you track performance?

3. What are your goals?

4. What do you do to ensure customer satisfaction?

5. How do you address the quality policy?

There is a difference, though, in the expected responses. Where the manager is a director and planner of the organization (department), the supervisor is the next in command and responsible for carrying out the plan; in other words, execution. When interviewing the supervisor, the auditors are looking for his or her understanding of the same processes but also their understanding of the plan and strategies, as defined by the manager. In other words, the supervisor will be explaining their understanding based on their interpretation of the manager's directives.

Is there miscommunication or misunderstanding between management and first-level supervision in the organization? This can be identified through the audit assessment process, not only through the questions, but also by overcoming some of the apprehensions of management when every one of their supervisors is "grilled" by the audit team. Is there little buy-in from manufacturing? This will also surface when auditing for understanding and implementation in the other areas of the department, and must be addressed by the plant manager and plant management team.

Supervisor Checklist

1. Process Overview

A. How does the manufacturing process (map) affect your area?

  • Describe the process, including the inputs and outputs.

  • What are the important interfaces (relationships) with other processes?

B. How do you track the performance of your process?

  • Are the measures reviewed?

  • (Do the measures match what the manager stated?)

C. What are the goals for your process?

  • Where are they documented?

  • Plans for improvement?

  • (Do the goals match what the manager stated?)

D. How do you ensure the satisfaction of your customer?

  • Are measures tracking favorably?

  • What actions have been taken to improve customer satisfaction?

  • (Discuss both internal and external customers, if applicable)

E. Describe the quality policy.

  • How does it relate to your area?

Figure 12.4 Supervisor checklist—Process Overview.

In the mind of the auditor, the following thoughts should be occurring for the supervisor checklist for process overview:

  • What is the depth of his or her understanding of the processes as defined?

    – Does the supervisor understand the process approach and quality management system?

    – Is their understanding of the process consistent with the manager's?

      ○ If well-structured, was this conveyed and practiced by the supervisor?

      ○ If it is a team environment, has the supervisor been given enough information to make decisions?

- ○ If relying on experienced personnel, is there indication of a strong training program?
- Are the objectives and measures known?
  - – Does the supervisor have enough understanding to convey them to others?
- Do the measures indicate the level of performance?
  - – Does the supervisor know where the measures are found?
  - – Does the department take or direct action based on the trends?
- Were realistic goals set based on analysis of the process?
  - – Does the supervisor understand the strategy for performance?
  - – Is there a negative trend that no one's reacting to, indicating lack of understanding, accuracy, or buy-in?
- Does the supervisor understand the customer satisfaction issues and take or direct action based on those results?
  - – Is there legitimate concern for the customer or is the focus more on getting product out the door?
  - – Can he or she describe efforts made to improve satisfaction and are they documented and evident in the measure?
- Does the quality policy really mean something to the supervisor?
  - – Can he or she define specific activities related to meeting it or is their response just a reiteration of the policy?

Manufacturing Engineer Checklist

Moving on in our discussion, the next checklist is for the manufacturing engineer (see Appendix D). This interview may take place after the supervisor, later in the audit during follow-up discussion on advanced product quality planning, or when auditing preventive maintenance programs. Although there is far greater focus on the technical areas in their checklist, it also includes discussion on the overall processes and systems. The Process Overview section of the manufacturing engineer checklist is shown in Figure 12.5.

In our organization, the primary role of the manufacturing engineer is related to maintaining and upgrading the equipment. They program the software, assist the setups when there are equipment breakdowns, develop the preventive maintenance programs, and provide the necessary technical support to keep production operations running smoothly. For this reason, they should have a good understanding of department and organizational goals because they operate as a support function. As a member of the process team, per the process maps, they should have an understanding of the key processes.

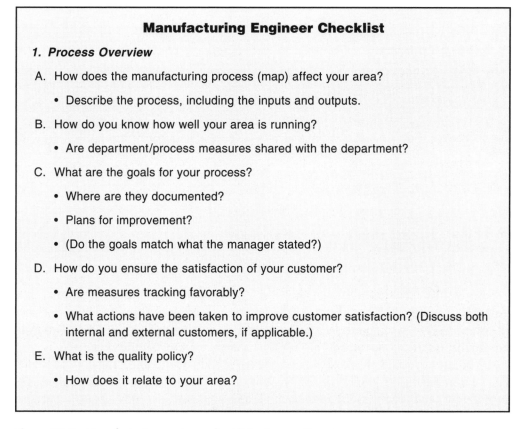

Figure 12.5 Manufacturing engineer checklist—Process Overview.

It is also expected that they have an understanding of customer satisfaction since they are a part of the team. They should also have an understanding of the quality policy as it relates to their area. There is far more detailed discussion relating to the operational side, defined in Management of the Process.

Setup, Operator, and Floor Checklist

The questions for both the setup and operator checklists (Appendixes E and F) for process overview are the same. See Figure 12.6.

Setup personnel are technical employees that work directly with the equipment. They are responsible for keeping it running, including supporting the operators. Operators work directly with the product, whether it is running a grinder or assembling components of an engine. Much of the information on the rest of the checklist will focus on product-related tasks, but there are also a number of questions pertaining to management of the organization. Even if it is limited, there must be communication of basic department measures and goals since the employees will contribute to their success.

Setup/Operator Checklist

1. Process Overview

B. How do you know if your area is successful?

C. What goals have been set for your area?

D1. Who is your customer?

D2. How do you know if you're doing a good job in terms of keeping your customers happy?

E. What is your understanding of the quality policy?

Figure 12.6 Setup/operator checklist—Process Overview.

Beside the setup and operator checklists, there is also one for the shop floor (see Appendix G). It includes specific instructions describing documents and control charts that must be reviewed and described by document number during the audit. This is to ensure that necessary documents are reviewed for correct revision and content.

Without a specific checklist, an audit team would have to understand what should be asked of the different areas of responsibility. Using a more generic checklist results in different teams asking different lines of questions between departments and also between seasons. The progressive audit methodology demands more up-front planning, so there are documents that clearly define what is expected and should be asked, providing a more consistent and repeatable audit process, even if auditors change.

INTERPRETING RESULTS

By the time the team has finished the audit interviews and tour, there are many notes to be reviewed in all the checklists. They are designed to audit all the necessary areas in the department and also provide enough supporting documentation to make a sound assessment of the level of implementation. From the manager's directives down to the understanding of the operators, the team can assess if information is properly developed, used, and communicated throughout the organization. In addition, the checklists provide enough detail to ensure an ability to determine audit effectiveness. This method reveals if the communication processes defined in the manager interviews are implemented and effective based on the responses from the shop floor. This also ties well into the Job Performance subsection.

There can be a situation where a manager provides many opportunities for communication of the message but the receiver still doesn't receive the message. For example, a manager presents charts in monthly meetings showing the performance of the business. He or she may explain objectives and goals on a regular basis, including posting them in common areas. However, the responses from the shop floor tour reveal that the employees don't understand or don't care. Is this a failure to communicate?

The way this is approached in the audit, partial credit is given but an opportunity for improvement is written up. Management has a responsibility to communicate important information to the workforce. If there is no understanding, the message is not being communicated properly. The opportunity here is for the message to be improved so it is easier to understand. In some cases, too much information is presented; this should be condensed to a few critical measures that relate to overall operations. Another possibility is that the process is not adequately defined or the measure is incorrect because those closest to the process don't see the connection. The important point is that the audit process extracts the truth from the operations so value is added to the organization.

In the progressive audit methodology, the Management of the Organization section would not be ready to score until interviews are completed for supervisor, manufacturing engineer, setup, and operator, and the shop floor tour is performed so that the team can rate the following questions in the scoring guide:

- Do the employees understand the measures and goals of management?

- Do they understand the requirements of the customer?

- Do they understand the quality policy?

- Are they involved in continuous improvement and decision-making activities and can they verify positive results?

- Are training programs or efforts taken to raise technical understanding?

- Are communication channels in place and effective, including change management for products and processes?

- Is there a level of understanding of the quality management system?

- Do they understand advanced product quality planning activities and are they involved in relation to new equipment and certification of operations?

- Is there training for new products, processes, and adequate supporting documentation such as instructions and standards?

- Are the involvement, training, and understanding of the employee appropriate to the employee's position?

- Is their understanding consistent with the direction provided by the management team?

The Management of the Organization section provides valuable insight for the audit team on management initiatives for current and future business activities in relationship to the quality management system. It also provides valuable insight for management since describing the various processes and reviewing the documentation reveals strengths and weaknesses just through the process of answering questions and recalling the logic of why it was developed that way.

Management of the Process as well as the final section on Nonconforming Product and Corrective Action require all interviews as well as the shop floor tour to be conducted prior to scoring. In this audit methodology, information gathered follows the flow of the audit to ensure that all necessary information is evaluated prior to making decisions on the effectiveness of the quality system.

The manager, supervisor, or both will serve as guides for the shop floor tour. They know what information was shared with the audit team so they can see firsthand if it was effectively communicated and implemented within their area of responsibility. The internal audit adds value through questioning techniques at various levels of management and staff because it reveals inconsistencies and opportunities within the interview process in terms of how well the policy is implemented on the shop floor. It verifies the processes of manufacturing, planning, and continuous improvement, where management sets direction for the business. It verifies that the methods for ensuring product and process quality have been properly developed. And finally, it verifies overall effectiveness through analysis of nonconforming material and corrective action activities.

13

The Auditors

Selecting auditor candidates with the necessary skills and establishing a sound training program to turn them into good auditors (Figure 13.1) is paramount to a successful audit program. I would define a successful audit program as one that doesn't need micromanaging; the program is self-sustaining, it verifies that systems are effective, and the results offer good suggestions for improvement. Given that it meets this definition, it should be well supported by management.

Prior to discussion of selection and training, it would be worthwhile to review the steps for implementing the progressive audit. From an overall perspective, the basic concepts and perceived value of the program should be presented to the management team and a commitment obtained to go forward with the program, defined as Step 1. The purpose and scope should be developed within the context of the quality management system, so the new audit format is a defined activity within the quality manual with agreement from the team. In addition, I feel it is important to have the purpose and scope in writing so the proposal is well thought out and clearly understood. This is Step 2.

Responsibility for managing the audit program, a key part of Step 3, should be established early on so that individuals can be actively involved in developing the scoring guide and defining the program. This can be a shared responsibility with the quality manager, but there are advantages when the quality manager takes the lesser role of merely providing support for the program, being an auditee, and setting direction as a member of the management team.

During the process of developing the scoring guide, the lead auditor given responsibility for the program should be working with the quality manager and management team to define the various processes and areas requiring an audit. Although developing the audit schedule is a later step, prior planning is required to ensure that all the necessary scoring guides are developed and adequate resources are available to complete the audit schedule.

Figure 13.1   Progressive audit Step 5.

SELECTING AUDITORS

Practically speaking, when implementing the program it is better to identify early on the lead auditor, who will be the one managing the program. This will allow the organization to select and train a smaller team, test out the scoring guide and checklists, and make modifications to the program to suit the environment. It also allows you to build confidence and credibility for the program.

Eventually you will want to have more than one lead auditor, especially if your organization is large. An internal audit program can require eight or more full audits during the year to complete an entire facility. This becomes quite demanding for one individual serving as manager of the program and lead auditor, unless this is their sole responsibility in the organization. Remember that two of the value-adding benefits of the progressive audit methodology are team-based auditing and increasing employee knowledge of the quality system. Although this decision must be made by the organization, the program does lend itself to multiple lead auditors.

This also allows them to divide up the audit schedule throughout the audit season. Overall, the goal should be having enough auditors so audit teams can be organized such that no one audits their own area of responsibility and the audit itself does not become a dreaded task because they get too far behind in their other duties. All of these individuals can have other responsibilities within the organization because the audit is a team-based activity, even for the lead auditor that manages the program. It does not require dedicating additional resources, which makes this a value-added activity.

Eventually, as the program expands and participants gain experience, the lead auditor/manager of the program moves into more of a program manager role. They still can serve as a lead auditor but less frequently. Instead, they may act as a team member, observing new lead auditors or team members and, afterward, offering suggestions for improvement. This works nicely because then they have time to update the scoring guide and checklist, develop the audit schedule, train new auditors, and facilitate the postseason planning meetings without being consumed with too many audits to conduct.

Developing the scoring guide is Step 4, described in the previous chapter. This is a very important tool of the internal audit, which is why you will want your lead auditor involved in this effort. Clearly, its usefulness lies in the thoroughness of its content. At a minimum, it should address the requirements of the relevant quality management system standard and the defined quality management system of the organization.

In addition, the flow of the audit process is also important and can be prescribed through the organization of the scoring guide sections. This is extremely important for inexperienced auditors and is helpful for seasoned ones as well. Proper flow puts the auditors in the best position to ensure ample coverage of the various aspects of planning, implementation, and effectiveness.

Selecting auditors can occur earlier in the process but the scoring guide should be completed prior to training, all of which represent Step 5. To field an audit team, you will need to find at least three auditor candidates so that during the audit you can divide the team in pairs (including the lead auditor). Over time, you will need to add more to maintain independence of the area in which they work and so you don't burn them out. There should be clear criteria for auditor selection although it need not be extensive. However, there are a few key attributes that should bear the most weight.

Key Attributes

Above all, a key attribute is that auditors should have a sincere interest in the company and have a desire to do things right. When we were first establishing our program, the managers referred to this as selecting participants that were good workers with a positive attitude. These employees were interested in learning something new and were willing to participate in an activity that would benefit the company and employees.

This is not to say someone slightly skeptical is bad because you want your auditors interested in digging for the truth and willing to report noncompliant situations. Care must be taken in this area because you don't want a negative person on the audit team nor do you want someone who has a vendetta against the company. This is disruptive to teams and there will be an obvious concern of bias because they have an axe to grind.

Another important attribute is that auditors must have integrity. Difficult issues may arise during the audit, such as a safety concern or possibly the intentional misreporting of information. This must be handled properly with the management of the area, but you must have auditors that will not tolerate any sort of cover-up, perhaps because the employee involved is a friend. There are defined systems, procedures, and work rules, and the auditors should take the position that their job is to report findings, whether positive or negative.

This approach also takes the personality out of the picture, which is very important in the audit. Questions asked during the audit, especially if they uncover something different than what is defined, can raise an auditee's defenses. If they realize they have responded incorrectly, they may try to explain, argue, or bully their way out. Both the auditor and the auditee can get into a real debate about what should be the right thing to do if personality gets in the way. Training covering how to deal with a situation like this helps, but an auditor that doesn't let personality get in the way will be better equipped to diffuse the issue.

One last point about integrity that must be discussed relates to the person. The audit should never be affected by any racial, gender, or ethnic bias. Audits are about people and they must not be influenced by internal prejudice or perceptions. Although there are federal regulations dealing with issues of discrimination in the workplace, we must be conscious of the potential of it subtly influencing decisions made during the audit and take actions to prevent it.

A third important characteristic of an auditor is the ability to listen and observe. In some respects, this also falls under the concept of being a good worker because they typically need to do this to do their job well. Without good listening and observing skills, the audit will become an exercise in asking a bunch of questions and recording an incomplete response. You simply do not obtain enough information unless you listen carefully and watch. While one of the team members is asking a question, the others should be studying the work area to obtain factual information to support or refute the particular line of questioning. When the auditee responds, everyone should be listening and watching, so they clearly understand what is stated and that the question was correctly understood.

A person who has the ability to listen and observe can stay focused on a task rather than become distracted and not pay attention to responses and actions. You don't want auditors involved in other conversations or mentally somewhere other than at the audit. This sends a wrong message that the audit is not important and also shows disrespect for the auditee.

Listening creates a positive atmosphere during the audit. When you listen carefully to what someone says it tells him or her that they are important and that you will shut everything else out until they are through. For that one moment in time, that operator or setup is the focus of attention, which may be one of the few times someone really listens to them talk about their job. The result of that brief interchange can send a powerful message about the audit and the company.

The ability to communicate well through questions and follow-up discussion is also important, but I don't necessarily consider that attribute as needing any special consideration for auditor selection. That is because the key points of discussion are already defined in the scoring guides and checklists. If you follow the format, they will be written in a way that allows the auditor to ask the leading question and follow with the bullet points to clarify and satisfy the intent of the question.

To explore this a little further, communication skills in this area actually relate directly to the knowledge of the subject and practical experience of the auditor. It is difficult to ask follow-up questions if you are unsure of the subject, so we train auditors to always follow the guides and checklists. The checklists become important in this regard because they represent the auditor's rewrite of the scoring guide questions into a flow of thought that fits nicely with the auditor's personal experience. In other words, they can simply read the question without trying to interpret the intent, allowing them to then listen carefully to the response.

The experience of other auditors and especially the lead auditor also plays an important role. When first introducing the program, it is extremely helpful to have individuals with auditing experience on the team. In our case, we enlisted the services of supplier quality, purchasing, and a manager with previous experience in supplier surveys. We also recruited a few individuals new to auditing. We performed training on the methodology of the scoring guides and reviewed key requirements of the quality system, but their experience was useful because they knew how to audit. The new team members learned quickly through observation and coaching.

As auditors are added, there is always a good mix of experience on the teams so new members learn quickly because they are always paired with experienced auditors. This ensures development of a sound audit program as well as preventing incorrect interpretations of the quality system. In my role as a divisional quality manager, I have served as an auditor on the team to show support. It also allows me to monitor the audits and generate strategies for improvement.

The attributes of a positive attitude, integrity, and ability to listen and observe are important for both auditors and lead auditors. Where inadequate communication skills can be overcome by good written questions for the auditor, the lead auditor must be skilled in this area. That means they must have knowledge and practical experience in understanding and interpreting the quality management system.

As their title implies, their primary role is to serve as the leader, meaning they are the source of knowledge and direction during the audit. When a situation arises, such as a difference in interpretation of a procedure, it is the lead auditor's role to intervene and ensure that a correct decision is made. This means they have a sound understanding of the system and an ability to hear all sides in order to make a correct call. It is the role of the lead auditor to have the final say. This person must have confidence in their ability, which comes from that knowledge and experience.

When the audit team and management are gathered together to begin the audit, they all look to the lead auditor to take charge of the meeting and explain the format and schedule of events. The same is expected during the closing meetings. They set the audit schedule, set up the audit teams, and make the arrangements for the meetings and tour. They also write up the reports and follow up on open issues, so they must have organizational skills.

TRAINING AUDITORS

One point of discussion prior to going into training is to review what the auditors will be auditing. The major emphasis in this book is auditing the manufacturing process using the manufacturing scoring guide and checklists. For this reason, auditor training requires less time because it is focused on manufacturing. There will be separate scoring guides for quality, human resources, product engineering, purchasing, and the plant manager. In our division, one lead auditor conducted these audits so teams were not used. This is changing since the audit program is fairly mature so more lead auditors have experience and knowledge to audit those processes. There is also the concern of maintaining independence of the area audited.

Auditor training should be formal and considered very important to the internal audit process. For new auditors, it opens their eyes to the depth and breadth of the quality management system, its importance to the organization beyond the department in which they work, and the necessity to verify that it is properly implemented. Training should not fall under the approach of setting up an hour meeting with the newly selected auditors and reading through key points of the audit and quality manual. This will send the wrong message to the auditors because it undermines the importance of the program.

The training program should consist of an overview of the audit purpose and scope, a fairly in-depth review of pertinent aspects of the quality manual, and a concentration on the specifics of the audit format and questions. For this reason, the scoring guide must be completed prior to the training. There is so much material covered that auditors come away both surprised and confused. They are surprised at all the effort and detail that goes into a good quality management system. They are confused because it appears too extensive for them to comprehend.

This is acceptable because we want them to appreciate the usefulness of the scoring guide and checklist. To a greater extent, we want them to depend on these documents during the audit as one depends on a road map during a long journey. We don't want improvising or second-guessing the intent of the system, but we still want to utilize a broad range of employees as part of the audit team. We want their practical experience and fresh ideas on what they see the system as trying to accomplish, but we want a thorough and complete assessment of the interpretation and use of various processes and procedures by management and the employees.

The auditor training takes approximately a half day. If it's the first time with new auditors, it may take the good portion of a day. In addition, as the audit scope expands to address areas beyond manufacturing, more training will be required to review additional quality systems such as engineering, purchasing, or human resources. The training is geared for new lead auditors and audit team members; the audit program manager conducts it. The training program in many ways is like a workshop, meaning open discussion should be encouraged, and typically follows this format:

- Overview of the internal audit

  - Purpose and scope

- Audit plan including opening/closing meetings

- Responsibilities

• Review of the quality management system

• Review of the scoring guide

• Review of the checklist

- Asking questions, listening to responses, and observing

- Taking notes

• How to score the audit

• Audit findings and reporting

In preparation for the training, copies of necessary documents are made so each participant can compile an auditor handbook for reference and to hold their notes. The audit manager makes copies of the pertinent quality system process maps and procedures for the processes the team will audit. They will also need copies of the scoring guide, checklist, and the slides or overheads used during the training.

Audit Process

The early stages of the training are focused at a higher level to provide perspective for the auditors. In a sense, we are laying a foundation of the basic structure of the audit, then the quality system, and building upon it with greater detail in the later training on the scoring guide and checklist.

Training should begin with a focus on the auditor through an overview of the audit, explaining what they are doing, why they are doing it, and what role they will play. It is important to establish expectations early on so everyone understands their role. Otherwise, you run the risk of spending a lot of time training, and possibly even initiating an actual audit, only to find one of the participants discovering they don't really want to be a part of the program. The selection process is not typically a formal interview but more a recommendation by a supervisor or manager for the employee to participate. You will see volunteered employees having little idea of what they are supposed to do.

There is another purpose for the general overview of the audit; it prevents the trainer from making the process so complicated that you run the risk of scaring good auditors off. Employees enjoy participating in the program because they learn something new and get an opportunity to do something different at work. If you overwhelm them with details of systems and audits too quickly, they may come away feeling ill-equipped for the task. Presenting the audit process in a simple structure, including the scoring guide and checklist, will make them realize that there are specific tools available to ensure their success and they will be less likely to make a mistake or be caught in an uncomfortable situation.

The audit can be described through a flowchart or basic diagram so they understand the overall method. Once a review of the audit process is completed, it makes sense to move to discussion of the purpose and scope, and then briefly review the tools of the scoring guide and checklist. This provides an opportunity to explain that the audit is a requirement, that the organization wants to expand the audit to obtain more benefit from the activity, and that the auditors have experiences that can add value to the process.

One point to make here is that you may have individuals in the training with fairly extensive experience in quality that want to move it along more quickly. On the other hand, there are employees with little understanding outside their own department. I would keep things at a basic level initially because you will move deeper into the systems and methods as the training progresses. You don't want to lose anyone, and you don't want to assume that someone knows as much as they think they do.

Although the opening review of the audit process can utilize basic bullet points and brief discussions, moving into auditor responsibilities requires a focus on certain key points of emphasis in relationship to the duties of an auditor. I believe those points are the same as the criteria for auditor selection: positive attitude, integrity, attentive listening, and careful observation. Even though candidates were hopefully selected with these attributes in mind, the auditors should clearly understand their importance during the actual audit.

Whether interviewing members of the management team, touring the floor, questioning setups and operators, or participating in the final scoring of the audit, those auditor attributes must be present at all times. There cannot be negativism, hidden agendas, or inattentiveness during any aspect of the audit process. It is a responsibility that must be willingly accepted and adhered too.

Quality Management System

Training on the quality management system must be logically approached so it doesn't appear to be a complicated mass of documents. I would recommend it be reviewed in two aspects: first the structure and then the systems. By structure, I mean physical makeup of the quality manual, process maps, procedures, work instructions, and working documents. Simply put, the auditors should be handed copies of these various documents so the key points and differences of each can be discussed and understood. They must know what makes up a process map versus a procedure because they will be questioning others about it.

On the systems side, there should be a review of the high-level processes pertinent to the audit and any related processes and procedures. This need not be extensive, because it will be addressed again in the context of the scoring guide, but the auditors must understand the key process maps defining the areas audited. For example, the manufacturing scoring guide has a focus on the manufacturing, continuous improvement, advanced product quality planning, and containment maps. In addition, they will review the highest-level plant processes and related measures so they have the perspective of how manufacturing fits into the overall plant environment.

In training, redundancy on key topics is important so they sink in. By following the recommended approach, the participants will review these processes in the context of the system and again in the context of the scoring guide. The auditors should see the quality manual as the defining document for the various quality activities. They should understand it as the approved way of conducting business and a point of reference should differences arise.

Interpreting Findings

Auditor training on systems must address defined versus practice. They need to learn that they are auditing for situations where the documentation doesn't match the activity. There may be minor differences or possibly quite significant ones. Although this creates a disparity from the approved method of doing something, there is an opportunity to improve on the systems and ensure that they are correct. The appropriate approach should be taught, which is to document the finding so a decision can be made to either update the manual or change the activity to what has been defined. If the nonconformity is significant, the lead auditor should be notified so that the situation is immediately addressed at that point in the audit. This should then be written up as a corrective action with required follow-up to ensure that it is resolved.

There is also a need to address the issue of excessive versus adequate detail in audit scrutiny. Auditors have gotten a reputation for being too "picky" during the audit because their findings create additional non-value-added work. If one sentence or a short phrase is not followed per the procedure, it is written up as a finding. The result leads to inadequate or vague procedures to avoid being caught in noncompliance rather than true improvement.

The ISO 9001:2000 standard has moved away from requiring numerous procedures to a focus only on key documents and allows training to suffice for other activities. In other words, it's up to the organization to determine what should be defined in writing. I believe it should be a management decision rather than a dictate from the standard, but most publications I have read state that there is as much, if not more, documentation now. This is the case in our organization.

I believe the reason for this is the quality culture. Raising the level of product and system quality requires increased discipline and more in-depth understanding of the employees. Within the organization, it means defining the proper methods and activities that have been refined over time and proven to be the best practices. This becomes a cycle of continuous improvement. The internal audit, and third-party audits for that matter, serve an important purpose in verifying that what is defined is matched by what is practiced. They also serve as regular and consistent reminders that these must be reviewed and updated.

How much detail is appropriate depends on the type of audit and the depth of the audit trail. The purpose of the internal quality systems audit is to verify that systems are followed and effective. The team is auditing the entire quality system and I believe this places it at a higher level. This means the team is working from process maps and procedures and pulling sample documents, not investigating every work instruction or procedural detail. If they find a working document is not completely followed or incorrect, it is noted and they go on. If they find the majority of the sample working documents with errors, they should follow that audit trail to other documents and determine the extent of the nonconformance.

Scoring Guide and Checklist

The scoring guide and checklist are discussed together because of the strong relationship between them. The training should first review the overall intent of the particular section in the guide and then move into each question so the auditors understand what is being asked. Examples are given from results of previous audits so the participants can discuss in detail the more difficult interpretations and pass over the obvious.

Since they have already reviewed the key processes and procedures in the quality system, they will have a basic understanding of what is supposed to occur. There is obviously more information than they could possibly comprehend, so the intent of the training is to provide basic concepts of the system so they understand the purpose of the questions. Some of it is intuitive because the auditors are familiar through their jobs. A broad background of auditors is important so that within the audit team, someone will be familiar with the procedure.

As each section in the scoring guide is reviewed with the related checklist questions, discussion should occur regarding what constitutes meeting the requirements so that they learn the scoring technique. The emphasis is on a team approach so during the actual audit there is open discussion to determine the score. Typically there is consensus as the team reviews their notes so it is not a difficult process. Finally, there is discussion on the format of the closing meeting and subsequent final report.

During this training, there must also be discussion on how to handle certain situations such as potential conflict during the audit. Challenges to interpretation will arise and auditors should understand they are on a fact-finding mission and are not there to correct a misunderstanding or challenge an auditee. Protocol should be discussed so in cases where there is an impasse, the lead auditor will be contacted to make the final call.

Working As a Team

The concept of teams is obviously important and discussed numerous times in this book. Training the team together builds consensus, as does the presence of experienced versus nonexperienced auditors. There should be discussion on working as a team, such as dividing up audit questions, so while one auditor is asking, the other is listening and looking for facts. Auditors also corroborate and build consensus in conclusions so the resulting score and comments are representative of the team. This does not mean everyone must always agree but instead that opposing views must be discussed so the best decision will be made.

As the audit program matures, there are opportunities for more-focused training, especially for lead auditors. This depends on the strategy of the organization and the size of the audit teams. Training can be expanded to have a session specifically focused on conflict resolution, team building, or questioning/listening techniques. In addition, lead auditors can serve as guides during the ISO or customer audits to learn new techniques.

There is little reason to believe that when the training session is finished, the auditors will have the necessary skills to perform a good audit. Although much of the system and audit format will make sense during the review, it may be difficult to recall any details or be able to put it in perspective. This does not take away from the fact that it is still important to train this way so familiarity with the audit process occurs.

Auditors can take notes on key points in addition to having copies of the slides or overheads for reference. Most important is the fact that they will have the checklist in hand during the audit as a guide to follow. They will also have an experienced lead auditor and eventually, experienced team members once the program becomes established. As the program expands and matures, training will expand to both teach new auditors the methodology and continue to expand the skill of experienced lead auditors and team members.

14

The Audit "Season"

Planning ahead is critical to the success of the internal audit (Figure 14.1). You clearly have options: time can be minimized, resulting in a last-minute audit, or much effort can be devoted to maintaining a strong program that can be expanded to increased levels of detail or other facilities. It's pure physics: put a little in and get a little out, or put a lot in and get a lot out.

Figure 14.1 Progressive audit Step 6.

What is the audit "season"? In my days as a last-minute auditor, auditing was an annual cycle of planning–conducting–documenting just prior to the ISO audit. Up-front planning was finding the checklist, which was a spreadsheet with rewritten ISO questions one of the quality managers had done some years back, and skim over it to make sure it was current. Sometimes I'd even get a call to send out the "latest" version to one of the other plants. Then a manager and I walked around on first shift, trying to interpret and ask questions from the sheet, finding opportunities for improvement. The report had some details and a couple of recommendations, but mainly documented that we did it.

Many good books and periodicals develop the concept of a thorough audit plan. All of the publications I have read reference an audit schedule, which means you need to plan ahead of time. It is obvious I didn't follow it in my last-minute audit days. There is also much detail on the stages of the audit itself, including examples of the working documents. Many suggest audits are ongoing, developing the necessary documents based on the immediate need. In my opinion, there should be greater focus on the concept of the audit season.

In the progressive audit methodology, we have a season when audits are conducted each year. This is when the teams are active, though it does not just mean the audit activity itself. The concept of season goes beyond the audit activity and suggests there is a preseason and postseason. Not unlike sports, preseason is preparation and postseason is analysis and strategy. There is also the concept of rest, meaning you take time off to clear your thoughts.

When initially developing the progressive audit, the preseason consists of Steps 1 through 5. Once the program is established, preseason comprises updating the scoring guide and checklists, selecting and training new auditors, and doing a "spring-training" refresher for everyone on methods and any changes. It may also mean expanding the scope of the program. Postseason means getting the teams together to review the program. This means discussions on areas that could be strengthened, expanding into other areas, improving training, and anything else related to the audit. This is the last step of the process but a very important concept in ensuring the success of the program, which I will detail shortly.

THE AUDIT PROCESS

The internal audit is a process and I have referred to it as such many times in this book. In the ISO standard, the internal audit is one of the required documented activities because Section 8.2.2 says it shall be defined. This means you must detail it in a procedure and I believe this is the correct approach. There is far too much that should be required of a sound program to simply create a process map. It really needs a procedure defining enough detail for the key aspects of preplanning, training, proper audit format, and postseason planning. However, this does not prevent us from defining it as a process, which makes it easy to see the important sequences and measures for effectiveness. The audit process assumes a mature program, with the previous five steps completed so that that the scope and all the necessary documents have been developed.

The progressive audit process (Figure 14.2) follows the cycle of preseason, audit season, and postseason strategic planning. The standards committee is a supplier of the process because they provide the ISO standard as an input of system structure and requirements. Management is also a supplier of the quality management system as well as supplying the resources to conduct the audit. Publications such as books and magazines are resources because there is information available (input) that will help improve understanding and methods.

Those involved with managing the audit should go outside the organization, including seminars and conferences, for information and new ideas. It is an important part of the postseason planning and strategy, which suggests actively seeking out new information and study. Although the audit is a learning experience in itself, it is also important to seek new approaches and ideas.

In the audit process, the customer is management as well as the stakeholders, who are represented by the management team in the context of the audit. Management is the recipient of the audit report, including specific areas identified as opportunities and corrective actions. The output also includes improved systems and processes by addressing the specific areas identified in the report. As customers, both management and employees benefit through greater understanding of the quality management system because of their involvement with the audit process.

Since the audit improves systems it will also improve performance, which benefits all stakeholders.[1] Employees are directly affected by participating in the audit and indirectly through presentations of results in management reviews and department meetings. Finally, as the general understanding of management and the workforce improves, the quality culture also benefits because of increased understanding and discipline within the organization. This ultimately benefits the remaining stakeholders: the investors and the community.

There are two overall measures for the audit process: compliance to schedule (date) and overall process or department rating based on the score. Meeting the schedule promotes planning and preparation and the overall rating promotes improvement. A rating such as excellent, good, and so on, will provide a quantitative assessment of the level of implementation in this particular area. In addition, the plant management team can develop strategies to address overall weaknesses in specific areas, such as advanced product quality planning, or containment if a problem surfaces as an issue in multiple areas.

You may ask how the rating is a measure of the audit process. One might conclude from the above statement that you are rating the department rather than the audit. As management gains experience in maintaining the audit program, the ratings will also provide a measure of the audit team's level of skill.

The ratings reflect the experience of the audit team because as the team's understanding of the process increases, they will have an improved vision of what they should be looking for, which will raise their skill level, resulting in improvements in

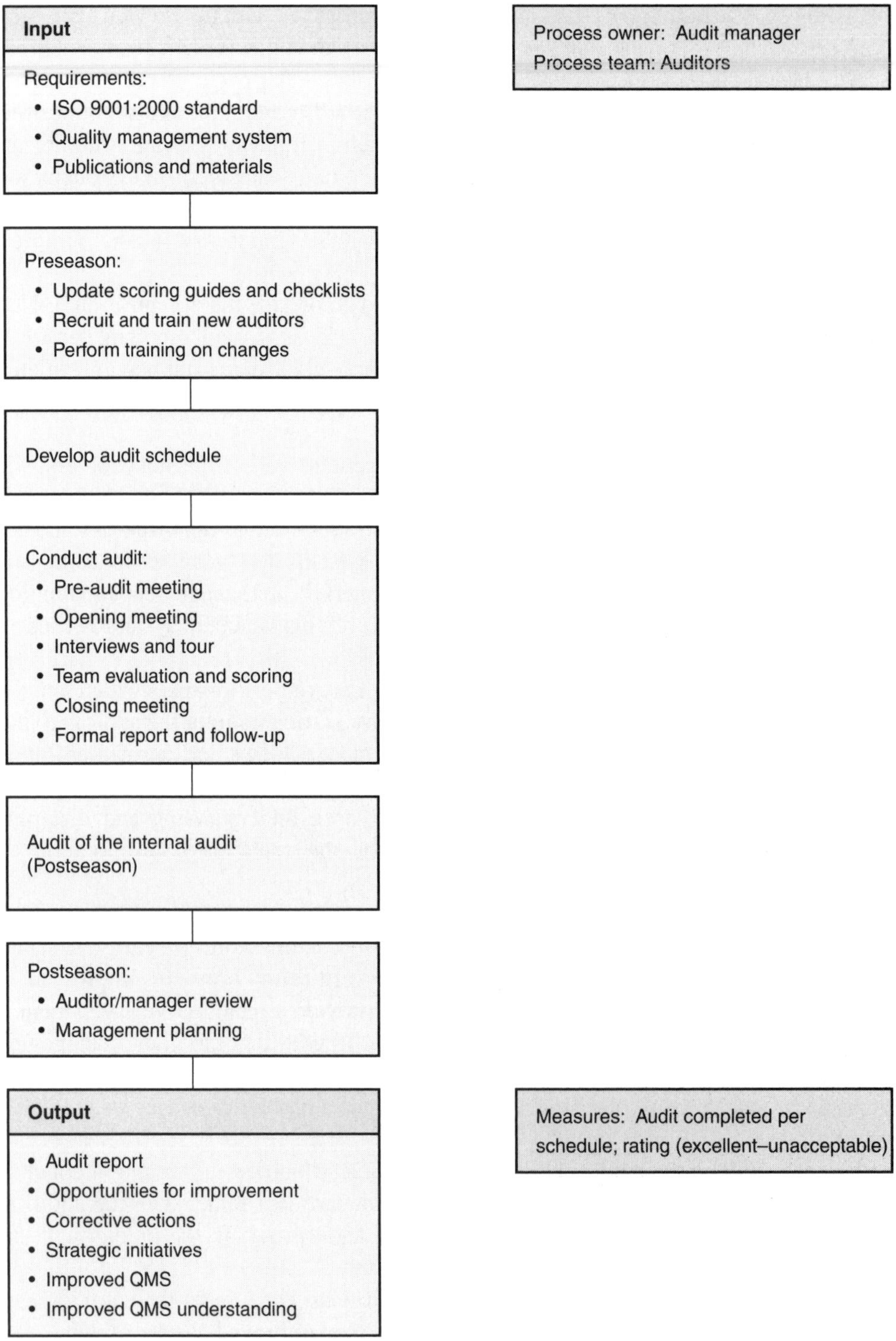

Input

Requirements:
- ISO 9001:2000 standard
- Quality management system
- Publications and materials

Process owner: Audit manager
Process team: Auditors

Preseason:
- Update scoring guides and checklists
- Recruit and train new auditors
- Perform training on changes

Develop audit schedule

Conduct audit:
- Pre-audit meeting
- Opening meeting
- Interviews and tour
- Team evaluation and scoring
- Closing meeting
- Formal report and follow-up

Audit of the internal audit
(Postseason)

Postseason:
- Auditor/manager review
- Management planning

Output

- Audit report
- Opportunities for improvement
- Corrective actions
- Strategic initiatives
- Improved QMS
- Improved QMS understanding

Measures: Audit completed per
schedule; rating (excellent–unacceptable)

Figure 14.2 The internal audit process.

the organization. This becomes a cycle of continuous improvement. In other words, as the team improves its understanding, they will audit in more depth. This will provide opportunities for improvement, and once management analyzes and implements, they will have a better system. The team audits to the new level of understanding and identifies new opportunities or additional refinements that raise the bar again. Equally important, there is the postseason planning that also impacts this process of improvement through analysis and development of strategies. Following are the steps of the audit process.

Preseason Updates, Recruiting, and Training

The sequence of process steps in the scoring guide and checklists is revised in the first step called preseason updates, based on the results of postseason planning activities. New auditors are selected, lead auditors identified if necessary, and the audit program manager or experienced lead auditors conduct the appropriate training. In addition, there is training for both experienced and new auditors on the updates and as an audit refresher for the entire team. In some instances, there may have been updates to the quality management system. These must also be included in the training if they affect any aspect of the internal audit.

Develop the Audit Schedule

The next step is for the audit program manager to develop the audit schedule for the season. Once developed, it is sent to the auditors and the management team so they can plan for it. This is simply a matter of identifying all of the areas requiring an audit and listing the month in which it should be conducted by the team. The schedule also includes the date of the preseason training, the audit of the internal audit at the end of the season, as well as the postseason planning and strategy session.

Important in the consideration of the schedule is the timing of the audit in relation to normal business operations. The audit should be scheduled during a period when all operations are running so important activities are not missed and to ensure that key personnel will be available. The lead auditor for each facility will work with the managers to select the actual date, and once the audit is completed, that completion date is also entered in the schedule. The audit schedule then becomes a time line for conducting all the necessary activities as well as a final document to show when those activities occurred. It provides useful documentation for the audit of the internal audit as well as the ISO audit.

The audit schedule is also important because it means planning for the audit season, which prevents it from being quickly thrown together to comply with an ISO requirement. To increase its effectiveness, it needs to be a well-planned and thorough process, so it becomes part of the culture and anticipated by the management team as a value-added activity that must occur each year. The audits are then conducted according to schedule. The schedule will obviously be adjusted during the season but audits should never be moved out so far that you end up with a last-minute audit program. There is flexibility but never complacency.

Conduct the Audit

The specific audit for a manufacturing department or process should have an audit schedule as well. It should be developed and sent out to the management of the area and the audit team with enough time allowed to make proper arrangements. Everyone should understand that it is an approximate schedule and will be adjusted based on need, but there must be a time commitment by management to ensure that the necessary individuals are available when needed. The actual audit date is arranged with management of the department prior to formalizing the schedule and should be done a week prior to ensure that necessary personnel are available.

The schedule should follow a format and content similar to the following:

7:30 AM	Pre-audit team meeting
8:00 AM	Opening meeting
8:15 AM	Manager interview
11:15 AM	Supervisor interview
12:15 PM	Lunch and discussion
1:15 PM	Manufacturing engineer interview
2:15 PM	Floor tour
3:15 PM	Operator and setup interviews (1 hour)
Second Day	
8:00 AM	Operator and setup interview (1 hour)
9:00 AM	Team evaluation and scoring meeting
12:00 PM	Closing meeting

When more than one shift is audited, the schedule will be expanded to include that as well. If more than one supervisor is interviewed, extra time must also be allowed. There is flexibility in the schedule for the lead auditor to allow for breaks. For example, usually after the manager interview, the team will take a 10-minute break. Regarding refreshments and lunch, we allow coffee to be available during the interviews to keep it more informal and relaxed. In addition, lunch is provided by the organization and brought in for the audit team. There is usually discussion about the audit during lunch, so although it is a break for the team, it also is a time to discuss comments and interpretations.

Pre-Audit Team Meeting

The pre-audit meeting is only for the audit team. Its purpose is for the lead auditor to hand out the checklists, pertinent process maps, and procedures from the quality manual and to review the schedule. In addition, it is important for the team to discuss strategies for accomplishing the audit such as how to divide the team for the floor tour. The departments in our organization are quite large, with numerous machining or assembly lines, each with dedicated personnel. The teams divide up in twos or threes, depending on the total number of auditors, putting one experienced person in each group to ensure that the audit is as efficient as possible.

The pre-audit meeting also allows the lead auditor to do a little coaching of new auditors as a refresher to their training. General comments are made on format and technique, in addition to a quick review of the process maps and procedures pertinent to the audit. The team must understand the responsibilities and sequence of events because once the audit has begun, there should not be coaching of auditors during the interviews and tour with the auditee present. The auditors can meet during a quick break to review an interpretation, but there should not be a practice during the audit of discussion on audit protocol.

Opening Meeting

The opening meeting should be attended by all audit team members, the management team of the area being audited, as well as any other interested parties. The plant quality manager and plant manager should also attend because it promotes greater understanding, demonstrates commitment and support, and also motivates the management team to have the key personnel attend. The lead auditor should circulate a sign-in sheet to document that the opening meeting has occurred and who attended.

The lead auditor is responsible for conducting the opening meeting. It begins with the formalities of welcoming everyone and formally opening the audit. The lead auditor should then hand out the schedule to all in attendance and review the times and activities, explaining who will be needed to attend and what topics will be covered. It is important to ensure that key personnel are available not only for the interviews but to conduct the tour. These individuals must have knowledge of the system and processes to answer questions during the tour because those responses will be reflected in the score.

The lead auditor also will review the audit methodology of the checklist and scoring guide, including a brief discussion of the rating method and final report. The auditees should understand that they will need to supply documentation to verify that certain activities have occurred and will need to explain the systems and processes during the interviews. It should be clearly communicated and stressed that the purpose is thorough assessment of the implementation of the quality management system and not to assess or rate individual performance.

There should also be discussion about audit findings. The lead auditor should explain that if during the interviews or tour the team should find certain areas are not in compliance, it will be discussed at that point with the appropriate individuals to ensure that the team and the auditee have a correct understanding. If more information is available, it should be presented for review to ensure that a correct assessment is made. If, in fact, it still is not found in compliance, it will be reported as such. Depending on the degree of noncompliance, it will be a corrective action, an opportunity for improvement, or simply reflected in a lower score.

All in attendance should understand prior to the actual audit the various roles of the lead auditor, audit team members, and the auditees. It should be explained that the lead auditor has the final say on interpretation to avoid unnecessary confusion and delay. The opening meeting should end with an opportunity for anyone to ask questions to clarify their understanding.

Interviews and Tour

Most of the details of this sequence of the process will be discussed in the sections dealing with the scoring guide and checklists. However, there are some overall comments that must be made. The interviews should be conducted in a meeting room that provides privacy and no distractions. The entire audit team should be present for the closed-door interviews.

Three hours are allotted for the manager interview because there is so much material to cover. The checklist contains all of the questions in the scoring guide. This means the manager is asked everything pertaining to his or her department. If advanced product quality planning or preventive maintenance is solely the responsibility of someone else, this area can be skipped. All other interviews are allotted one hour except for operators and setups because the audit team will meet with more people.

If more than one supervisor is interviewed, they should be separate although we allowed the manager to be present the first year. The manager and supervisor will need to provide evidence of activities so an available computer is useful since most reports today are electronic. Much of the manufacturing engineer interview deals with advanced product quality planning and preventive maintenance so he or she must have supporting documentation as well.

The setup and operator interviews are limited to two people for each position. The manager provides a list of candidates from which the auditors randomly select the individuals for the interviews. This allows some preselection by management since there must be some screening of individuals that may not have the experience to answer questions covering all areas of the department. It also reduces the chance of someone coming in with bias that may negatively impact the results.

Interviews should be complete, which means no questions skipped unless they do not apply to that particular area. If the auditee does not understand, one of the audit team members should explain. If the response is somewhat vague, additional probing questions should be asked.

There are several approaches that can be used for the interviews. The lead auditor could ask all the questions as the team sits quietly and takes notes. However, this makes for a stagnant process and encourages mental "drifting" by the team. It is better if the team divides up the various sections to allow each team member to ask questions. It comes across more spontaneous because it is more informal and encourages all to ask follow-up questions. It also moves the focus of attention of the auditee around the room rather than remaining on one person.

The interviews really should be in a relaxed but respectful atmosphere. It should not come across as a "grilling" by the team but more an informal discussion prompted by a series of questions to keep the team on track. The reality is that team members still read the questions off and listen for the answer but the format of the questions simulates discussion and encourages dialogue. There is often joking during the process, especially after a somewhat detailed discussion, and this should also be acceptable.

The shop floor tour occurs after the completion of the interviews, although operator and setup interviews usually come afterward. This improves understanding of observations made on the tour. The team needs a good understanding of the management directives and interpretations of the staff prior to verification of activities on the floor. The team usually divides up so the entire department can be efficiently covered. Each member has the shop floor checklist that is used to provide direction for the necessary questions, activities, and documents that must be audited.

The tour should represent the flow of the department so they should start with how raw materials or components are received and finish with shipping. In our organization, receiving inspection is addressed as part of the quality assurance audit because it is performed for the entire facility. During the tour, usually a supervisor or manager leads the team through the process, questions are asked from the checklist, and documents are pulled and recorded. The auditors should ask for the appropriate personnel to demonstrate the inspection plan, gauge techniques, and to explain their interpretation of a control chart. They should expect to see no hesitancy on the part of the employee to perform the requested activity, which would indicate a lack of training, unless it is not in their area of responsibility. They will also ask for work instructions and explanation of the training process, which should verify job responsibility and requirements.

During the tour, the auditors will also ask employees about their job responsibilities and how they relate to the customer. This is to verify earlier interview points from management. It will demonstrate whether these responsibilities are communicated and if the communication process is effective. It will also identify if the message sent is the message received.

The checklist is very specific in describing the necessary documents, gauges, and control charts that should be reviewed during the tour. There are spaces for noting titles and revisions and for a minimum quantity to be reviewed. This is important to ensure that the team documents this information and that they actually review it. It is correct audit protocol and provides a reference for the closing meeting and final report should any findings result from it. The teams will complete the tour when all questions have been adequately answered and required documentation reviewed.

Team Evaluation and Scoring Meeting

Once the interviews and shop floor tour have been completed, the audit team meets privately to evaluate the results and score the audit. The team will review all questions and the lead auditor will add up the points for an overall score and rating. In addition, positive comments, opportunities for improvement, and any corrective actions will be noted for the closing meeting. This sequence of the process is very important and will be discussed in detail in the next section.

Closing Meeting

The lead auditor will facilitate the closing meeting, which typically lasts about 30 minutes. At this point, a rough draft of the scoring guide, with an overall rating and score, is handed out in the meeting. The scoring guide is maintained in a database and lead auditors can have a laptop or computer available to update it during the team rating session. All the auditors, department management, the plant manager, and quality manager should attend. The lead auditor should circulate a sign-in sheet to document that the meeting has occurred and who attended. Typically, it is the same document as the opening meeting with check-boxes identifying each meeting.

The protocol is for the lead auditor to open the meeting with some comments of appreciation for the time spent with the team by the department. It is important to recognize efforts made to ensure the success of the audit because it promotes the benefits of the process for everyone and opens lines of communication. The lead auditor does not want to convey the impression to the department that pulling people away from a busy schedule is something they have to do.

Because the audit is a team effort, the lead auditor may elect to divide up the sections so each auditor covers a section of the scoring guide. The auditor will state the question without the bullet points, give the score and briefly summarize the finding at the end of the subsection. This format is followed as the team reviews the entire guide. The purpose is twofold: to review the results, allowing discussion on findings specific to each aspect of the quality system, and to provide a review of the system for the attendees. When we first initiated this approach, reading the questions was done for the entire management team but we came to realize that the ones who benefit most are in the department concerned.

This approach is somewhat detailed but it encourages open discussion on specific aspects of the system rather than something more generalized. Should a concern from management arise, it is better to identify a challenge to a score within the context of the specific section rather than have it occur during the discussion of overall rating. This makes it easier to explain in its proper context. In addition, there is the possibility that the team did not see all the necessary documents so this issue can be addressed prior to the final report.

The other advantage of this approach is education and training. Although the scoring guide is a series of questions, it does reflect the quality management system. Reviewing the results in this method also reviews the relationships of aspects of the system and encourages greater understanding of its purpose and intent. It may be redundant since the questions were asked earlier in the day, but it also puts the results in the context of the understanding of the department team and how they are interpreted and implemented.

After all the sections are reviewed, the lead auditor will present the overall score and rating (excellent, good, and so on), summarize the positive aspects of the system, opportunities for improvement, and any corrective actions issued. Sometimes this is done first, but I find doing this at the end results in fewer surprises and promotes the idea that decisions are made on facts.

The lead auditor should explain that opportunities for improvement do not require a response but should be investigated. He or she should also explain that some issues left unaddressed could escalate to corrective actions in future audits. When reviewing corrective actions, if any, the audit team and department should agree on a due date and person responsible. This decision can be delayed pending a short investigation but is required for the audit report, which usually follows within one week of the audit. There should be enough time allowed for any additional questions and clarifications and then the closing meeting is ended.

Should there be any corrective actions issued, they will be the responsibility of the person assigned to resolve. The lead auditor is responsible for monitoring progress and closure, so he or she will need to be kept abreast of the corrective action efforts and provide verification that they have been successfully implemented.

TEAM EVALUATION AND SCORING

We have reviewed and discussed some general aspects about the audit process. One important activity that needs further explanation is the team evaluation and scoring meeting. This occurs after the team has interviewed all the auditees and completed the shop floor tour.

First on the agenda is for the lead auditor to verify with the team that all open issues and questions have been resolved. By open issues I mean that sometimes during the audit, additional personnel must be contacted or information reviewed and this is noted on the checklist. If these items have not been resolved, the appropriate personnel should be contacted or information gathered so the open items can be closed. The team cannot complete the evaluation until they are resolved. If during the evaluation process an issue should arise, the lead auditor will contact the appropriate personnel to ensure that the necessary information is gathered so the audit can be completed. For this reason, it is important that a contact for the department be defined should an issue arise.

During this scoring meeting, the auditors should have all of their checklists and appropriate process maps and procedures available. In addition, if copies of the appropriate scoring guide have not been handed out, this now occurs. The lead auditor is responsible for the final report, so he or she will write up the summary comments on their scoring guide during the evaluation process and maintain the final scores.

The evaluation process follows the format of the scoring guide, working through each section and related questions. The lead auditor begins with Section 1 of Management of the Process, which is Process Overview. He or she reads the first question, and the audit team discusses their findings in regard to meeting the required items of the question and bullet points.

Each question or group of questions represents a specific aspect of the quality management system. In thinking through the particular aspect of the system, the audit team must consider the responses of the manager, supervisor, manufacturing engineer, setups, and operators to determine how well the department meets the requirement for the question. In many cases, it goes beyond their comments to include notes on observations and pertinent documentation.

Four Basic Questions to Answer

Although there is much to consider, the thought process can be organized around four basic questions:

1. How is it defined?

   a. In the manual

   b. By the manager

   c. By the supervisor(s)

An organization should have control over its systems and operations. You really don't want employees "inventing" new methods on the shop floor without some thought and planning, which should include management. To demonstrate that there is control, there should be someone in authority and/or a document, such as the manual, that can define it. In some organizations, there may be empowered teams running the operations, but someone in a position of authority will still have the responsibility to define how things are done.

2. Is it consistently and correctly interpreted?

   a. By the manager

   b. By the supervisor as directed by the manager

   c. By the setups and operators as directed by the manager and supervisor

A defined process or procedure must be interpreted, and that is important for successful implementation. It also tells us about the quality of the defining process; in other words, is there a good process for updating the manager? If the defining authority is the manual, the interpretation should be consistent from the manager on down. If there are gaps, are they due to inadequate training or communication? This should be reflected in the comments and score of that section in the guide.

3. Is it consistently and correctly implemented as defined?

   a. By management for their area of responsibility and control

   b. Within the department (engineering, setups, operators) for their area of responsibility and control

If all is done right, you will have a well-defined procedure, correctly interpreted and implemented. There is a relationship between interpretation and implementation because the latter verifies the former. However, you may also have a case of correct interpretation but for some reason it has been implemented differently or there is a lack of discipline within the organization to do it right. For example, you may have a good understanding of APQP as it is defined, but there just wasn't enough time to do it correctly and meet the deadline.

    4. What are the results?

        a. Are they positive or negative (effectiveness of system)?

The last consideration is results and whether the process or procedure is effective based on its intent. There could be a situation where trends are negative for reasons out of department management control, such as a temporary drop in sales, yet it is an effective measurement and process. The team could also find a situation where it is not an effective process or procedure for accomplishing its intent. For example, there may be a defined and implemented system for project management but the results show delays or over-budget projects.

This rating process would seem like quite an involved and time-consuming methodology, but in fact, the teams move through most of the sections at a reasonable pace. The reason we have all team members participate in the manager and supervisor interviews is because we don't want to have explanations of management interpretations and directives during the evaluation process. They all know what was said during the interview, although there may be discussion on interpretation of the comments. Also, at times, one astute auditor may share a comment picked up in the interview the others missed that becomes pertinent to the evaluation.

As the team moves further into the scoring guide, a team dynamic always develops. The question is read; one of the auditors will share their opinion on the score with the group and support it with facts. There is consensus or further discussion, but it is always a group decision. There are areas that will require more discussion and these relate to the shop floor tour when the teams divide up responsibilities. In this case, there may be differences in interpretation between various areas of the department so these must be shared and discussed. This difference is compounded when the audit scope is more than one shift because you tend to find additional differences in supervision and interpretation.

In the progressive audit methodology you must score, and scoring each question comes down to four basic points:

    1. Did they completely meet the requirement? (2 points)

    2. Did they meet some of it? (1 point)

    3. Is there little evidence it exists? (0 points)

    4. Can the team support its position based on fact?

All of the discussion comes down to the score and the ability to provide a quantitative analysis of whether the intent of the requirement is met. One important point to keep in mind is whether the finding was an isolated incident or widespread. For example, if during the floor tour you find one document not at the correct revision but no other documents found in this state, it should be noted in the comments but still receive some credit, with no corrective action written because the system is not in compliance. The audit is fact-finding but should not overwhelm a department with action items. This is obviously a decision of the organization and depends on the importance of the finding to quality, but I believe the intent of improving the system should be paramount to the audit.

During this evaluation process, the lead auditor should be noting the scores for each question and summarizing the related comments in the appropriate space at the end of each section. He or she should read back what was written to the group to ensure agreement with the statements made. This is important because the scoring guide and the comments within become a historical record of the audit, defining why certain areas were rated at that score and to provide a statement of the level of implementation as a reference for future audits. It is important to note both the positive as well as negative findings in the area.

After all sections have been evaluated, the overall score is calculated and the rating noted. At this point, the team must develop an overall summary of the audit to be presented at the closing meeting. This is also noted on the summary page of the audit report in the form of bullet points. The format for the summary page, which follows directly after the cover page in the report, is as follows:

- Positive aspects

- Opportunities for improvement

- Corrective actions required

Positive Aspects

Positive aspects provides a brief summary of things that go above and beyond the system or stand out in the way they are implemented. It is good to note what the department has done well in the closing meeting, but this statement also provides some potential benchmarking for others should they be looking for ways to improve in this particular aspect of the system.

Opportunities for Improvement

Opportunities for improvement identify certain aspects of the system that may be adequate but need further attention. In some cases, opportunities turn into corrective actions in subsequent years if nothing is done to improve. These may relate to a need for improved training, better communication, procedures not defining all requirements, or a process that needs additional measures because the ones defined are not sensitive enough. Opportunities for improvement are not used for outright violations of procedures or procedures that do not reflect operations. Opportunities for improvement represent findings that do not require an action plan or time frame for implementation.

Corrective Action

A corrective action is issued for a finding that must be corrected. In other words, if it weren't issued, the system would be noncompliant. It also means putting it in writing to make sure it gets addressed. It covers a range of issues from serious violations of a procedure or directive to details in the manual that must be updated. It is a formal directive whereas an opportunity for improvement is informal. One might suggest that a preventive action could also be written, such as a case where an action response would prevent future problems from occurring. I view opportunities for improvement as preventive actions while corrective actions are for noncompliance to a defined system, process, or procedure.

One important point is that a corrective action must be written against some stated authority such as a specific ISO standard clause, a quality manual process or procedure, or a statement by management that this is what should be done. The reference to this must state the specific document or management directive and the finding showing it is noncompliant. This prevents the team from issuing one based on opinion.

The corrective action should also have a reasonable date it is due for completion, agreed to by the management team during the closing meeting. It should also state a person responsible for carrying out the investigation and initiating the action to correct it. If corrective actions carry a negative connotation of failure, the lead auditor should address it. The management group should understand that it is a documented finding that must be addressed and not the auditors finding fault with the people audited. It is an important tool of the audit to ensure that issues are resolved.

I have told teams that corrective actions can have two responses: management will fix it or they will choose not to. Either way, it is important to document the results and clean up the system. Some things must be addressed because they are required by the ISO standard or are important to the quality of the product or system. The management team may discuss other findings and decide it is not in the best interests of their business to implement. In this case, procedures should be revised to reflect the decision.

For example, the procedure may say all rework requires a written instruction. The audit team found during the floor tour that some areas had rework performed without instructions or visual aids available. There was more than one occurrence so it was not an isolated incident. The management team decided it was too labor intensive to write instructions for all rework. Since this is a corrective action, a response is required but ignoring the procedure is not an option.

The result could be a clause added stating that when rework is part of an employee's job description and not unique to the operation, such as deburring trimmed die cast parts, proper training will be used instead of written instruction. In other cases, rework instruction will be required. The management team recognized the importance of written instruction for many areas of operation, yet did not want to require needless documentation for normal rework.

RESULTS REPORTING AND FOLLOW-UP

The final internal audit report should be completed within a few business days after the audit, a week maximum. Copies should be distributed to the management team of the department audited, as well as the plant manager and quality manager, and a copy maintained for records by the lead auditor.

In our organization, the scoring guide and checklists are maintained in our document control system so copies can be readily accessible for future audits. The scoring guide is also maintained in an access database along with the actual records of all the audits, including corrective actions, as defined by our record retention procedure. Since it is in a database, the lead auditor uses a laptop in the evaluation and scoring meeting. This is a very efficient process because the scoring and notes go right into the database at the time of the evaluation. Writing up the final report then becomes a matter of the lead auditor reviewing the information to ensure that spelling, grammar, and content are correct. This also eliminates errors in calculation since the program does it. An alternate approach is a spreadsheet, which can be saved as a template and serves the same purpose, including formulas for calculating the score.

The lead auditor should also save the hard-copy checklists from the auditors for the previous audits that season. The time period for maintaining the records should be chosen to ensure that if an issue should arise, all the necessary documentation is available for review. This may occur when investigating a corrective action or during a department review of the audit. It would be expected that this would occur within a few months after the audit so we maintain three previous sets of audit checklists. Keep in mind that the scoring guide records are not deleted but maintained within the database. This is a decision to be made by the organization.

Present the results of the audit to the entire management team at each facility. Not in the detail of the closing meeting but a review of positive aspects, opportunities, and corrective actions is presented, including the overall rating. Positive aspects identify particularly good systems to the management team that other areas may benchmark for improvement initiatives. Opportunities and corrective actions identify common areas within the facility that are weak and should be addressed by the management team. This information is also presented during the management review to identify strategies for the facility and to ensure that follow-up has occurred on corrective actions. The management team may also see common themes within the opportunities for improvement and possibly suggest actions be taken based on that. This is a requirement of the ISO standard.

Formalized Corrective Action

If there are corrective actions, the responsibility for resolving the issues is the person designated on the report. To provide accountability, it should always be an individual and not a department. A corrective action will contain the following information:

- Header information (filled in by lead auditor at closing meeting)
  - Date issued

- – Issued by (lead auditor)

- – Quality manual clause(s) affected

- – Reason for noncompliance

- – Category—major/minor (optional)

- – Department issued to

- – Person responsible

- – Date due

• Body of report (filled in by person responsible based on analysis)

- – Action response (details conclusion and action to resolve)

- – Date implemented

- – Implemented by

• Verification (filled in by lead auditor after action is implemented)

- – Verification activity (what was done)

- – Verified by

- – Verification date

The header information is completed during the closing meeting. Within the database we use, only the lead auditor has security rights for the header information and the verification activities. If that is not available, it is still important to maintain that control. This prevents key information from being changed or issues closed out without proper authority to do so. If information should change, such as the responsible party, it should be the lead auditor's responsibility to update.

Once the department begins its analysis of the issue, they may request additional time added on to the due date. The lead auditor should make this decision. If there is a good reason, such as more time to train on an updated process, it should be extended. In my experience, changing a process or procedure can be difficult because it may affect other areas in the organization that are less willing to change. For instance, if it is a corporate procedure, there may not be the sense of urgency since it was written up for the plant. I would rather push the date out to ensure it is done right than maintain the date and have it haphazardly implemented.

The key point is preventing complacency because no one wants to work on it. If this occurs, it should be brought to the attention of the manager or elevated to the plant manager's attention. The inability to obtain closure on issues can become a systemic issue. It may be caused by other priorities in or outside the departments, but also can also occur because there is not a good system for monitoring open corrective actions. The lead auditor should be responsible for monitoring open issues and reporting back to the management team. If there is not a good mechanism, this should be presented to management during management review so a better system can be developed. This could also be an opportunity or corrective action issued during the audit of the internal audit.

In some cases, a department may need the assistance of the quality manager or lead auditor for suggestions on a good strategy for resolving the issue. I feel this is acceptable because you want to correct the finding with the best solution. I do not see a conflict of interests or lack of maintaining independence, suggesting the auditors are also serving as consultants. The lead auditor will have a thorough understanding of the quality system and be able to share that for the benefit of the organization. However, you do run the risk of the lead auditor becoming so involved that they are doing all the work. This also must be monitored closely.

Once the actions are implemented and noted in the corrective action, the lead auditor should perform the verification activities. They have the option of doing it themselves or asking one of the team members to verify that it was implemented if that person has more knowledge of the issue. He or she should note a brief description in the corrective action report with enough detail to explain what was done. The name of the person that verified the activity should be noted and the date verified entered. This completes the document. In the database, this closes the record as completed.

AUDIT OF THE INTERNAL AUDIT

This is an important activity as an overall evaluation of the audit program and to provide necessary information for the review and planning sessions. Defined in the audit schedule to occur after the audit season, the purpose is to review all the required audit activities against the audit schedule to ensure that all were completed and there are no outstanding issues.

The person responsible for this activity should be independent of the audit; in our organization, I perform this audit as the divisional quality manager. Although I participate in the planning sessions, I still maintain an independence of the process. Auditing the internal audit requires a review of the audit schedule against the actual audits so records must be available for each internal audit conducted the most recent season. Since preseason activities like updates and training are part of the schedule, they are also reviewed as well as notes from the previous season's planning and review sessions.

Following are the steps:

- Verify audit schedule has all required activities.

- Verify training has occurred for updates and for new auditors.

- Verify updates were made based on planning and review meeting.

- Verify all required audits were conducted according to schedule.

  – Dates may be different than original but verify audit was completed.

- Verify all listed auditors were properly trained.

- Verify all audit reports were properly documented with the necessary notes.

- Verify all corrective actions were properly verified and closed per date due.

- Write up audit report and submit to plant quality manager for management review.

POSTSEASON REVIEW AND PLANNING

The last sequence in the audit process is the postseason review and planning session but one could also think of it as the first step in overall system improvement. As part of the audit schedule, this last step ensures management the opportunity to review the results of the audit season and set direction for the coming year. This should not be confused with the audit of the internal audit, the purpose of which is to verify that all necessary activities and requirements have been met. In the review and planning session, management is more focused on the facility as a whole and how it can be improved.

The meeting should be organized and facilitated by the audit manager. The management personnel invited should be the ones responsible for the overall facility so that they are focused on the bigger picture. In our organization, the vice president of the division represents overall operations, plant managers and quality managers represent their respective plant operations, and I represent quality from a divisional perspective. Our vice president has attended some of the closing meetings as well, but this session provides an opportunity for top management to review overall strengths and weaknesses and develop improvement strategies with the plant teams that are consistent with overall organizational strategies. This encourages a vertical integration of initiatives from the highest level down to the shop floor.

In preparation for the meeting, the audit manager conducts postseason meetings with the lead auditors and teams from each facility. The agenda for these meetings is to review the overall findings of the all the audits and find common reoccurring themes within the organization. Some of these may or may not have been addressed as corrective actions or opportunities for improvement, but the goal is to summarize strengths and weaknesses within the organization. In addition, the audit process itself is discussed, and suggestions for improving the scorecard and checklists are documented.

After these meetings have been completed for each facility, the audit manager summarizes the information and reviews it in the context of overall divisional strengths and weaknesses, both of systems and the audit process itself. During this phase, both of us will meet to discuss overall results and potential courses of action that could be taken to address a specific area that needs improvement.

It is at this stage that we will also review related articles and books, an input to the audit process. The purpose is to better understand the issues and possibly benchmark other organizations to find a course of action. In addition, we will review current information related to the standard because the knowledge base changes as others write about their experiences and understanding of quality systems. Although the focus here is analysis and research, throughout the year we read periodicals and books to find reference information that can be pertinent to improvement initiatives.

It is important to allow ample time after the close of the audit season to conduct the review meetings with the team, summarize the data, perform your research, and conduct the planning meeting. We usually allow at least two months for this process. This meeting should not be approached lightly because the outcome can provide excellent strategies for organizational improvement. Keep in mind that preplanning begins the next audit season and usually requires updates to the audit documents and training based on those updates, so there must be enough time allowed in the schedule to complete one season, give the auditors a break, and begin the next.

During the review and planning meeting, the audit manager will present the overall summaries to management in addition to information gathered during the research activity and any recommendations for action. One purpose of this meeting is to review the overall results of the audits and discuss the implications of the findings. It's quite possible that although some areas are identified as candidates for improvement, management may decide they are adequate for the near future and no additional actions need to be taken.

A second purpose of the meeting is to move an aspect of the organization that may currently be compliant according to the quality system in another direction because greater demands in the future necessitate an upgrade. For example, you may find that your organization has an adequate system for change management. However, top management notes that there will be significant changes coming in the future so it must be more detailed and formalized. You should have the opportunity to compare the departments within the facilities to determine if one has a better system, so you could benchmark ideas from within. You could also do a literature search to read articles on how other organizations handle this process, and possibly contact one and even tour them to learn other approaches.

Management may determine that the best scenario will require a significant time commitment to upgrade the systems. In preparation for the upcoming changes, a short-term response could be to upgrade the quality manual and demand more detail of the current system. The audit for the next season would then be updated to require more detailed activities and increase the focus on this activity. As the current process is upgraded, it also prepares the organization for a new system in the future with greater demands for change management.

Finally, if we look at this step in the context of the process, management is the customer. The customer must have the opportunity to review, make recommendations, and approve the scope, requirements, and execution of the audit. The review and planning meeting provides an avenue for this as well as determining customer satisfaction. Management, as the customer, reviews all the pertinent information and determines if the audit process effectively meets the needs of the organization. This then becomes a formal process where the customer approves the audit program. This is done through management perceptions of the audit season, improvements generated, and a general review of the ratings and scores.

As I stated in the process map, meeting the schedule and the ratings are measures of the process. A review of the audit of the internal audit will determine if the schedule was met. Reviewing overall scores will give an understanding of the experience of the teams, how different departments and facilities are improving, and if more intervention is necessary to improve.

ENDNOTE

1. Martin E. Smith, "Changing an Organization's Culture: Correlates of Success and Failure," *Leadership and Organizational Development Journal* 24, no. 5 (2003).

15

Ensuring an Effective Audit Program

Management is concerned about costs. Controlling them is not only part of the budget process but in most cases it is also part of their performance evaluation. They review reports on department productivity and investigate labor variances to trim the fat out of them because they try to run lean. Management has been working from a process perspective for years, although they never really called it that: improve your input, improve your process, and increase your output.

Quality comes along and says we need to audit our systems and management agrees, though sometimes they are kicking and fighting along the way. A compromise usually is made and the result is a last-minute audit because they don't want to add resources for a full-time auditor. The problem is the input versus output mentality because they just aren't going to devote resources to achieve an output that merely tells them that everything's okay. It's their perception of value, which they have been living by for many years.

Internal audits are a cost. I believe management considers them a sunk cost, meaning it's something you have to do anyway, so you just accept it. The compromise comes to play in the fact that management will accept it but you still must minimize the costs. In other words, go ahead and do your audits but don't spend too much time on it because we have work to do. Sometimes I think the quality managers believe this as well. We have to do it, but let's just minimize the pain.

If we look at the audit through the input versus output mentality, we distort it so that rather than look at increasing the input to increase the output, we focus on minimizing resources or costs. In fact, most of the publications on audits are focused on improving the process, but even here most of them deal with training and education on audit details. I would suggest that ensuring an effective audit program means you will follow a proven process strategy of improving your inputs, improving your process, and increasing your output.

Approaching the audit program from a process strategy is also important because it starts to align our thought process with that of management. Instead of looking at it in the traditional quality mind-set of compliance to requirements, we look at it in terms of resource allocation, providing quality input tools, and improving our process to achieve a high-quality output. When we present the audit program as an improvement to the old way of doing things, we must also discuss the value of those added resources we are asking them to reassign and how they relate to attaining a higher output.

EFFICIENT AUDITS

If we want to speak the language of management, one measure for input versus output is efficiency, and the audit should be an efficient process.[1] Efficiency, as defined in the ISO 9000: 2000 standard, is the "relationship between the result achieved and the resources used." In manufacturing, we use the term productivity, which is a measure based on a set standard in organizations of a specific amount of labor hours to achieve an output, or make one unit. Although somewhat similar in concept, we can't view the audit in the same light as productivity by saying we need six auditors to get one audit report. If we approached it this way, next audit season manufacturing would eliminate one auditor and improve productivity by 16 percent.

To understand what we mean by the term efficiency, we need to understand what we mean by resources used and what results we expect to achieve. If we view the term *resource* as employees, to execute the progressive audit means we are taking employees temporarily away from their normal job and reassigning them to a quality function, whether or not they actually charge the labor to quality in the system. Operators are taken out of the direct labor account so there is less impact on daily productivity, but the department still carries an extra body so the meter is still running in the mind of that manager. Auditors from engineering are indirect labor, so the impact on productivity is not as immediate, but you still lose a day's work when they are auditing instead of working on an engineering project.

With this in mind, audit efficiency should mean that those resources are used well. We must make sure they are properly trained so they will add value to the process. We must also find a way of ensuring that each team member contributes to the audit process. In fact, each time an audit is conducted we must make sure the process is efficient, so time will be considered a resource.

From the opening meeting to the closing meeting, there should not be waste in the process. Meetings should be well organized and purposeful, without time spent in meaningless discussion. They should be informal but the lead auditor must ensure they are efficient. During the audit interviews, the checklist questions should be asked at a steady and reasonable pace, allowing enough time for follow-up questions but preventing side discussions that waste time and accomplish nothing. During the shop floor tour, the auditors must be about their business and not involved with activities not related to the audit.

The lead auditor has full responsibility for the audit process and must maintain control at all times. The auditors also have a responsibility to the team and the lead auditor to take the job seriously. Managers, supervisors, engineers, setups, and operators are not only being interviewed but also developing perceptions about the program during the audit. They will see waste if it's present because that is part of their manufacturing mentality. If they see too much, it will reflect on the audit program and management will return to last-minute audits.

The other important aspect of efficiency is the results achieved. If we view the results of an audit as meeting requirements, the last-minute audit is efficient because all areas are audited and it does offer a few suggestions for improvement. However, I realized as a last-minute auditor that I couldn't possibly audit all the key departments in enough detail. I felt we were missing a huge benefit by not having teams performing a thorough audit of management and staff, not to mention expanding the audit to all shifts. If I wanted more output, I needed to expand the input of the audit process. My concept of results had expanded.

In the progressive audit methodology, we are not only analyzing the quality system but also educating management and employees to better understand that system. We also are increasing the buy-in to the system because it is a team effort and since more people are involved, it creates credibility. The output is increased because it is not only an audit that meets requirements and offers suggestions for improvement, but also a means to increase employee understanding and involvement.

This philosophy is similar to the marketing tool of offering people reduced rates on a hotel stay if they will sit through a two-hour sales pitch on a vacation condominium package. Marketing experts know that they get far better results from their investment if they can have prospective buyers see and touch the product rather than read about it in a flyer. This same technique works for training; if you can get the participants directly involved with the subject, they will learn much more than by just sitting through a class. In other words, we teach them about the quality system and then we go analyze it in the audit. Since you periodically add new auditors to the program, more employees obtain a deeper understanding of the system and can take that back with them to their jobs. They will look at the tasks and processes in a different light and offer far more suggestions for improvement than employees that do not have a good understanding of systems and processes.

Efficiency is a term not often used when describing internal audits, unless you view audits in terms of a process. In that light, you must satisfy the customer and because that customer is management, it is important to measure the program in ways that they will understand and support. Efficiency is an important part of evaluation, but that concept alone is not adequate to determine how well a process is doing. Just as productivity is one of many measures for manufacturing performance, the effectiveness of the audit process must also be addressed.

EFFECTIVE AUDITS

According to ISO 9000:2000, effectiveness is the "extent to which planned activities are realized and planned results achieved." Where efficiency measures a relationship between resources and results, effectiveness measures how well those planned activities were carried out and whether or not we got the results that we wanted. In other words, efficiency measures the quantity of work and effectiveness measures the quality of the work; one looks at the output against the input and the other looks at the output details against the details of the plan.

If we look at the first half of the definition, "extent to which planned activities are realized," effectiveness would mean we have met the requirements of the audit schedule. There is more to this than just making sure we audited all the areas in the time frame defined. Audit scope comes into play, so if we determined that all shifts in all areas would be audited, then an effective audit would mean we have accomplished this task. The audit schedule also includes preseason activities like training and the postseason planning activities, so these areas must be reviewed as well.

Determining audit effectiveness, the extent that activities meet the plan, is part of the audit schedule as the audit of the internal audit. It is during this activity that we determine if everything went according to plan. This is an important activity because it tells you if there is a real commitment to the audit program. If audits are cut short or postponed, it indicates a serious problem that the management team must address. This would be a good topic of discussion in the management review because the reasons behind the problem must be reviewed and resolved or the program will be jeopardized.

Determining effectiveness, the other half of the definition, "planned results achieved," is also part of the audit schedule and occurs during the postseason review and planning session. One obvious point in determining effectiveness is the fact that you must have a plan. In the case of audit activities, the plan is the audit schedule. In the case of results, the plan is defined when you develop the audit purpose. The plan must occur prior to any action because it determines what you need to accomplish based on requirements and management objectives.

The ISO standard, regulations, or other internal directives will determine requirements for the plan. In the case of the ISO standard, the quality management system must address all the pertinent clauses in the standard, all areas must be audited, the audit must verify system implementation, and the audit must also verify effectiveness.

The customer, in this case management, will determine objectives, which are additional tasks or desired accomplishments in addition to or beyond the requirements. The progressive audit methodology, for example, has objectives of team-based auditing and increasing the knowledge base of the organization.

During the postseason review and planning session, management will verify through review of the audit of the internal audit that all activities occurred according to plan. They will then review a summary of the audit season to verify that they have achieved the results that were part of the plan. If areas were lacking, they must go back to the plan to determine where they need to put more effort. There may be training programs that need to occur, improved tools for better accomplishing the tasks, or resources devoted to analyzing the situation and recommending a solution. An action may be to revise the scoring guide and checklist so a particular aspect of the system is covered in more detail. They can revise the audit schedule for more coverage in areas found weak, or go to a surveillance audit for areas that are strong.

In the review and planning sessions, we must also consider the element of risk in ensuring an effective audit program.[2] The intent of the audit program is probably not to find every noncompliance to the system, but we do want it to uncover issues that could have a significant impact on the organization. Those issues should be identified by management and addressed. Management should ask itself if the audit scope is broad enough to cover all the key areas of our organization, yet have sufficient focus to ensure thorough coverage of the key processes and procedures.

Team-based auditing has its risks. There is a trade-off between using one or two auditors with much experience in systems and technique versus teams made up of inexperienced individuals from outside of quality. The selection and subsequent training process is very important in reducing this risk, and management must evaluate the audit results in this context.

Risk assessment may or may not be a formalized method that is part of audit planning, but it must be considered. The extent of it depends on your organization, but management must clearly identify its objectives so they can be assessed. You do not want a situation to arise where management had expectations that were unrealistic based on the scope of the program. Firestone was subject to huge liability and recall costs due to sport-utility rollovers and tire thread failures. During the proceedings, Firestone's top management implicated their registrar because he failed to identify the problem.[3]

Planning is critical for an effective audit program, and going back and reviewing results against the plan is equally important. That is why this should be part of the audit schedule. It is as important to the effectiveness of the audit program as the audit itself. As the organization learns from the audit process, its planning activity will develop or upgrade the resources and tools that will ensure the continued effectiveness of the audit program.

RELIABLE AUDITS

One last point of discussion is the reliability of the audit program. A measurement system must be repeatable and reproducible in order for the user to have confidence in the results. In this same regard, an audit program must provide a high degree of reliability in its results in order for management to consider the program credible. If the audit report for a given area is inconsistent with the results from the previous year, it creates conflict because your audit may be considered unreliable. Recommendations for improvement or possibly even corrective actions may be open for debate if the audit teams cannot provide trustworthy results year after year.

We have all read about and probably experienced some inconsistency by the registrar during ISO audits. It can be a frustrating experience to implement an improvement, based on the result of an audit, only to have next year's auditors find fault with what was recommended to do. All quality managers can recite the commonly used argument for this: the audit is a "snapshot in time" and will vary between years and different auditors. In fact, the same auditor may have a different opinion on an issue based on a changed perspective from one year to the next.

If not properly planned for, this potential problem is compounded when a rating system with a quantified result is applied, such as recommended in this book. With a reliable rating system, not only is there an opportunity to compare findings between auditors and years, but quantified results also allow you to compare scores. In previous chapters, I recommended up-front discussions with management to explain the benefits of rating but also that direct comparisons of scores should not be made. Try as you might, the reality is that management will compare results until they have made up their mind that the program is a good one. Once they are convinced it is sound, you will even catch yourself comparing scores.

Recently one of the managers at the Poplar Bluff facility was discussing their audit with me. He explained that they had implemented a number of improvements based on last year's opportunities. He felt the efforts were successful because he raised his score a half point (1 to 10 scale with one decimal) and they also audited all the shifts this season. In his mind, the ratings are a valuable tool because he believes the auditors were thorough and he has a measure to compare against and set improvement goals. The key point is the ability to compare results to determine if your efforts are paying off. You may try to explain away some inconsistencies but reliability is still an important issue that will impact the expectations and results of the audit. How can we ensure reliability and what is a reasonable expectation for the audit?

There is research available to review. In a two-year study of state quality award examiners that I will refer to later, it was found that reliability between auditors was low to moderate.[4] Reliability in this study was defined as score similarity among different auditors for the same applicant. The state quality awards are modeled after the Malcolm Baldrige National Quality Award and rate organizations based on eight categories (1998 criteria), each worth a specified total number of points. Organizations submit a detailed report to the examiners who in turn review and rate it. The scoring range for the award, based on scoring guidelines defined in the criteria, was zero to 100 percent.

In this study, the researchers commonly found variation between examiners of 50 percent for the same applicant within the same year. The highest range varied from a low of 20 percent to a high of 85 percent. Using the scoring guideline criteria, a 20 percent overall score means significant gaps in deployment exist, while an 85 percent score means a sound, systematic approach exists.

The training programs for examiners increased from four hours the first year to five the second. Training methods for both years included presentations and handouts, and the second year also included a case study with scoring and class discussion. Examiners were either experienced or if first-timers, in most cases from organizations that had won the award previously. It is interesting to note that even with using the case study and increasing training time, examiner reliability did not improve from one year to the next.

There are some key takeaways from this research that will support the progressive audit program. First is the fact that there will always be variation in the rating process so the solution is to minimize it. Even though examiners received more training the second year plus the benefit of a case study with discussion, variation did not improve. Training auditors will improve their understanding of the systems and methods, but they will still have differences in perception and interpretation. The way to reduce variation is to reduce the possible choices of scale. If you allow 10 selections (examiners choose in 10-point increments) versus three as in the scoring guide, the reliability of the result is greatly improved. The questions are also written to be more direct and focused, which reduces variation and error in interpretation.

The second point is that rather than individually rate, more consistent results are achieved as a team. The state quality awards attain consistency because there are examiner teams reviewing and discussing the aggregate results, so conclusions are not reached from the individual scoring. In the same sense, the internal audits maintain consistency because the audit teams discuss and score the audit, weighing all the facts and interpretations of the individuals. Even if you have the same experienced auditor year after year, I believe teams will provide better and more reliable results. One person can fall into a pattern and even believe they hear or see something that they did not. Audit teams will have a far better chance of seeing and hearing reality, and that will result in an honest assessment through the team evaluation and scoring process.

I believe the progressive audit methodology is successful because it is well planned and many people are involved. There is also a common goal of improvement and the program is efficient and effective. In my experience over the past four seasons, we have had challenges over interpretation, suggestions that we were too tough in some areas, various interpretations of the intent of a procedure or process, and numerous suggestions for improvement. I have rarely heard that teams were ineffective or a waste of time.

From my perspective as a divisional quality manager, I feel I have detailed knowledge of the level of implementation of the quality systems at all our facilities, with information helping us to define where we need to go as a division. I can go into any plant and discuss systems and they will know what I'm talking about because it is part of the culture. I believe that is an effective internal audit program.

ENDNOTES

1. I. A. Beckmerhagen, H. P. Berg, S. V. Karapetrovic, and W. O. Willborn, "On the Effectiveness of Quality Management System Audits," *The TQM Magazine* 6, no. 1 (2004).
2. Ibid.
3. Ibid.
4. Garry D. Coleman, Eileen M. Van Aken, and Jianming Shen, "Estimating Interrater Reliability of Examiner Scoring for a State Quality Award," *Quality Management Journal* 10, no. 3 (2002).

16

The Progressive Audit: Where Are We Headed?

If a business doesn't make money, it can't reinvest in upgrades so it falls behind compared to the competition. In fact, many organizations move facilities even when they are profitable because costs, especially labor, are so much lower in China that it offers them a great business advantage over what they have currently. An interesting paradox I read is that with all the debate and discussion about overseas ventures, more companies than ever are investigating their feasibility because all the publicity has made them feel they will be left behind.

Organizations are all focused on lowering costs, increasing efficiencies, and improving profits any way they can to remain competitive. If they're big enough, they do it through squeezing the margins of their suppliers, forcing them to relocate, or they resource to someone overseas to obtain those cherished lower costs. Companies purchase software to improve systems and technology to streamline processes, making more with fewer resources. Most also run very lean in the parts of the organization where the employees work directly with the product. Productivity is at an all-time high yet all of us need only look to the next neighborhood, or possibly our own backyard, to feel the stress and anxiety of global competition.

The competitive spirit of America is great, and we have proven ourselves time and time again as we have overcome obstacles and conquered the competition, or at least held our own. Much of that was due to innovation and finding new and better ways of doing things. But innovation and new concepts come at a price, and that price is the risk of investing in the wave of the future only to find that success could have come from improvements in the methods of the past.

Management is amazingly aggressive in pursuing profits yet hesitant in understanding the truth about their own internal systems outside of accounting. Business books continue to preach the importance of upper management involvement, just like they have proclaimed for the last 50 years, yet upper management continues to not get involved unless it affects profits. Millions of dollars are spent at seminars and in training sessions to hear new ideas with the same underlying themes: how to have better systems, how to make better numbers, and how to change our culture. Management would rather go outside to hear what "should" be done than go inside to hear what "needs" to be done. I believe both are important.

Organizations live by their systems, yet they seem to trust more in quantitative financial measures and results than in an analysis of all the other activities that are critical to organizational performance. A great assumption is made that the systems are good because the results are satisfactory, yet they really don't know if those systems are efficient. They could be inefficient even while the numbers look good. Case studies are written for MBA programs about organizations that failed in their initiatives because they didn't realize that their underlying systems were inefficient and ineffective. By the time it showed up in the numbers, it was too late.

One problem is the generally accepted concept of a leader. Leaders that live high in the organization need the freedom from systemic control to lead and be creative. They are known for cutting corners and doing what it takes to get the job done. They are empowered by the organization to use but be above many of the systems, unless controlled by legislation; even then some try to find ways around it. The concept of a leader says they operate on a higher plane than the rest of us; they create the systems but don't necessarily live by them.

Another problem is corporate politics. Leaders have political power in the organization so it is difficult for others to tell them what they need to do, such as having their systems audited. For one thing, since they're encouraged to go beyond many of the systems, they would get a corrective action. Can you imagine writing a corrective action to an executive vice president? The other problem is that since they are empowered by the organization with the ability to override the system, you couldn't audit them to it anyway.

I know there are many great leaders that are firm believers in systems, and they hold themselves accountable to policy directives like anyone else in the organization. But I also know that is not commonplace because these individuals are written about because of the fact that they are unique. Because of this, I believe the internal audit is one of the most underutilized tools in the corporate arsenal. I am referring to the quality systems audit because internal audit usually means accounting systems audit to management.

The concept of a quality system is rapidly expanding. With the introduction of the ISO 9000:2000 standard and the process approach, quality has reached out and pulled in financial and performance measures as we define our processes. Since organizations must plan, the standard defines project management activities related to the end product. Both have a direct relationship to upper management, and in the case of big projects and large investments, the standard reaches to the boardroom.

Because quality is in a sense expanding into upper management activities, it is just a matter of time before an audit trail takes you into the executive office. The concept of the leader and corporate politics must be overcome, but slowly those invisible walls will be broken down. This surely won't happen overnight, but as we continue to redefine our systems through improvement efforts, we can only go one of three ways: broader and more in depth at the middle-management level in which the majority of the activities occur, further down into the organization where they are closer to the manufacture of the product, or up to executive levels where they are closer to the decision-making and resource allocation activities. In my estimation, we are two-thirds there.

This won't occur because ISO says so or because it is a requirement since, as I argued previously, those upper-management levels operate at a higher plane. That philosophy is cultivated not only by the leaders themselves, but also bred within the culture of the organization. Instead, it must evolve gradually with the expansion of the progressive audit methodology as we learn more about ourselves through the execution of the audit process.

In a sense, this methodology can lead a change from within. As we continue to expand the audit scope outward and downward, audit trails will start chipping away at the walls preventing us from going upward. Since the methodology is really an audit of your peers, we can expand the audit team to start including those middle-level managers who may one day move to the top. As we expand the knowledge base of those team members that are closer to those higher levels within the organization, the realization that this is a good way of doing business will sink in and all levels of the organization will actively and willingly participate in the progressive audit.

Just think about it. Executives, especially potential candidates for the position, would have the opportunity to be on the audit team. They could learn firsthand some of the systems within their organization and how they really operate. No longer would they have to assume that they know those processes because they would have seen them in action. More importantly, they could see the opportunities and risks within the organization from a better vantage point and create new systems that would truly add value and integrate with the culture.

It shouldn't take a revolt to get upper management to realize the benefits of the internal quality systems audit. There should be a strong desire to know that the systems are operating as planned and that if inconsistencies exist, they will be uncovered and presented so a decision can be made. They should also know that the audit brings with it a reality check that systems don't get implemented just because an executive says they should, or that an extensive training program is all that is needed. The best practice is to train, implement, audit, revise, train, implement, audit, revise, and so on, in a cycle of continuous improvement that propels the organization forward based on the reality of the present.

Implementing the progressive audit throughout your organization will not keep the competition at bay, nor prevent jobs from relocating overseas. It will, however, provide critical insight into how your systems really operate so decisions can be made based on direct knowledge rather than assumption or the opinion of others too far removed to truly understand what's going on.

Expanding the audit does not mean that everyone must operate within rigid procedures and processes and that "thinking outside the box" is wrong. A critical and detailed assessment of the systems that drive the organization does not mean that management should stop thinking "outside the box" but rather that they will truly understand first what the "box" is.

Part IV

Appendixes[*]

The purpose of the progressive audit is to help organizations improve their internal audit programs. Though copies of the working documents are included in the following pages, printable versions will be needed for actual use. For this reason, the CD-ROM in the back of the book contains the Manufacturing Scoring Guide and all the related checklists. Your organization will be different than mine. To implement this program, you will need to adapt the files to suit your organizational needs.

In the grand scheme of things, it is my hope that the concepts and materials presented in this book can be effective in improving the quality culture of your organization as it has in ours. Happy auditing!

Appendix A

Manufacturing Internal Audit Scoring Guide

Internal Audit Scoring Guide

Audit scope: Manufacturing process

Date: _____

Shift: _____

Audit team:
(Include name and area employed)

_____

_____

_____

Process audited

_____

Area/business manager:

_____

Area supervisor:
1st shift
2nd shift
3rd shift

_____

Discipline	Score/base	Rating
Management of the Organization	/ 44	Excellent (10–9.5)
Management of the Process	/ 37	Very good (9.4–8.5)
Nonconforming Product and Corrective Actions	/ 16	Good (8.4–7)
		Conditional (6.9–5)
Total Quality Points	/ 97	Unacceptable (4.9–0)

$$\text{Rating} = \frac{\text{Total score}}{\text{Total base}} \times 10 = \boxed{}$$

Audit Guidelines

The internal audit will be conducted by an audit team consisting of representatives from various areas of the plant. The team should be independent of the area, meaning no member should currently be assigned to that area during normal operations. Team members should receive training in general auditing concepts and techniques by the lead auditor, facilitated by the QA department. Each team will have a lead auditor chosen by the plant manager and quality manager and report their findings to the plant management team which will request, monitor, and verify necessary corrective actions.

Prior to the audit, the team should familiarize themselves with the quality management system in regard to procedures and processes related to the areas being audited. It is good auditing practice to make copies of important procedures, process maps, and work instructions to have readily available during the internal audit. It is also recommended that the team print out the operation sequence (flow) for the particular line(s) being audited, if available.

The internal audit is a detailed review of department operations at a particular point in time. Personnel being audited (the auditee) should be given ample opportunity to respond to questions and if unclear, it is the auditor's responsibility to ensure that the questions are clearly understood. The purpose of the audit is to determine if the department is in compliance with quality procedures and related work instructions and determine if the systems and methods are effective for the area. Any issues found not in compliance should be discussed at the time of the finding to ensure that all information was properly reviewed. The area must demonstrate compliance through proper responses and current documentation to verify that activities have occurred.

Finally, the audit was not developed to classify nor rate departments but to provide a means to benchmark our operations and establish goals for continually improving our operations.

Audit Scoring Guidelines

This questionnaire is to help guide the audit team when evaluating the quality system. Each numbered element is worth 2 points with the exception of housekeeping. The general housekeeping score is subjective based on the team's overall impression at the time of the audit. The auditor should note certain details during the audit for documentation purposes, such as document numbers or dates that were reviewed and gauge numbers that were verified for calibration. Comments are encouraged in each area to detail the auditor's findings.

Note: Each section has a letter question (A, B, C, and so on) followed by additional questions designed to expand on the original question. To award full points, the area personnel must have responded appropriately to all questions. In many cases, this will also require documentation to verify that activity has occurred.

Scoring the audit is a simplified process to provide consistency between the audit teams and to some extent between audit seasons for each major process. It is represented by the following requirements:

- 2 Points. All requirements met; satisfactory responses/activities

- 1 Point. Requirements partially met; some question details not fully addressed

- 0 Points. Little evidence of activity in area of questioning

Management of the Organization

1. Process Overview

A. Is there an understanding of the manufacturing process (map) as it
   relates to your area?   _____

   • Is there a consistent understanding of process, inputs,
     and outputs?

   • Are the interfaces of the other key processes understood?

B. Is there an understanding of the process objectives and measures?   _____

   • How do you analyze your measures?

C. Have goals been established for each measure?   _____

   • Are the goals documented?

   • Do plans exist for improvement based on this information?

D. Is customer satisfaction managed?   _____

   • Is the customer known? (Internal and external)

   • Are there measures in place to gauge and track customer
     satisfaction?

   • Are the measures tracking favorably?

   • Have actions been taken to improve customer satisfaction?

E. Is there a general awareness of the quality policy?   _____

   • Can the area personnel show how they are meeting their
     commitment to the quality policy?

Comments: _____

_____

2. Commitment to Improvement

A. What is the process for continuous improvement?   _____

   • What are the objectives, measures, and goals?

   • Have actions been taken to achieve the goals?

   • Have improvement initiatives been addressed in long-range plans?

B. Is there evidence of improvement in the area?   _____

   • Were improvements made as a result of process measures?

   • Is there evidence of improvement projects in the capital budget?

   • Have goals been met?

C. Does management involve the employee in decision making? _____

  • Are team and board meetings held on a regular basis?

  • Is there recognition of the employee?

D. How does the area obtain knowledge in the latest technologies? _____

  • Are employees encouraged to attended seminars and best-practices meetings?

Comments: _____

_____

3. Communication

A. Does management communicate its policies, objectives, and measures for the organization? _____

  • Are department meetings held and suggestions encouraged?

  • Is there a flow of information from management?

  • Have goals been communicated to the area?

B. Is there a system to inform manufacturing that a print/part has been changed by product engineering? _____

  • Are responsibilities defined for updating the prints and the related process?

  • Are the audit sheets and SPC changed and gauging updated?

  • Are all related personnel informed of the change?

C. Is there a system to inform all shifts that a process/machine has been changed by manufacturing engineering? _____

  • Are all related personnel informed of the change?

D. Are revisions recorded on all working documents related to quality? _____

  • Are you using the latest revision?

  • How do you know it's the latest revision?

E. Is there an understanding of the quality management system? _____

  • Was there training or orientation in its use?

  • Are relevant personnel able to locate the quality manual?

Comments: _____

_____

4. Advanced Product Quality Planning

A. What is the APQP process as it affects your area? _____

- Are the performance measures effective?

- Is there an understanding of important interfaces?

B. When new equipment was purchased, were steps taken to ensure its performance? _____

- Was a qualification plan written and approved prior to receiving the equipment?

- Was a process FMEA conducted?

C. Did the qualification plan include the appropriate requirements? _____

- Were critical features identified and capabilities measured?

- Were critical performance requirements, such as cycle time, verified?

- All other items required by relevant procedures?

D. Are advanced product quality planning techniques being used for current projects and improvements? _____

- For current projects, is APQP being conducted?
  (See capital budget, APQP map.)

- Are certified operations current?

- Are all production processes defined in the system?

E. Are setup instructions established and available for use? _____

- Are the instructions current?

- Has training occurred on the procedures?

- Do they contain key process variables?

- Have process parameters been established?

F. Are there written operator instructions for each process? _____

- Do they adequately describe the operation performed?

- Are they available at the workstation and understood by the operators?

G. Are FMEAs being used to prevent possible defects? _____

- Were FMEAs completed for all major process and product changes?

- Is there a system or plan to review previous FMEAs to verify effectiveness and completion?

H. Are there provisions for first-piece inspection at setup, process change, die change, or shift change?   _____

Comments: _____

_____

Total for Management of the Organization   / 44

Management of the Process

1. Statistical Process Control

A. Are there initiatives to ensure capable processes?   _____

- Do the SPC charts provide useful information about the process?

- Is there good evidence that this information is used?

- Is there a good understanding of the results? (Interpreting control charts, Cpk, CP, Ppk, histograms)

B. Is there management direction to ensure that the process is stable and in control?   _____

- Does management actively review process information?

C. Does manufacturing understand out-of-control and take appropriate action to correct?   _____

- Are they reacting to out-of-control processes?

- Is there evidence of appropriate responses?

- Can setups analyze historical data to investigate issues?

D. Have processes been improved based on analysis, and appropriate actions taken from interpreting SPC results?   _____

- Is there evidence of this improvement (report cards, and so on)?

- Have processes with classified features that do not meet requirements been identified for improvement?

Comments: _____

_____

2. Product and Process Audits

A. Are there regular inspections by operators and/or setups to verify compliance to specifications?   _____

- Is inspection made according to the audit sheets?

- Is there an acceptable procedure for addressing nonconforming product?
- Does the person performing the inspection know the quality requirements?
- Do they have the appropriate tools, visual aids, standards, and instructions to perform the activity?

B. Are the audit sheets to the current revision? _____

- Do they reflect the gauges and techniques correctly?

C. Do setups regularly verify process parameters? _____

- Are processes running to parameters stated in setup instructions?
- Do they verify autodetection equipment to be working correctly?

D. Is the gauging equipment adequately protected from damage and _____
appropriate for the environment in which it is used?

Comments: _____

_____

3. Job Performance

A. Are operators adequately trained on the job responsibilities? _____

- Do they understand the purpose of the operator instructions and are the instructions current?
- Do they know where operator instruction cards are?
- Do they know what nonconforming product is and do they know what action to take if it is found?
- Have training needs been identified?

B. Are setups adequately trained on the job responsibilities? _____

- Have they been trained in statistical techniques?
- Do they understand the deviation process?
- Have training needs been identified?

C. Has management (managers/supervisors/engineers) been trained _____
in their job responsibilities?

- Have they been trained in statistical techniques?
- Do they understand the quality management system?
- Is there a structured training/orientation program to cover all training requirements?

D. Do employees understand the safety requirements of the job?   _____

Comments: _____

_____

4. Material Status

A. Is material clearly identified per procedure?   _____

  • If not on overhead, is product identified by WIP or completed tickets?

B. Is nonconforming material clearly identified to ensure that it cannot   _____
be mixed with acceptable product (reject, hold, and so on)?

Comments: _____

_____

5. Preventive Maintenance

A. Have PM programs been established for new equipment?   _____

  • Is the PM schedule an output of APQP?

B. Is there an established PM program for the existing equipment?   _____

  • Does it identify the required activities and are they performed?

  • Was it established based on an analysis of defects or downtime?

  • Does it identify responsibilities for PMs?

C. Is there a PM program for the tooling?   _____

  • Is there a satisfactory tracking system?

  • Is the tooling corrected when parts do not meet quality requirements and are these corrections verified through a layout inspection report or first-piece inspection?

Comments: _____

_____

6. General Housekeeping

A. Are all areas neat and orderly? (Scale 0–5)   / 5

  • Are the floors clean relative to the process?

  • Is there management direction regarding a housekeeping policy?

Comments: _____

_____

Total for Management of the Process   / 37

Nonconforming Product and Corrective Actions

1. Analysis of Nonconforming Product

A. Is there a system for reviewing nonconforming product and determining its disposition?   _____

  - What is the procedure when stock is rejected?

  - Who is responsible for disposition of product?

B. Does nonconforming product require engineering or quality approval prior to release to production?   _____

  - Are formal deviations or written approval required?

  - When this occurs, are corrective actions issued to ensure that the problem does not repeat?

C. Is there a system for reworking nonconforming product?   _____

  - Do rework operations require reinspection?

  - Are rework instructions written, available, and in the document control system?

D. Are steps taken to reduce the number of defects produced?   _____

  - Is there evidence of an initiative to reduce defects?

  - Is root cause identified for top defects?

  - Is permanent corrective action implemented?

  - Is data from monthly summaries, scrap reports, and significant internal quality complaints used to drive improvement?

E. Are QA daily reports used to monitor performance on a regular basis?   _____

  - Is this information reacted to in a timely manner?

  - Are corrective actions issued/implemented for reoccurring issues?

F. Are customer (OEM) complaints and returns analyzed and corrective action and feedback given in a timely manner?   _____
Note: (For parts relative to the area.)

  - Do the setups receive this complaint information and are they involved in corrective action activities?

  - Is this a customer feedback measure?

Comments: _____

2. Corrective Actions

A. Are corrective actions verified for effectiveness? _____

- When corrective actions are issued for repeat issues, are previous corrective actions reviewed and verified?

- Are PFMEAs updated as a result?

B. Has appropriate and timely action been taken as a result of previous internal audits? _____

Comments: _____

_____

Total for Nonconforming Product and Corrective Actions / 16

Appendix B

Manager Checklist

Manager Checklist

Date: _____ Name: _____

Process: _____

Management of the Organization

1. Process Overview

A. How does the manufacturing process (map) affect your area?

  • Describe the process, including the inputs and outputs.

  • What are the important interfaces (relationships) with other processes?

  _____

  _____

  _____

  _____

B. How do you track the performance of your process?

  • Are the measures reviewed?

  _____

  _____

  _____

  _____

  *Identify documents reviewed and key measures for tracking.

  _____

_____

_____

_____

C. What are the goals for your process?

  • Where are they documented?

  • Plans for improvement? (Auditor note: should have action plans if negative results)

_____

_____

_____

_____

D. How do you ensure the satisfaction of your customer?

  • Are measures in place? (Need to see chart)

  • What actions have been taken to improve customer satisfaction? (Discuss both internal and external customers, if applicable)

_____

_____

_____

_____

E. Describe the quality policy.

  • What role does it play in your area?

  • Are you meeting your commitment to the policy? (Should see measures)

_____

_____

_____

_____

2. Commitment to Improvement

A. What is your process for continuous improvement?

  • What are the measures and goals?

  • Are there actions in place to achieve the goals?

- Were initiatives developed in long-range plans based on the measures?

_____

_____

_____

_____

B. What improvements have been made to the areas over the past year? (Process or equipment)

- How were these projects identified?
- Does your capital budget contain items relative to improvement projects?
- Have goals been met for the past year? If not, why?

_____

_____

_____

*Identify capital budget items reviewed including specific tracking number.

_____

_____

_____

C. How do you incorporate the ideas and suggestions of your employees in decision making?

- How can employees become involved or voice suggestions?
- When employees contribute, are they formally recognized?

_____

_____

_____

*Identify meeting minutes or projects reviewed including dates or tracking number.

_____

_____

_____

_____

D. How does the area find out about new techniques?

  • Are "best practices" meetings or seminars attended?

_____

_____

_____

_____

3. Communication

A. How do you communicate with your employees?

  • What type of items? (Policies, measures, or goals)

_____

_____

_____

_____

B. How are product changes communicated in your area?

  • Who is responsible for updating prints and information related to specs?

_____

_____

_____

_____

C. How are equipment (manufacturing engineering) changes communicated?

  • Who is responsible for updating setup instructions and related documents on the shop floor?

_____

_____

_____

_____

D. How do you control working documents on the shop floor?

  • How do you know what the latest revision is?

_____

_____

_____

_____

E. What aspects of the quality management system do you use on a regular basis?

   • What expectations do you have for your area to use the QMS?

   • What kind of training has been provided and how have you supported it?

_____

_____

_____

_____

4. Advanced Product Quality Planning

A. What is the APQP process as it affects your area?

   • What measures do yo use to track performance?

   • What are the important interfaces (relationships)?

_____

_____

_____

_____

B. When new equipment is purchased, how do you ensure that it will perform acceptably?

   • Was a qualification written and approved prior to receiving equipment?

   • Was a process FMEA conducted?

_____

_____

_____

_____

C. What was included in the qualification plan?

   • Critical features? Required capabilities? Performance requirements such as cycle time?

   • Were capabilities measured?

   • (See procedure for all requirements.)

_____

_____

_____

_____

D. How do you ensure that operations get certified for production in your area?

   • Does this reflect current projects?

   • Are all processes defined? (Ask to see capital budget. Can APQP be demonstrated for each of the items?)

   _____

   _____

   _____

   _____

E. Describe how setup instructions are handled in your area?

   • Do they contain process parameters?

   • Is there a defined process for keeping them up to date?

   • Are setup instructions part of the training program for new setups?

   _____

   _____

   _____

   _____

F. Describe how operator instructions are handled in your area?

   • Do they contain all the important information?

   • How do you ensure that they are available at the workstation?

   • Are instructions part of the training program for new operators?

   _____

   _____

   _____

   _____

G. When are process FMEAs conducted?

   • Were they completed for all major changes?

- Is there a system to review previous FMEAs?

_____

_____

_____

_____

H. When a changeover (either a new part, shift change, or process change) occurs, how do you ensure the quality of the first parts produced?

- How do you know if this procedure is effective?

_____

_____

_____

_____

Management of the Process

1. Statistical Process Control

A. Are there initiatives to ensure capable processes?

- Is the information reviewed and used?
- Is there understanding of the results (Cpk, Cp)?

_____

_____

_____

_____

B. What policies have you put in place to ensure that processes are controlled and capable?

- Ensure that charts are monitored?

_____

_____

_____

_____

C. How do you ensure that manufacturing understands out-of-control and takes appropriate action?

- Ensure that charts are monitored?

- Reacting properly to out-of-control data?

_____

_____

_____

_____

D. What efforts are in place to improve process capability?

- Do report cards show improvement?
- Have classified features been identified?
- Is there an effort to get those processes to required Cpks?

_____

_____

_____

_____

2. Product and Process Audits

A1. How do you ensure that the required inspections by operators and setups are made?

- On time?
- Correctly?

_____

_____

_____

_____

A2. Do the ones making the checks have the appropriate tools and information?

- Visual aids and standards?
- Do they understand how to react if a "bad" part is found?

_____

_____

_____

_____

B. How do you ensure that the audit sheets are current and correct?

_____

_____

_____

_____

C1. Besides checking a part, how do you ensure that the processes (lines/machines/presses/ovens) are running correctly?

  - Is there a plan to verify the process parameters?

  - Are setups encouraged to run the processes to the parameters? How?

_____

_____

_____

_____

C2. How do you ensure that auto-detection equipment is always working correctly?

  - When it is not running, are additional checks made? Is this documented?

  - When it is found to be not working correctly, was product previously run, verified?

_____

_____

_____

_____

D. Is the gauging equipment adequately protected from damage and appropriately protected?

_____

_____

_____

_____

3. Job Performance

A. How are operator training needs identified and addressed?

_____

_____

_____

_____

B. How are training needs of setups identified and addressed?

_____

_____

_____

_____

C. Describe the process for training new supervisors.

   • Does it cover all necessary areas, such as quality system, HR policies, safety, software?

   _____

   _____

   _____

   _____

D. Describe the process for training on safety.

   • How are safety requirements enforced?

   _____

   _____

   _____

   _____

4. Material Status

A. What is the procedure for identifying material status?

   • Production-ready?

   • Work in process (WIP)?

   _____

   _____

   _____

   _____

B. How is nonconforming material identified to ensure that it cannot be mixed with production?

   • What is the reject versus hold procedure?

   _____

   _____

   _____

5. Preventive Maintenance

A. If you bought new equipment this year, how and when did you set up the PM program?

- Was this part of the FMEA?
- Was it set up before the equipment started running production?

_____

_____

_____

_____

B. How do you measure the effectiveness of the PM program?

- Is it tracking favorably? (Need to see chart)
- If not, have changes been made?

_____

_____

_____

_____

("C" is only for Die Cast, Machining/Grinding, and Press areas)

C1. How do you maintain your tooling?

_____

_____

_____

_____

C2. When tooling is corrected/adjusted during a PM, are the first parts verified?

_____

_____

_____

_____

C3. How do you measure the effectiveness of the tooling PM program?

- Is it tracking favorably? (Need to see chart)
- If not, have changes been made?

_____

_____

_____

_____

6. General Housekeeping

A. What is the housekeeping policy in your area?

_____

_____

_____

_____

Nonconforming Product and Corrective Actions

1. Analysis of Nonconforming Product

A. Describe the process for the handling of nonconforming product after it has been rejected.

- How do you keep it isolated?
- Who makes the decision to use, rework, or scrap?

_____

_____

_____

_____

B. When nonconforming product will be shipped to the customer "as-is" (meaning no rework), what is the approval process?

- Does is require engineering and quality approval? Is it documented?
- Are corrective actions issued to ensure that the problem doesn't repeat?

_____

_____

_____

_____

C. What is the process for reworking nonconforming material?

- Are rework instructions written and available?

• Does inspection occur prior to release for production?

_____

_____

_____

D. Is there an initiative to reduce the overall number of defects produced?

  • What is used to drive this initiative? (Scrap, quality complaints, or ppms)

  • Is root cause identified for top defects?

  • Are corrective actions implemented?

  • Is there evidence of improvement? (Need to see chart)

_____

_____

_____

E. How are QA daily reports reacted to?

  • Are feedback or responses given in a timely manner?

  • Are corrective actions issued or implemented for recurring issues?

_____

_____

_____

("F" is only for the areas that have had a customer return for a part they produce.)

F. What is the process for responding to customer (OEM) complaints?

  • Is feedback to the customer given in a timely manner?

  • Is the info passed on to the setups?

  • Is this info turned into data, and used as a customer feedback measure?

_____

_____

_____

2. Corrective Actions

A. How do you monitor corrective actions for effectiveness?

   • How do you know if they were successful? Long-term?

   • Are repeat corrective actions reviewed and analyzed?

   _____

   _____

   _____

   _____

A1. Are process FMEAs reviewed when corrective actions are issued?

   • Is this noted in the corrective action form?

   _____

   _____

   _____

   _____

B. How have you addressed issues raised in previous internal audits?

   • What were some of the previous issues?

   • Have they been successfully addressed?

   _____

   _____

   _____

   _____

Appendix C

Supervisor Checklist

Supervisor Checklist

Date: _____ Name: _____

Process: _____

Management of the Organization

1. Process Overview

A. How does the manufacturing process (map) affect your area?

- Describe the process, including the inputs and outputs.
- What are the important interfaces (relationships) with other processes?

_____

_____

_____

_____

B. How do you track the performance of your process?

- Are the measures reviewed?
- (Do the measures match what the manager stated?)

_____

_____

_____

_____

C. What are the goals for your process?

   • Where are they documented?

   • Plans for improvement?

   • (Do the goals match what the manager stated?)

   _____

   _____

   _____

   _____

D. How do you ensure the satisfaction of your customer?

   • Are measures tracking favorably?

   • What actions have been taken to improve customer satisfaction? (Discuss both internal and external customers, if applicable)

   _____

   _____

   _____

   _____

E. Describe the quality policy.

   • How does it relate to your area?

   _____

   _____

   _____

   _____

2. Commitment to Improvement

A. What is your process for continuous improvement?

   • What are the measures and goals?

   • Are there actions in place to achieve the goals?

   _____

   _____

   _____

   _____

B. What improvements have been made to the areas over the past year? (Process or equipment)

- How were these projects identified and communicated?

- Have goals been met for the past year? If not, why?

- Do improvement projects agree with capital budget projects from manager?

_____

_____

_____

_____

C. How do you incorporate the ideas and suggestions of your employees in decision making?

- How can employees become involved or voice suggestions?

- When employees contribute, are they formally recognized?

_____

_____

_____

_____

D. How does the area find out about new techniques?

- Are "best practices" meetings or seminars attended?

_____

_____

_____

_____

3. *Communication*

A. How does communication flow in your area?

- What type of items? (Policies, measures, or goals)

- How are they communicated from your manager?

- How are they communicated to your employees?

_____

_____

_____

B. How are product changes communicated in your area?

  • Who is responsible for updating prints and information related to specs?

  _____

  _____

  _____

  _____

C. How are equipment (manufacturing engineering) changes communicated?

  • Who is responsible for updating setup instructions and related documents on the shop floor?

  _____

  _____

  _____

  _____

D. How do you control working documents on the shop floor?

  • How do you know what the latest revision is?

  _____

  _____

  _____

  _____

E. What aspects of the quality management system do you use on a regular basis?

  • What kind of training have you been given?

  _____

  _____

  _____

  _____

4. Advanced Product Quality Planning

A. What is the APQP process as it affects your area?

  • What measures do yo use to track performance?

  • What are the important interfaces (relationships)?

  _____

_____

_____

_____

B. When new equipment is purchased, how do you ensure that it will perform acceptably?

   • Was a qualification written and approved prior to receiving equipment?

   • Was a process FMEA conducted?

_____

_____

_____

_____

D. How do operations get certified for production in your area?

   • Does this reflect current projects?

   • Are all processes defined?

_____

_____

_____

_____

E. Describe how setup instructions are handled in your area.

   • Is there a defined process for keeping them up to date?

   • Are setup instructions part of the training program for new setups?

_____

_____

_____

_____

F. Describe how operator instructions are handled in your area.

   • Do they contain all the important information?

   • How do you ensure they are available at the workstation?

   • Are instructions part of the training program for new operators?

_____

_____

_____

_____

G. When are process FMEAs conducted?

• Were they completed for all major changes?

• Are previous FMEAs reviewed?

_____

_____

_____

_____

H. When a changeover (either a new part, shift change, or process change) occurs, how do you ensure the quality of the first parts produced?

• How do you know if this procedure is effective?

_____

_____

_____

_____

Management of the Process

1. Statistical Process Control

A. Are there initiatives to ensure capable processes?

• Is the information reviewed and used?

• Is there understanding of the results (Cpk, Cp)?

_____

_____

_____

_____

B. What policies have you put in place to ensure that processes are controlled and capable?

• Reviewing charts?

• Reacting to out-of-control data?

_____

_____

_____

_____

C. How do you ensure that manufacturing understands out-of-control and takes appropriate action?

- Ensure that charts are monitored?
- Reacting properly to out-of-control data?

_____

_____

_____

_____

D. What efforts are in place to improve process capability?

- Do report cards show improvement?
- Have classified features been identified?
- Is there an effort to get those processes to required Cpks?

_____

_____

_____

_____

2. Product and Process Audits

A1. How do you ensure that the required inspections by operators and setups are made?

- On time?
- Correctly?

_____

_____

_____

_____

A2. Do the ones making the checks have the appropriate tools and information?

- Visual aids and standards?

_____

_____

B. How do you ensure that the audit sheets are current and correct?

C1. Besides checking a part, how do you ensure that the processes (lines/machines/ presses/ovens) are running correctly?

- Is there a plan to verify the process parameters?
- Are setups encouraged to run the processes to the parameters? How?

C2. How do you ensure that auto-detection equipment is always working correctly?

- When it is not running, are additional checks made? Is this documented?
- When it is found to be not working correctly, was product previously run, verified?

D. Is the gauging equipment adequately protected from damage and appropriately protected?

3. Job Performance

A. How are operator training needs identified?

- How are operators trained?

_____

_____

_____

_____

B. How are training needs of setups identified?

- How are setups trained?

_____

_____

_____

_____

C. Describe the training you have received.

- Does it cover all necessary areas, such as quality system, HR policies, safety, software needs?

_____

_____

_____

_____

D. Describe the process for training on safety.

- How are safety requirements enforced?

_____

_____

_____

_____

4. Material Status

A. What is the procedure for identifying material status?

- Production-ready?
- Work in process (WIP)?

_____

_____

_____

_____

B. How is nonconforming material identified to ensure that it cannot be mixed with production?

   • What is the reject versus hold procedure?

   _____

   _____

   _____

   _____

5. Preventive Maintenance

B. What role do you plan in the PM process?

("C" is only for Die Cast, Machining/Grinding, and Press areas)

C1. How do you maintain your tooling?

   • How do you decide when to PM tooling?

   _____

   _____

   _____

   _____

C2. When tooling is corrected/adjusted during a PM, are the first parts verified?

   _____

   _____

   _____

   _____

6. General Housekeeping

A. What is the housekeeping policy in your area?

   _____

   _____

   _____

   _____

Nonconforming Product and Corrective Actions

1. Analysis of Nonconforming Product

A. Describe the process for the handling of nonconforming product after it has been rejected.

- How do you keep it isolated?
- Who makes the decision to use, rework, or scrap?

_____

_____

_____

_____

B. When nonconforming product will be shipped to the customer "as-is" (meaning no rework), what is the approval process?

- Does is require engineering and quality approval? Is it documented?

_____

_____

_____

_____

C. What is the process for reworking nonconforming material?

- Are rework instructions written and available?
- Does inspection occur prior to release for production?

_____

_____

_____

_____

D. Is there an initiative to reduce the overall number of defects produced?

- What is used to drive this initiative? (Scrap, quality complaints, or ppms)
- Is root cause identified for top defects?
- Are corrective actions implemented?
- Is there evidence of improvement?

_____

_____

_____

_____

Appendix D

Manufacturing Engineer Checklist

Manufacturing Engineer Checklist

Date: _____ Name: _____

Process: _____

Management of the Organization

1. Process Overview

A. How does the manufacturing process (map) affect your area?

- Describe the process, including the inputs and outputs.

_____

_____

_____

_____

B. How do you know how well your area is running?

- Are department/process measures shared with the department?

_____

_____

_____

_____

C. What are the goals for your process?

- Where are they documented?

- Plans for improvement?

- (Do the goals match what the manager stated?)

_____

_____

_____

_____

D. How do you ensure the satisfaction of your customer?

- Are measures tracking favorably?

- What actions have been taken to improve customer satisfaction? (Discuss both internal and external customers, if applicable.)

_____

_____

_____

_____

E. What is the quality policy?

- How does it relate to your area?

_____

_____

_____

_____

2. Commitment to Improvement

A. What is your process for continuous improvement?

- What are the measures and goals?

- Are there actions in place to achieve the goals?

_____

_____

_____

_____

B. What improvements have been made to the areas over the past year? (Process or equipment)

- How were these projects identified?

- Have goals been met for the past year? If not, why?

- Do improvement projects agree with capital budget projects from manager?

_____

_____

_____

_____

D. How does the area find out about new techniques?

_____

_____

_____

_____

3. Communication

A. How does communication flow in your area?

- What type of items? (Policies, measures, or goals)
- How are they communicated from your manager?

_____

_____

_____

_____

B. How are product changes communicated in your area?

- Who is responsible for updating prints and information related to specs?

_____

_____

_____

_____

C. How are equipment (manufacturing engineering) changes communicated?

- Who is responsible for updating setup instructions and related documents on the shop floor?

_____

_____

_____

_____

D. How do you control working documents on the shop floor?

   • How do you know what the latest revision is?

   _____

   _____

   _____

   _____

E. What aspects of the quality management system do you use on a regular basis?

   • What kind of training have you been given?

   _____

   _____

   _____

   _____

4. Advanced Product Quality Planning

A. What is the APQP process as it affects your area?

   • What measures do yo use to track performance?

   • What are the important interfaces (relationships)?

   _____

   _____

   _____

   _____

B. When new equipment is purchased, how do you ensure that it will perform acceptably?

   • Was a qualification written and approved prior to receiving equipment?

   • Was a process FMEA conducted?

   _____

   _____

   _____

   _____

C. What was included in the qualification plan?

- Critical features? Required capabilities? Performance requirements such as cycle time?
- Were capabilities measured? (See procedure for all requirements.)

_____

_____

_____

_____

D. How are operations certified for production in your area?

- Does this reflect current projects?
- Are all processes defined? (Ask to see capital budget. Can APQP be demonstrated for each of the items?)

_____

_____

_____

_____

E. Describe how setup instructions are handled in your area.

- How do you define process parameters?
- Do they contain process parameters?
- Is there a defined process for keeping them up to date?

_____

_____

_____

_____

G. When are process FMEAs conducted?

- Were they completed for all major changes?
- Is there a system to review previous FMEAs?

_____

_____

_____

_____

Management of the Process

1. Statistical Process Control

A. Are there initiatives to ensure capable processes?

- How is the information reviewed and used?
- Is there understanding of the results (Cpk, Cp)?

_____

_____

_____

_____

D. What efforts are in place to improve process capability?

- Do report cards show improvement?
- Have classified features been identified?
- Is there an effort to get those processes to required Cpks?

_____

_____

_____

_____

2. Product and Process Audits

C. Besides checking a part, how do you ensure that the processes (lines/machines/presses/ovens) are running correctly?

- Is there a plan to verify the process parameters?
- Are setups encouraged to run the processes to the parameters? How?

_____

_____

_____

_____

3. Job Performance

C. Describe the process for training new manufacturing engineers.

- Does it cover all necessary areas, such as quality system, HR policies, safety, software?

_____

_____

_____

_____

D. Describe the process for training on safety.

  • How are safety requirements enforced?

_____

_____

_____

_____

5. Preventive Maintenance

A. If you bought new equipment this year, how and when did you set up the PM program?

  • Was this part of the FMEA?

  • Was it set up before the equipment started running production?

_____

_____

_____

_____

B. How do you measure the effectiveness of the PM program?

  • Is it tracking favorably? (Need to see chart)

  • If not, have changes been made?

_____

_____

_____

_____

("C" is only for Die Cast, Machining/Grinding, and Press areas)

C1. How do you maintain your tooling?

_____

_____

_____

_____

C3. How do you measure the effectiveness of the tooling PM program?

- Is it tracking favorably? (Need to see chart)

- If not, have changes been made?

_____

_____

_____

_____

6. General Housekeeping

A. What is the housekeeping policy in your area?

_____

_____

_____

_____

Nonconforming Product and Corrective Actions

1. Analysis of Nonconforming Product

D. Is there an initiative to reduce the overall number of defects produced?

- What is used to drive this initiative? (Scrap, quality complaints, or ppms)

- Is there evidence of improvement?

_____

_____

_____

_____

Appendix E

Setup Checklist

Setup Checklist

Date: _____   Name: _____

Process: _____

Management of the Organization

1. Process Overview

B. How do you know if your area is successful and what are the measures?

_____

_____

_____

_____

C. What goals have been set for your area? Are there plans for improvement?

_____

_____

_____

_____

D1. Who is your customer? (Internal and external)

_____

_____

_____

_____

D2. How do you know if you're doing a good job in terms of keeping your customers happy?

_____

_____

_____

_____

E. What is your understanding of the quality policy?

_____

_____

_____

_____

2. Commitment to Improvement

C1.. Are team meetings held to gather input?

_____

_____

_____

_____

C2. Is your input requested when decisions are made in your area?

_____

_____

_____

_____

C3. What avenues do you have to make suggestions?

_____

_____

_____

_____

D. Are setups encouraged to attend seminars and "best-practices" meetings?

_____

_____

_____

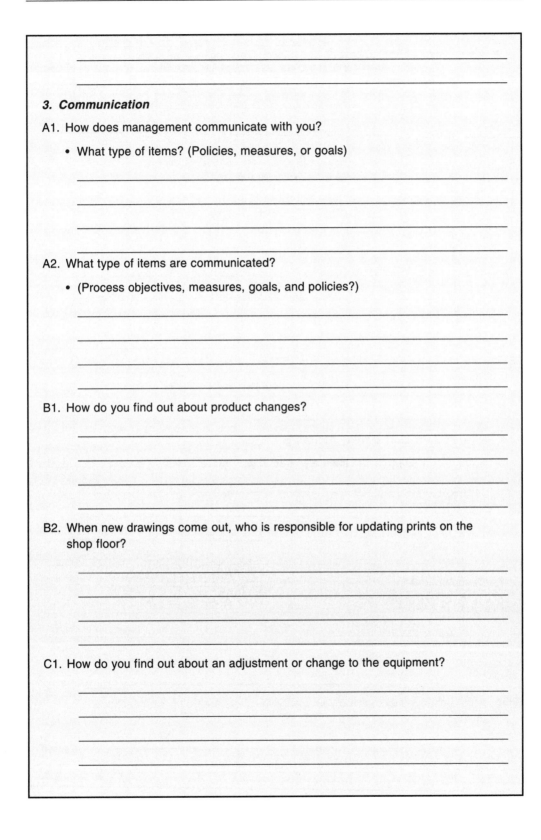

_____

_____

3. Communication

A1. How does management communicate with you?

  • What type of items? (Policies, measures, or goals)

_____

_____

_____

_____

A2. What type of items are communicated?

  • (Process objectives, measures, goals, and policies?)

_____

_____

_____

_____

B1. How do you find out about product changes?

_____

_____

_____

_____

B2. When new drawings come out, who is responsible for updating prints on the shop floor?

_____

_____

_____

_____

C1. How do you find out about an adjustment or change to the equipment?

_____

_____

_____

_____

C2. If you make a change, how do you inform everyone? On all shifts?

_____

_____

_____

_____

D. How do you control working documents on the floor?

• How do you know what the latest revision is?

_____

_____

_____

_____

E. If you needed to look something up in the quality manual, where would you look?

_____

_____

_____

_____

4. Advanced Product Quality Planning

D. Explain how setup instructions are used in your area.

_____

_____

_____

_____

F. Describe how operator instructions are handled in your area.

_____

_____

_____

_____

H. After a changeover, how do you ensure the parts are being manufactured to spec?

_____

_____

_____

_____

_____

Management of the Process

1. Statistical Process Control

A. What are the initiatives to improve the process/equipment?

_____

_____

_____

_____

B. What are your responsibilities with respect to SPC?

_____

_____

_____

_____

C1. When you see a point beyond the control limits, what do you do? (Are notes recorded?)

_____

_____

_____

_____

C2. How has your area benefited by using SPC?

_____

_____

_____

_____

2. Product and Process Audits

A1. When you are checking a part, how do you know if it is good or bad?

_____

_____

_____

_____

A2. While making a check, what happens when you find a bad part?

_____

_____

_____

_____

B. How do you know the audit sheets are current and correct?

_____

_____

_____

_____

C1. How often do you verify that your equipment is running within the parameters stated in the setup instructions?

_____

_____

_____

_____

C2. How often do you verify that the auto-detection equipment is working correctly?

_____

_____

_____

_____

D. Is the gauging equipment adequately protected from damage and appropriately protected?

_____

_____

_____

_____

4. Job Performance

A. What kind of training do you provide the operators?

_____

B1. What kind of training did you receive when you started your current job?

_____

_____

_____

_____

B2. Have you been to SPC training?

_____

_____

_____

D. What are the safety requirements of your job?

_____

_____

_____

_____

4. Material Status

A. How is production versus WIP material identified?

_____

_____

_____

_____

B. What is the rejected stock procedure? Hold procedure?

_____

_____

_____

_____

5. Preventive Maintenance

B1. Explain how PMs are handled in your area.

_____

_____

_____

_____

B2. Are PM schedules ever adjusted for equipment that has more downtime or causes more defects?

_____

_____

_____

_____

C. When an adjustment is made to tooling during a PM, is a layout conducted to verify that it is correct?

_____

_____

_____

_____

6. General Housekeeping

A. What is the housekeeping policy in your area?

_____

_____

_____

_____

Nonconforming Product and Corrective Actions

1. Analysis of Nonconforming Product

A. When a product has been tagged as nonconforming, what must happen before it can be used in production?

_____

_____

_____

_____

B. What approvals are required prior to use of nonconforming product?

_____

_____

_____

_____

C. When rework is being completed, are written instructions provided?

_____

_____

_____

_____

D. What kind of initiatives are there to reduce scrap, rework, and so on?

_____

_____

_____

_____

F. What kind of action is taken when customer complaints are received?

_____

_____

_____

_____

Appendix F

Operator Checklist

Operator Checklist

Date: _____   Name: _____

Process: _____

Management of the Organization

1. Process Overview

B. How do you know if your area is successful and what are the measures?

_____

_____

_____

_____

C. What goals have been set for your area? Any plans for improvement?

_____

_____

_____

_____

D1. Who is your customer? (Internal and external)

_____

_____

_____

_____

D2. How do you know if you're doing a good job in terms of keeping your customers happy?

_____

_____

_____

_____

E. What is your understanding of the quality policy?

_____

_____

_____

_____

2. Commitment to Improvement

C2. Is your input requested when decisions are made in your area?

_____

_____

_____

_____

C3. What avenues do you have to make suggestions?

_____

_____

_____

_____

3. Communication

A1. How does management communicate with you?

_____

_____

_____

_____

A2. What type of items are communicated?

- (Process objectives, measures, goals, and policies?)

_____

B1. How do you find out about product changes?

C1. How do you find out about a change to the equipment?

F. Describe how operator instructions are used in your area.

4. Advanced Product Quality Planning

D. Explain how operator instruction cards are used in your area?

Management of the Process

2. Product and Process Audits

A1. How do you know that the parts you are making are good?

A2. When you find a part that is bad, what do you do?

_____

_____

_____

_____

3. Job Performance

A1. What kind of training did you receive when you started your current job?

_____

_____

_____

_____

A2. Were operator instruction cards part of your training?

_____

_____

_____

_____

D. What are the safety requirements of your job?

_____

_____

_____

_____

4. Material Status

A. How is production versus WIP material identified?

_____

_____

_____

_____

B. What is the rejected stock procedure? Hold procedure?

_____

_____

_____

5. Preventive Maintenance

B. Explain how PMs are handled in your area.

_____

_____

_____

_____

6. General Housekeeping

A. What is the housekeeping policy in your area?

_____

_____

_____

Nonconforming Product and Corrective Actions

1. Analysis of Nonconforming Product

A. When product has been tagged as nonconforming, what must happen before it can be used in production?

_____

_____

_____

_____

D. What kind of initiatives are there to reduce scrap, rework, and so on?

_____

_____

_____

_____

F. What kind of action is taken when customer complaints are received?

_____

_____

_____

_____

Appendix G

Floor Tour Checklist

Floor Tour Checklist

Date: _____ Team: _____

Process: _____

1. Identify three part prints on the shop floor. Are they to the latest revision levels?

    Print # _____ Rev. _____ Correct?_____

    Print # _____ Rev. _____ Correct?_____

    Print # _____ Rev. _____ Correct?_____

    Comments: _____

    _____

    _____

2. Identify three work instructions related to quality. Do they have revision levels? Are they current?

    Doc 1) _____ Rev. _____ Correct?_____

    Doc 2) _____ Rev. _____ Correct?_____

    Doc 3) _____ Rev. _____ Correct?_____

    Comments: _____

    _____

    _____

---

3. Identify three setup instructions. Do they have revision levels? Are they current?

   Doc 1) _____ Rev. _____ Correct?_____

   Doc 2) _____ Rev. _____ Correct?_____

   Doc 3) _____ Rev. _____ Correct?_____

   Comments: _____

   _____

   _____

4. Does each document have key process parameters established? (List one parameter per document)

   Doc 1) _____ Value at Machine _____

   Doc 2) _____ Value at Machine _____

   Doc 3) _____ Value at Machine _____

   Comments: _____

   _____

   _____

5. Are operator instructions available at all workstations? Yes/No _____

   List stations where operator instruction cards are not available or not correct.

   _____

   _____

   _____

6. Identify three SPC control charts.

Feature	Yes/No Process in control?	Yes/No Notes if out	Cpk
Chart 1: _____	_____	_____	_____
Chart 2: _____	_____	_____	_____
Chart 3: _____	_____	_____	_____

   Comments: _____

   _____

   _____

7. Identify three audit/inspection sheets.

   Audit sheet 1: _____

   Audit sheet 2: _____

   Audit sheet 3: _____

	Sheet 1	**Sheet 2**	**Sheet 3**
Are the audit sheets to the correct revision? (Y/N)	_____	_____	_____
Do they match what is inspected at the station? (Y/N)	_____	_____	_____
Do they identify the appropriate gauging? (Y/N)	_____	_____	_____
Do personnel use the proper technique? (Y/N)	_____	_____	_____

8. Identify five gauges used on the shop floor (note ID #):

   Gage 1: _____   Gage 4: _____

   Gage 2: _____   Gage 5: _____

   Gage 3: _____

	Gage 1	**Gage 2**	**Gage 3**	**Gage 4**	**Gage 5**
Are the gauges in the calibration system? (Y/N)	_____	_____	_____	_____	_____
Are the gauges properly calibrated? (Y/N)	_____	_____	_____	_____	_____
Are they clean and suitable for use? (Y/N)	_____	_____	_____	_____	_____
Do personnel use the proper technique? (Y/N)	_____	_____	_____	_____	_____

9. Is all material clearly identified? Yes/No _____

   If not, list basket and location.

   Comments: _____

   _____

   _____

Glossary

advanced product quality planning (APQP)—Referred to as one of the five pillars of quality used by Ford, DaimlerChrysler, and General Motors, it defines a method for identifying the process flow and corresponding quality requirements for each process utilizing a formal document called a control plan. This methodology or some variant of it is commonly used in industry.

audit/internal audit—A method or technique by which a quality requirement, standard, or defined activity is reviewed against practice to verify that it is properly followed; this is accomplished through interviews, observations, and review of documentation.

- First-party audits: internal audits

- Second-party audits: customer audits; supplier audits

- Third-party audits: independent audits; registrar audits for ISO 9001 certification

audit season—In the progressive audit methodology, there is a season or period of time each year when internal audits are conducted. There is also a preseason period where new auditors are identified and trained and the audit scoring guides and checklists are updated. Postseason is when review occurs, including developing strategies for the next audit season.

audit schedule—Approximate dates for conducting audits of the various major processes, departments, and functions during the audit season.

auditee—The person, department, or organization that is audited.

auditor—The person that is performing the audit, asking the interview questions, and observing activities.

best practice—For the purpose of this book, identifying and implementing the best method used between shifts, within a facility, or within an organization. This concept is often expanded in publications to a defined methodology of benchmarking (reviewing best methods) across industries.

closing meeting—Presentation of audit findings by the audit team at the conclusion of the internal audit. The lead auditor facilitates this meeting to summarize the results and issue corrective actions, if necessary.

corrective action—In regard to the audit, a formal document that is issued when the auditor determines the activity is not in compliance with the procedure or defined method; it should not be issued for minor details. Corrective actions should describe the noncompliance, the procedure or defined activity, person responsible, and due date.

checklist (audit)—A formal document that contains specific questions or activities that must be asked or performed during the audit. The auditor uses this to document the interviews, observations, and specific records or items reviewed.

failure mode and effects analysis (FMEA)—One of the five pillars of quality used by Ford, DaimlerChrysler, and General Motors, it defines methods for reviewing designs (design FMEA) and processes (process FMEA). Using a standard format, the FMEA document leads teams in rating potential failures, effects of failures, causes, and current controls or inspection to prevent occurrence. This methodology or some variant of it is commonly used in industry.

findings (audit)—Documented results of audit interviews, observations, and record review.

interface—Relationship of one process to another process, typically defined in the quality management system.

ISO 9001:2000—The international quality system standard, published by ASQ, that defines requirements for a quality system.

lead auditor—Person with overall responsibility for the audit team, including setting the audit schedule, issuing checklists and scoring guides, making decisions on findings, issuing corrective actions, and publishing the audit report.

manager—For the purposes of this book, a person reporting to the plant manager responsible for overall operations in a specific department such as machining, quality, or production control. They will have direct reports such as manufacturing engineers and supervisors, who have as direct reports setups and operators.

management review—Required for ISO 9001 registration, this is the management group's review of specified quality activities to verify that the quality management system is adequate, suitable, and effective for the organization.

manufacturing engineer—Highly technical personnel responsible for developing and maintaining manufacturing equipment, including attaining operating efficiencies and meeting specific quality requirements.

measurement system analysis (MSA)—One of the five pillars of quality used by Ford, DaimlerChrysler, and General Motors, it defines methods for analyzing measurement equipment to verify that it is acceptable for production; it utilizes gauge repeatability and reproducibility studies, which incorporate proven statistical methods. This methodology or some variant of it is commonly used in industry.

opening meeting—Introduction of audit team and auditee, including review of the audit scope, purpose, and agenda. The lead auditor facilitates this.

operators—Personnel responsible for machining and assembling product, including operating equipment.

opportunity for improvement—Documented audit findings that do not require a corrective action but provide thoughts and activities that offer improvement to the area audited.

process—A sequence of activities initiated by certain inputs that work together to provide an output that adds value to an organization through defined process objectives. There is a supplier, customer, and process owner, and typically process measures with corresponding goals. Defining major processes is a requirement of ISO 9001:2000.

process map—A document in the quality management system that depicts the process.

production part approval process (PPAP)—One of the five pillars of quality used by Ford, DaimlerChrysler, and General Motors, it defines methods for approving components and assemblies for production, whether new designs or changes. It requires inspection layout reports, control plans, capability studies, and gauge studies included with the PPAP packet in the form of a warrant by the supplier that it meets requirements. This methodology or some variant of it is commonly used in industry.

quality management system (QMS)—A group of processes, procedures, and work instructions that comprise the quality system used by an organization, compiled in the quality manual.

scoring guide (audit)—In the progressive audit methodology, the scoring guide is a document that defines all the requirements for the internal audit of a specific major process/department; it includes a scoring system that results in an overall rating of the area audited.

setup—Personnel directly responsible for changeovers, adjustments, monitoring control charts, maintaining equipment on a day-to-day basis, and ensuring that operations are running as planned.

statistical process control (SPC)—In general, a proven method utilizing process control (behavior) charts to monitor process performance based on the statistical standard deviation. There are various rules applied to alert when nonnormal variation occurs so it can be addressed. This is also one of the five pillars of quality used by Ford, DaimlerChrysler, and General Motors as a requirement for suppliers and addressed through AIAG.

supervisor—Directly reporting to the manager, the supervisor is responsible for production activities and has setups and operators as direct reports.

TS 16949—A collaborative work involving American and European automotive groups based on ISO 9001:1994 to which are added auto industry supplements, such as APQP, PPAP, FMEA, and MSA. This motor industry–specific "standard" replaces the existing American and European industry standards QS-9000 (3rd ed.), VDA-6.1, EAQF, and AVSQ.

Bibliography

Adams, Larry. "More Work, More Pay." *Quality* (July 2003).

ANSI/ISO/ASQ Q9001:2000. *Quality management systems requirements.* Milwaukee: ASQ Quality Press, 2000.

Beckmerhagen, I. A., H. P. Berg, S. V. Karapetrovic, and W. O. Willborn. "On the Effectiveness of Quality Management System Audits." *The TQM Magazine* 6, no. 1 (2004).

Beeler, Dewitt L. "Internal Auditing: The Big Lies." *Quality Progress* (May 1999).

Cameron, Kim, and Wesley Sine. "A Framework for Organizational Quality Culture." *Quality Management Journal* 6, no. 4 (1999).

Cianfrani, Charles A., Joseph J. Tsiakals, and John E. (Jack) West. *The ASQ ISO 9000:2000 Handbook.* Milwaukee: ASQ Quality Press, 2002.

Coleman, Garry D., and C. Patrick Koelling. "Estimating the Consistency of Third-Party Evaluator Scoring of Organizational Self-Assessments." *Quality Management Journal* 5, no. 3 (1998).

Coleman, Garry D., Eileen M. Van Aken, and Jianming Shen. "Estimating Interrater Reliability of Examiner Scoring for a State Quality Award." *Quality Management Journal* 10, no. 3 (2002).

Dusharme, Dirk. "ISO 9001 Survey." *Quality Digest* (July 2004).

Forsman, Theresa. "Dark Days for Detroit's Suppliers." *Business Week* (March 5, 2001).

Garvin, David A. *Managing Quality.* New York: The Free Press, 1988.

"ISO Survey Reports Registration Growth." *Quality Digest* (September 2003).

Ittner, Christopher D., and David F. Larcker. "Coming Up Short on Nonfinancial Performance Measurement." *Harvard Business Review* (November 2003).

Kerwin, Kathleen, and Joann Muller. "Reviving GM." *Business Week* (December 1, 1999).

Mills, Charles A. *The Quality Audit.* Milwaukee: ASQ Quality Press, 1989.

Mintzberg, Henry. "The Manager's Job." A paper published in *The Organizational Behavior Reader,* 7th ed. Joyce S. Osland, David A. Kolb, and Irwin M. Rubin. Upper Saddle River: Prentice Hall, 2001.

Naish, Phyllis. "Why Companies Aren't Making the Change." *Quality Progress* (September 2002).

Ozgur, Ceyhun, Gary E. Meek, and Aysegul Toker. "The Impact of ISO Certification on the Levels of Awareness and Useage of Quality Tools and Concepts: A Survey of Turkish Manufacturing Companies." *Quality Management Journal* 9, no. 2 (2002).

Schonberger, Richard J. "Is the Baldrige Still About Quality?" *Quality Digest* (December 2001).

Smith, Kennedy. "The Baldrige Revisited." *Quality Digest* (March 2004).

Smith, Martin E. "Changing an Organization's Culture: Correlates of Success and Failure." *Leadership and Organizational Development Journal* 24, no. 5 (2003); referenced the works of E. H. Shein, *Organizational Culture and Leadership*, 2nd ed. San Francisco: Jossey-Bass, 1992.

———. "Changing an Organization's Culture: Correlates of Success and Failure." *Leadership and Organizational Development Journal* 24, no. 5 (2003); referenced works of J. P. Kotter, "Leading Change: An Action Plan from the World's Foremost Expert on Business Leadership." Boston: Harvard Business School Press, 1996.

———. "Changing an Organization's Culture: Correlates of Success and Failure." *Leadership and Organizational Development Journal* 24, no. 5 (2003); reference to K. Troy, "Change Management: An Overview of Current Initiatives." New York: The Conference Board, 1994.

———. "Changing an Organization's Culture: Correlates of Success and Failure." *Leadership and Organizational Development Journal* 24, no. 5 (2003); referenced P. Mourier and M. E. Smith, "Conquering Organizational Change: How to Succeed Where Most Companies Fail." Atlanta: CEP Press, 2001.

Stern, Joel M., John S. Shiely, with Irwin Ross. *The EVA Challenge.* New York: John Wiley & Sons, 2001.

Trottman, Melanie. "Southwest Seeks Mediation in Talks with Attendants." *Wall Street Journal* (September 16, 2003).

Walker, Marlon A. "The Day the E-Mail Dies." *Wall Street Journal* (August 26, 2004).

Webster's New Millennium Dictionary of English. Long Beach: Lexico Publishing Group, 2003.

Webster's Revised Unabridged Dictionary. www/dictionary.com, Wordnet ® 2.0, Princeton University: MICRA, 1996, 1998.

"Welch's March to the South." *Business Week* (December 6, 1999).

West, John E. (Jack). "Is There Time?" *Quality Progress* (March 2003).

Whitmore, Karen, and Caria Kalogeridis. "ISO/TS 16949: Here at Last." *Quality Digest* (October 2002).

"Why Apply?" www.Baldrige.nist.gov.

www.dictionary.com. Lexico Publishing Group, 2003.

Yahya, Salleh, and Wee-Keat Goh. "The Implementation of an ISO 9000 Quality System." *International Journal of Quality and Reliability* 18, no. 9 (2001).

Zimmerman, Ann, and Marin Fackler. "Wal-Mart's Foray into Japan Stirs a Retail Upheaval." *Wall Street Journal* (September 19, 2003).

Index

A

accountability, 42

action level, managing on, 87

advanced product quality planning, 131–34, 142
    failure mode and effects analysis, 134
    internal operations, 134
    new production equipment, 133
    process, 133
    process failure mode and effects analysis, 134

American industry, 12–13

American Society for Quality, 56

assessment teams, 21

assumptions, making, 66–68

attendance system, 83

attitude, 73

attribute checks, 137

audit
    conducting, 184
    last-minute, 65
    scoring, 90–91
    standardizing, 113

audit checklists, 76–77, 80, 109, 149–66
    accurate and consistent scoring, 153
    ISO-based, 111, 112
    key points, 150–53
    manager, 151, 155–59
    manufacturing engineer, 151, 162–63
    methodology, 153–64
    note taking, 151
    operator, 151, 163–64
    purpose, 150
    questions, 151
    results, interpreting, 164–66

    setup personnel, 151, 163–64
    shop floor, 164
    specific by responsibility, 151
    supervisor, 159–62

audit guidelines, 114–16

audit manager, postseason review and planning, 197

audit process, 180–89
    audit, conducting, 184
    audit schedule, developing, 183–84
    closing meeting, 188–89
    interviews, 186–87
    opening meeting, 185–86
    ownership, 81
    pre-audit team meeting, 185
    preseason updates, 183
    recruiting, 183
    team evaluation and scoring meeting, 187–88, 189–93
    tour, 187
    training, 183

audit program, successful, 167

audit program manager, 107–8, 183

audit purpose, 99–102, 116
    identification, 100–101
    increasing knowledge, 101–2
    verification, 99–100

audit question format, 116–17

audit schedule, 93
    developing, 183–84

audit scope, 76, 82, 99, 102–6

audit scoring guidelines, 116

audit season, 98, 179–99
    audit of internal audit, 196–97